A WORLD BETWEEN WAVES

EDITED BY FRANK STEWART

ISLAND PRESS
Washington, D.C.
Covelo, California

Library of Congress Cataloging-in-Publication Data

A World between waves / edited by Frank Stewart.
        p. cm.
     Includes bibliographical references.
     ISBN 1-55963-207-0. — ISBN 1-55963-208-9 (pbk.)
     1. Natural History—Hawaii. 2. Ecology—Hawaii. I.
Stewart, Frank, 1946-
QH198.H3W67 1992
508.969—dc20   92-14458
                                                     CIP

Reprinted on recycled, acid-free paper

Manufactured in the United States of America
10 9 8 7 6 5 4 3 2 1

CONTENTS

PREFACE

The Hawaiian Islands comprise one of the most fascinating eco-logical regions on earth—every bit as dramatic and profound, from an evolutionary viewpoint, as the Galápagos Islands, where Charles Darwin in his youth formed his insights into the origins of life on earth. Large areas of the islands are as breathtakingly beautiful as any place on the planet—with razor-sharp cliffs that soar into the clouds; cool, verdant rain forests; iron-red deserts; living volcanoes; pristine coral reefs; and snow-capped moun-tains. For many of the native Polynesian people, the islands are also profoundly sacred, each part of the land and sea essential to the life of the spirit and to the well-being of the mind and body.

Located over 2,500 miles from any continent, the Hawaiian Islands are isolated but not protected from ecological destruction. Amid the great beauty and diversity of the islands, it's distressing to realize how much of the natural environment has been de-stroyed and how many of the native species that still exist are on the verge of extinction. For example, of all the native birds that existed when the Polynesians first arrived, in about 500 A.D., at least 50 percent are now extinct; another 41 percent of the remaining species are classified by the U.S. Fish and Wildlife Service as either endangered or threatened. Hawai'i has a higher rate of species extinction than any other place in the United States.

There are various reasons for what has happened to the natural environment of the Hawaiian Islands. Because of its very isolation, the delicately balanced ecological system has been especially vulnerable to human disturbance—including large-scale farming, toxic pollution, and the importation, accidental or otherwise, of alien mammals, insects, and plants. In the past, such destruction was often the result of ignorance and poor management. Why destruction of the islands' environment continues is more complex. Primary among the reasons is our inadequate understanding of how to balance conservation biology with the needs of increased human populations and the failure of citizens and policymakers to recognize how swiftly they must act to save the remaining critical habitats that support the native species.

The essays in this book represent a hope—if not always an optimism—that accurate and articulate natural history writing about the Hawaiian Islands may contribute to focusing attention on the wonder and fragility of the Hawaiian environment, and to awaken us to our obligations to protect this and similar places. There is still much that can be saved in Hawai'i.

All the essays gathered here are contemporary and fall within the broad and generous category now called "nature writing"; at the same time, they represent a variety of styles and approaches to their subjects. Throughout the book, the reader meets remarkable people, through whose informed eyes we are better able to see this richly varied world between waves.

The prologue is meant to place the islands in the context of the early voyages of exploration and the Western naturalists who first came to the Pacific. Section one, "Islands from the Blue Abyss," contains essays that describe the geologic origins and veg-

etation zones in Hawai'i, from coastal beaches to volcanic summits. Essays here take us into the islands' forests, deserts, and rift
zones. Section two, "The Living Ocean," turns our attention to
the sea that surrounds the islands—the shoreline, waves, coral
reefs, and marine creatures. The epilogue, a meditative essay on a
young artist who sailed with Captain James Cook, reminds us of
the limits of what we know about nature, and how we form ideas
of what we think we know.

Each of the writers in this book—whether scientist, poet,
novelist, or essayist—relishes hard facts, but each is after something else as well: the spirit of the land. Each writes out of the
effort to love, understand, and protect this place and, by extension, all places that require our care and attention.

The intent of this book, then, is to introduce the natural
history of Hawai'i to many people. Most will never live in the
islands or even visit. Nevertheless, what is left of the endangered
beauty in Hawai'i will be protected only if concerned people,
including those who may experience Hawai'i primarily in these
pages, become aware of the true nature of the islands—of the vital
mysteries still to be discovered here, and the tragedy for all of us
if we continue to tolerate the destruction of this irreplaceable
island world.

—F.S.

A WORLD BETWEEN WAVES

The Hawaiian Islands

Map by Laurel Lynn Indalecio

PROLOGUE: EARLY NATURALISTS AND NATURE WRITING IN THE PACIFIC

FRANK STEWART

THE island of Hawai'i is the largest in the chain of islands collectively called by that name. Hawai'i is the home of the most powerful gods, the most devastating earthquakes, the most barren deserts, and the highest mountains. It is also "the darkly verdant one" in Hawaiian epithets, home of lush, dense rain forests. Rivers of lava set the seas on the southern coast to boiling and snowstorms blow across its cold, high peaks.

Having hiked this island during the past week, from the coastal deserts to the freezing uplands, I'm ready to go home to the more moderate temperatures of O'ahu. The little island commuter airplane shudders as it climbs through 6,000 feet, and the rising air currents from the warm land mass below bounce the half-empty DeHaviland side to side. The plane banks sharply, giving a last look at a long volcanic plume billowing into the upper atmosphere. The plume rises from just west of the village of Kalapana, buried during the past month under a steaming plateau of black lava. As the plane banks again, the island's volcanic peaks dominate the view for the last time and are left behind. This winter morning, they are snowcapped in the early light.

The bay at Kealakekua, where I spent part of the previous week, is particularly well sheltered and shaped like a fishhook. The longer part is rocky, lying below a steep cliff called Pali-kapu-o-Keōua, where the early Hawaiians buried the remains of great chiefs. A little calcareous sand beach, called Nāpōʻopoʻo, nestles in the narrow, inner part of the hook's barb. Here, bathers spread their blankets; these days there are usually more visitors than there is beach to lie on.

From this spot, I have often stood and looked at the cliffs and deep ocean, the vegetation and fauna, and the remnants of human history that comprise Kealakekua. So much is here that I know I cannot see, or don't yet know how to see, despite having lived several decades in the islands. When I try hard to take everything in together, hold the expanse, the detail, and the history all in the eye, as if they were one thing, a vertigo sweeps them into a blur. For a while, then, I go back to the parts one at a time: the hillside of ēkoa, kiawe, and ʻopiuma; a school of spinner dolphins, glimpsed far out at the point; a wandering tattler skimming low over the water.

The smallness of the bay belies its historic importance. At the northwest end, clear in the sunlight, is a white monument to Captain James Cook, who landed here and was killed in 1779. And here at the beach's edge looking seaward is an ancient heiau, or Hawaiian temple. Embedded in a low cairn in front of the massive heiau is a weathered marker bearing the name of William Watman, a crewman on Captain Cook's final voyage. The remains of both Cook and Watman are still here, though no one is sure where.

When I first came to Kealakekua, I was intrigued by the cairn for William Watman. Of all the significant occurrences and presences in this bay, many of which profoundly shaped the fate of the Hawaiian Islands, why was Watman's life and death so prominently marked and not the lives of the others? Why wasn't there something here about the great Hawaiian temple that looks out at the bay, and why wasn't it preserved like the one just south at Hōnaunau, which has become a national park? No one I asked seemed to know.

You have to go to Captain Cook's journals to find out about William Watman. An ordinary seaman, he was old when he sailed with Cook to Hawai'i in July 1776; he had also sailed on Cook's previous voyage, around the world along the high southern latitudes of the Antarctic. Despite his age, he seemed in sound shape, which explains why Cook and the other crewmen were surprised when Watman was suddenly seized with a paralytic stroke and died ten days after the expedition's ships had reached Kealakekua Bay. The priests of the heiau shared Cook's sadness and agreed at once that Watman should be buried in sacred ground, within the temple compound.

During the burial ceremony, Cook solemnly pronounced the ritual of the Church of England over Watman's remains. Then the Hawaiian priests slaughtered animals and performed their own ritual service, placing the burned carcasses of the animals into Watman's grave with great solemnity; the site was marked with a stake. Cook earlier had committed the same indiscretion of mixing two religious services. Almost as soon as he had arrived in the bay, he participated in a service in which he, a Christian, had allowed himself to be treated as a native deity. This behavior earned him the everlasting scorn of the New England missionaries who later arrived to convert the Hawaiian people. It set a bad example, they said, for the kind of work they were trying to do—separating error from true faith.

Less than a month after Watman died, Cook participated in mixed services a third time, though involuntarily. After he was killed by the Hawaiians, his body was dismembered: a few parts were buried at sea by his crew in a Church of England ritual; other parts were used in a Hawaiian service somewhere on the high bluffs of Pali-kapu-o-Keōua.

*   *   *

THE actions of many early Western travelers to the Pacific, like
Cook, are discredited or controversial now, or else their lives and
deaths are all but forgotten, like Watman's. Some, like William
Dampier or Abel Tasman, were privateers and buccaneers who
seized territory and searched for islands of gold and silver. Many
brought a culture of command and submission, willing to torture
and murder in order to proliferate their political and religious
convictions. Others, though, came because they were awed by the
miraculous plenitude of the natural world, and were willing to
undertake dangerous Pacific voyages for the chance to see and
record as many of the earth's plants and creatures as possible.[1]

The great majority of the early naturalists in the Pacific, especially in Cook's era, were amateur collectors and observers, not
what today we would call scientists. Nevertheless, they laid the
groundwork for natural science in the region, and the skilled writers among them wrote descriptions that are often of equal value to
the specimens they collected.

Neither their descriptions nor their collections were obtained
easily, however. Early voyagers into the South Seas entered an
uncharted region larger than all of Europe, Africa, Asia, and the
Atlantic Ocean combined. To sail there in crowded wooden ships
required enormous bravery and ambition. So large and unknown
was the region that before the 1760s few Westerners made trans-
Pacific voyages without becoming almost hopelessly lost—their
ships became wrecked on far-off reefs and their crews died of starvation or disease. Many of the best-equipped expeditions in this
period were simply never heard from again.

With the aid of new navigational technology and with the
first, primitive means to combat scurvy and other diseases, more
and more explorers ventured out in earnest to discover countries
hitherto unknown by Westerners. Part of the mission of these
explorers was, increasingly, to bring back as much of the undis-

covered natural world as possible, usually "curious objects" and specimens preserved in jars or dried between pages. They also brought back beautiful illustrations from life, however, and first-hand descriptions of plants, insects, fish, and mammals.

Captain Cook was such an observer. On his three voyages into the Pacific he scrupulously measured and described every phenomenon he encountered. Self-disciplined and precise, he knew very well his journals would be read by his superiors, then published for a public as eager to hear about natural history as about adventure. The account of his second voyage, into the Antarctic, sold out on the day after its publication in 1777; the account of his third and last voyage sold out in three days. At their best, the accounts are careful narratives by an explorer of the first rank, recording the human as well as the nonhuman world. Of his initial glimpse of the Hawaiians on Kaua'i he wrote, in admiration:

> They are vigorous, active, and most expert swimmers; leaving their canoes upon the most trifling occasion; diving under them, and swimming to others though at a great distance. It was very common to see women, with infants at the breast, when the surf was so high that they could not land in the canoes, leap overboard, and without endangering their little ones, swim to the shore, through a sea that looked dreadful.

The British public was not interested in Cook, though, but in the collections brought back by the expedition's gentlemen naturalists, Joseph Banks and Daniel Solander. They, not Cook, were given heroes' welcomes, audiences with the king, grand parties, and honorary doctorates from Oxford. For a long time, Cook's first voyage was known popularly as "Mr. Banks's Voyage" or "The Banks and Solander Expedition." The specimens Banks and Solander collected were extensive: 3,000 plants, about 1,300 of which had not previously been seen by Europeans; plus, according to Banks, "500 fish, as many Birds and insects Sea and Land innumerable." The collections were so extensive that Banks was never able—despite all his personal wealth and resources, and his long tenure as president of the Royal Society—to complete a full account of his findings, nor to have his journal published in his lifetime.

Even the most level-headed and scientific-minded of the early naturalist-explorers registered unrestrained wonder at what they saw. As Christians, these rational gentlemen scientists were encouraged by their faith, as well as by their time and culture, to see a theological design in nature and to respond to it with awe. The pioneer naturalist and taxonomist John Ray had admonished his readers in 1691, in *The Wisdom of God Manifested in the Works of Creation*:

> Some reproach methinks it is to learned men that there should be so many animals still in the world whose outward shape is not yet taken notice of or described, much less their way of generation, food, manners, uses, observed. If man ought to reflect upon his Creator the glory of all His works, then ought he to take notice of them all and not to think anything unworthy of his cognizance.

*   *   *

ABOUT seven thousand feet up the side of Mauna Loa, on the island of Hawai'i, I am in a small grove of māmane trees, hiking one of my favorite places and watching for i'iwi and other endemic birds. The i'iwi have flame-like crimson feathers and long, salmon-colored beaks that curve downward in a crescent fitting exactly the corolla of certain native lobelias. A local scarlet flower that resembles the bird's beak is called nukui'iwi (bill of the i'iwi). The early Hawaiians made brilliant red capes for their chiefs from the breast feathers of the little honeycreepers, and they gave such a cape to Captain Cook when he landed at Kealakekua. The Hawaiians also ate the i'iwi, and used their feathers to pay taxes and for barter. Unlike the still, silent creatures in the field guides, in life they are raucous, swift, and aggressive. Their powerful calls have been likened to everything from a police whistle to the creaking of a wheelbarrow, from gurgles and squawks to the sound of a child playing a rusty harmonica and the barking of a dog. More than one person has also found the call "sweet and plaintive." In any case, the wild i'iwi are nothing if not exuberant, singing while they feed and darting from flower to flower.

Here also is the Hawaiian 'elepaio, a small, reddish brown bird, curious and approachable. Each of several Hawaiian islands has its own subspecies. I used to hear them whistling deep in the forest, often hidden in the treetops, before I ever saw one. I searched without luck for them until one day my hiking companion brought an inexpensive bird caller along and screeched with it in the grove. The 'elepaio came from all over; they swooped into the trees above us, darted among the low branches, and finally landed next to us, nearly close enough to touch. Some mysteries you have to search for a long time to see, my friend said; others fly to you.

*　*　*

MANY of the early Pacific naturalists, though "gentleman travellers," endured formidable hardships while pursuing their scientific observations. Even Charles Darwin, on his first voyage into the Pacific, was more a "gentleman" than a scientist. Twenty-three years old when he joined the crew of the *Beagle* in 1831, he intended to become a parson when he returned to England. Nevertheless, his work was astonishing and precise. While the books and papers he wrote much later are models of scientific argument, the *Voyage of the Beagle* is a model of literary natural history at its best: a combination of close observation of nature, personal narrative, well-written travelogue, and speculation.

Darwin's lifetime coincided roughly with the decades of the first systematic exploration of the Pacific, and with the years that have been called the golden age of literary natural history, 1770 to 1880. Just prior to this time, anyone attempting to write seriously about nature was quickly discouraged by an awareness of how little was known about the natural world. In contrast, by 1880 so much new information had been collected that the subject was even more daunting and unmanageable; the natural world became the domain of specialists, to be studied in laboratories only, and not to be written about by amateurs.[2] Nonspecialists by 1880 were regarded by professional scientists as lowly, contemptible "species hunters."

What made the golden age of literary naturalists possible was a large rural audience of readers with a practical use for first-hand accounts of landscapes, plants, and creatures. Many readers were themselves amateur naturalists. They expected accuracy and hard information, but also something from the long-standing tradition that recognized elements of spirit, or at least wonder, in the natural world. Even academically trained scientists of the period were free to write about nature using the methods of the literary essay, and when individuals appeared whose skills for writing matched their skills of observation, it was more than fortunate. Their books educated an avid public and altered that public's understanding of the natural world.

THE early Pacific explorers often had a tremendous capacity to find, collect, and organize what they came upon, but they were not always skillful writers. Those that were gathered a particularly rare treasure—first-hand accounts and descriptions of flora, fauna, and ways of life that, in many cases, no longer exist. When their works were lost, or their lives cut short, we can't help feeling that human history and natural science both have suffered.

An example of such a loss involves the first professional botanist ever to journey into the Pacific, Philibert Commerson. Commerson sailed under the command of Louis-Antoine de Bougainville, on an expedition intended to demonstrate France's strong maritime presence in the Pacific; the journey was also designed, however, to be a serious scientific enterprise. On board were new devices for astronomy and navigation plus the men to operate them. In addition, Bougainville's ships were richly equipped to study natural history.

Commerson suffered violent seasickness from the very beginning of the voyage. But with the help of his young servant, Jean Baret, he managed a stormy crossing of the Atlantic. The overloaded *Étoile* and her sister ship, *Boudeuse*, were nearly sunk more than once reaching the coast of South America. The expedition rounded the Cape, anchored when it could, and eventually arrived in Tahiti, eighteen months after leaving France. At each landfall, Commerson and Baret combed the countryside for specimens of plants, fish, and mammals, and they sent back to Paris an enormous collection. Relatively few of the plants Commerson collected reached their destination, however. And some specimens that did arrive were largely ignored, such as the fish specimens that were stored in an attic unopened until well after Commerson's death. But among the flowers that survived the journey to Paris was a genus he named after his captain, the *Bougainvillea*.

Everywhere the ship anchored, Commerson and Baret gathered specimens with untiring zeal. Baret in particular, according to Bougainville, was seen "accompanying his master in all his expeditions amidst the snows, on the frozen peaks of the Straits of Magellan, carrying, even on those laborious excursions, provisions, arms, and bulky portfolios of specimens with a perseverance and a strength which gained for him from the naturalist the nick-name of his 'beast of burden.'"

Tahiti overwhelmed the naturalist with wonder, and when the expedition reached the islands he redoubled his efforts to botanize and explore. Tahiti had been discovered by Europeans less than a year before and almost everything was new to Commerson. Unfortunately for him, however, his personal life was about to get more attention from the captain and crew than his botanical discoveries. The crew had found Commerson to be high-strung and aloof, standoffish even with the officers. And they had developed suspicions about the naturalist's relationship to Baret—ever attentive, always with him, even sleeping in Commerson's cabin. Shortly after dropping anchor in Tahiti, these suspicions were finally confirmed. The first Tahitian men who boarded the ship circled Baret several times, then shouted gleefully, "It's a girl!"

The Tahitian men were delighted at their discovery of Baret's true gender. To her consternation, however, it was soon clear they expected from Baret the same favors the Tahitian women were granting to the French sailors. The captain, for his part, could only be philosophical about the deception. For a time, Baret—Jeanne, not Jean—tried to convince Bougainville that she was an orphan who had come aboard to escape her poverty, and that Commerson had had no idea of her gender and thus should not be blamed for smuggling a woman aboard a vessel of the French navy. There is no record that the captain or anyone else believed her.

After nine days in Tahiti, the expedition sailed on, a new relationship having been established between the crew and the naturalist couple. The captain's disapproving clerk noted dryly in his log, "I believe that this girl will be the first of her sex to have circumnavigated the globe." When the ship reached Mauritius, its Pacific journey all but over, Commerson and Baret decided to disembark rather than sail back to France. There, Commerson died five years later—without ever having told the fascinating tale of his travels.

FROM the 1780s to the 1810s, many gifted naturalists from Europe and the West explored the Hawaiian Islands. Among the most prominent in this period was Archibald Menzies, who sailed with George Vancouver in 1789, reaching Kealakekua Bay in 1792. Menzies, a tireless collector, climbed both Hualālai and Mauna Loa on this trip. The expedition returned to England with the first geographical survey of the Hawaiian Islands.

Several years earlier, Nathaniel Portlock and George Dixon, both of whom had sailed with Cook, had been the first Europeans to enter Kealakekua Bay following Cook's death there. Both published extensively on what they saw. Others from this period included Adelbert von Chamisso, who along with the expedition's artist, Louis Choris, published rich accounts of the natural history of the Hawaiian Islands.

These men were followed by Louis Claude de Saulces de Freycinet. Like Commerson, Freycinet smuggled a woman aboard his expedition—his twenty-two-year-old wife, Rose. Before this harrowing voyage, which included being shipwrecked in the Falkland Islands, she referred to herself as "the gay, the thoughtless madcap Rose." After Rose returned to France—perhaps the second woman to circumnavigate the globe—her friends remarked that she had become more subdued. Though she had kept detailed notes along the way, Rose's journal from the voyage was not published for more than 100 years, out of consideration for her husband's reputation.

The next important expedition to reach Hawai'i arrived in 1825. Naturalists Andrew Bloxam and James Macrae, along with the artist Robert Dampier, arrived aboard HMS *Blonde*, commanded by George Anson Lord Byron, grandson of "Foul Weather Jack" and cousin of the English poet. While ascending Mauna Loa, Macrae became the first European botanist to collect and describe the rare silversword plant, which he called "truly superb, and almost worth the journey of coming here to see it on purpose." On this expedition, at Hōnaunau village just south of Kealakekua, Byron was given permission by the local chiefs to carry away every artifact he wished to have from the heiau at the City of Refuge—which he and his crew promptly did. Bloxam then drew and wrote a description of the heiau which, just before it was stripped, was the last known in the islands to be still in perfect condition.[3]

*   *   *

IT GOES without saying that the natural history of Hawai'i was thoroughly and intimately a part of the lives and culture of the native Hawaiian people long before Western travelers reached their shores. Without a written language, Hawaiians communicated this knowledge through oral means—in chants, songs, prayers, rituals, and sayings—as well as in formal instruction. Where the subject was the natural world, the knowledge was sacred, just as words themselves were sacred and powerful; misuse of words could create havoc just as misuse of nature could unleash destruction and death. Moreover, the spoken Hawaiian language, replete with beauty and subtlety, was a sophisticated form of expression, and whatever was said of importance was firmly retained without loss in the memory of trained listeners. For these reasons alone, it's not surprising that traditional Hawaiian knowledge about the natural world, for the most part, was not immediately written down after the establishment of a standard Hawaiian alphabet in 1829. To a great degree, that knowledge continues to be unwritten.

Some Hawaiian scholars in the nineteenth century, however, did choose to record a portion of traditional island history and natural science. Among the first native Hawaiians who contributed significantly to written natural history was the educator and historian David Malo. Born near Kealakekua Bay in about 1795, Malo was a man of impressive intellect and character who managed to record—in a written language less than twenty years old—important aspects of his culture and of the natural history of Hawai'i, both of which were quickly being eroded by foreign contact. Malo's work was first published in English in 1839.

Another important Hawaiian writer of the period was John Papa 'I'i, who was born in 1800 on O'ahu. 'I'i was at various times an attendant to King Kamehameha, a representative to the Hawaiian legislature, and finally associate justice of the Supreme Court of Hawai'i. A selection of his articles written from 1866 to 1870 for

the Hawaiian newspaper *Ku'oko'a* (Independence) has been translated into English and has become a valuable contribution to the
written natural history of Hawai'i. Scholar and legislator Samuel
Kamakau, fifteen years younger than John 'I'i, wrote in the late
1860s. For his books and articles, Kamakau drew from his own
considerable learning and also wrote down the accounts that he
collected from older Hawaiians about a range of historical and
cultural subjects. The works of Samuel Kamakau, John Papa 'I'i,
and David Malo are the most important written resources from
the nineteenth century that we have, in English, for understanding traditional Hawaiian ways of regarding nature. Among contemporary Hawaiians, George S. Kanahele has contributed a great
deal through his book *Ku Kanaka: Stand Tall—A Search for Hawaiian Values.*

BY THE 1830s, Hawai'i did not seem as distant to many Westerners as it once had. Honolulu had become essentially an international harbor, according to one amazed traveler, populated by
foreigners from Asia, Europe, and America. But Hawai'i was still
not entirely safe for avid Western naturalists, and its natural history remained essentially unexplored.

Among those who attempted the exploration in this period
was David Douglas, who was the very embodiment of a century
of intrepid naturalists, and was perhaps the most adventurous of
them all. His life illustrates again the missing stories of many naturalists in this era who, like him, left only a fragmentary written
record of their lives. Douglas's early and untiring love of natural
history lead him from his birthplace in Scotland to a grisly death
on the slopes of Mauna Kea on the island of Hawai'i, mutilated
by a wild bull at the bottom of a pit dug to capture feral cattle.
How he came to die in this way is still a mystery.

Though he didn't like school, the young Douglas seems to
have loved the Scottish countryside and its creatures, owls and
hawks especially, which he kept as pets. At age eleven he was

removed from school and apprenticed to a gardener at the palace of the Earl of Mansfield. There, Douglas found his vocation and his element. So suited was he for this new life that, by the time he was eighteen, he had risen to the post of first gardener. At twenty-four he was appointed botanical collector to the Horticultural Society of London, now the Royal Horticultural Society. It was a remarkable ascent for a rural Scottish boy born of low means and with no connections. Even more remarkable, he would soon have more plants named in his honor, including the Douglas fir of North America, than perhaps anyone in the history of botany—though many of these would be renamed later.[4]

Douglas was the first botanist systematically to explore the Pacific Northwest and California, as well as many parts of the Hawaiian Islands. As a solitary explorer gathering seeds and new plant specimens, he was perhaps the most well traveled of a century of tough field naturalists known for unbelievable perseverance and bravery. He may have been the first nonnative to have climbed any of the Cascade Mountains, the Blue Mountains of Oregon, both Mauna Loa and Mauna Kea in Hawai'i, and the first to attempt Mount Hood. Douglas was sometimes seen traveling with a wild eagle in a cage on his pack and his pockets filled with reptiles, to whom he whistled tunes to keep them quiet. The dangers he faced alone, or with one or two Indian companions, are almost beyond belief—Indian wars, grizzly bears, descents over waterfalls, starvation, frostbite, drowning, infections, and disease are just the beginning of the list. Often subsisting on berries, ground rats, and wild game, or sucked into whirlpools or blinded by snow and sandstorms, he wrote of his worst adventures, "On such occasions I am very liable to become fretful."

THOSE who examined Douglas's corpse on Mauna Kea described it as "mangled in a shocking manner." The missionaries Joseph Goodrich and John Diell reported to the British Consul in

Honolulu, Richard Charlton, "There were ten to twelve gashes on the head, a large one over the left eye, another, rather deep, just above the left temple, and a deep one behind the right ear; the left cheek bone appeared to be broken, and also the ribs on the left side." In addition to being gored, Douglas had also been trampled badly by the wild bull that stood over his body at the bottom of the pit where he was found. After an investigation—and continuing suspicions that Douglas had been murdered and thrown into the pit by a former convict from the Botany Bay penal colony—Douglas's body was buried in the churchyard of Kawaiaha'o in Honolulu on August 4, 1834. The grave was unmarked except for a layer of bricks placed over it by Charlton, and soon its location was forgotten. Perhaps it lies somewhere now beneath the pavement of Punchbowl Street in downtown Honolulu. At the time of his death, Douglas was thirty-five years old.[5]

Douglas wrote very little for publication—only fourteen papers are listed in the Royal Horticultural Society's catalog, and only eight were published. But he did leave a rough journal, which was printed by the society in 1914 and reprinted in 1959. The North American portions were edited and republished in 1980. They are not literary, but between the clumsy lines and hastily written fragments is an exciting and harrowing story of adventure in the cause of natural science. In a letter describing his ascent of Mauna Loa, for example, he wrote:

> A sight of the volcano fills the mind with awe—a vast basin in a state of igneous fusion, throwing out lava in a thousand forms, from tortuous masses like large cables to the finest filamentous thread. Some places in large sheets, some in terrible rolled masses, like the breaking up of a large river with ice—of all colors and forms, showing the mighty agency ever existing in its immense laboratory. The strongest man is unstrung; the most courageous heart is daunted, in approaching this place.

*   *   *

BY THE time Douglas died, the American government had yet
to send any scientific explorations into the Pacific, despite successful voyages by other nations which had been costly both in
human life and in money. American ships and citizens visited the
Pacific in great numbers, but the visitors were mainly whalers,
traders, and missionaries. The respectability of American science
suffered from the absence of exploratory voyages. The maritime
prestige of America was in doubt as well, especially since several
challenges to U.S. naval authority in the region had gone unanswered. What was needed was a show of force—and there were
economic advantages still to be gained for whaling and trading if
new lands or new routes to older trading destinations could be
discovered.

Some years before Douglas's death, a retired army captain
from Cincinnati named John Cleves Symmes formulated the notion that the globe is not round at all but like a doughnut, with
big holes in the top and bottom. When birds migrate north, he
reasoned, they reach these holes and fly down inside the earth's
hollow center, where it's warm and pleasant and "stocked with
thrifty vegetables and animals."

Some people called it the "Holes in the Poles Theory"; others called it "Symmes's Holes." However fantastical the idea was,
it did not prevent lobbyists from trying to persuade Congress to
mount an expedition, at government expense, to prove Symmes's
theory. This revolutionary notion was going to show the world
the kind of scientific genius that nineteenth-century America could
produce.

By 1838, ten years after Congress had authorized the expedition (Symmes's believers had by then dwindled in number), the
first American government scientific adventure into the Pacific
and around the world was finally launched—the largest expedition mounted by any country up to that time.

The United States Exploring Expedition, commanded by Lt. Charles Wilkes, set out in 1838 with six ships. Commercial and pragmatic, the expedition nevertheless carried nine scientists—or "Scientifics," as they were called. Wilkes did not particularly like the "clam diggers and bug catchers" he took along, and during the expedition he managed to stir up animosity between the crew and the small band of Scientifics. Even after the expedition, Wilkes caused trouble over their collections.

Eventually, the botanical specimens that were gathered in Hawai'i and elsewhere were sorted and described by the preeminent American botanist of the time, Asa Gray, whose methods of handling the collection transformed natural science into an academic profession in America. The expedition's five-year voyage, ending in 1842, yielded more than fifty thousand plants, insects, and animals—which were described in twenty-four volumes and atlases.

American citizens avidly followed newspaper accounts of the progress of the expedition. Among those interested was a young naturalist who would alter literary natural history in America as much as Asa Gray would alter botany: Henry David Thoreau. Though Thoreau never traveled far from his native Massachusetts until just before his death, Hawai'i and the South Pacific became important metaphors for him.

In 1840, Thoreau was just out of Harvard and still wondering what he should do with his life. One of his classmates, Horatio Hale, was on the Wilkes voyage as an expert in linguistics; as an undergraduate, Hale had already published a pamphlet on the language of the Penobscot Indians. Thinking of the many scientists on the voyage who were young, like himself, Thoreau must have felt keenly his own position—at home, helping out with his family's pencil factory. Having already failed as a teacher, he seemed destined, in the opinion of many, to become no more than the village handyman.

But Thoreau had greater plans, even if they were still vague. That year, he began taking notes on the life of Sir Walter Raleigh and writing an essay titled "A Chapter on Bravery." In a youthful journal entry written on March 21, 1840, thinking of Hale and of the Pacific expedition, he mused on his own prospects: "By another spring I may be a mail-carrier in Peru, or a South African planter, or a Siberian exile, or a Greenland whaler, or a settler on the Columbia River, or a Canton merchant, or a soldier in Florida, or a mackerel-fisher off Cape Sable, or a Robinson Crusoe in the Pacific, or a silent navigator of any sea." Or, he added, "go on a South Sea exploring expedition."

Even at age twenty-three, however, Thoreau was already concluding that it was the spirit and imagination, not the globe, which were still uncharted and in need of strong-willed explorers.[6] "Our limbs, indeed, have room enough," he wrote, "but it is our souls that rust in a corner. Let us migrate interiorly without intermission, and pitch our tent each day nearer the western horizon."

Going toward the western horizon would come to represent for Thoreau the essence of renewal and expansiveness—but always in this metaphorical sense. Written some years later, the opening paragraphs of *Walden* turned to Hawai'i and the Pacific, where Thoreau remarks on the great geographical distance between himself and the "Sandwich Islander"—literally a distance in miles, but figuratively an expanse he felt neither he nor his New England readers needed to cross in order to experience life's essential phenomena. The reference is followed by a self-mocking comment on Thoreau's own style of adventurousness, "I have travelled a good deal in Concord."

The concluding chapter of *Walden*, culled from that same journal entry of March 21, 1840, returns to a concern with the Pacific. *Walden* thus is framed by references to the far western horizon, reaching specifically to Hawai'i but then beyond to the farthest shore imaginable—a shore that can never be explored in literal ships. In this final chapter, Thoreau cites the Pacific expedition as an example of how much easier—and how much more readily undertaken—are voyages to explore the exterior world than those into our own interiors. His imperative to the reader is to "be a Columbus to whole new continents and worlds within you, opening new channels, not of trade, but of thought." Then he adds, referring to the Wilkes voyage,

> What was the meaning of the South-Sea Exploring Expedition, with all its parade and expense, but an indirect recognition of the fact, that there are continents and seas in the moral world, to which every man is an isthmus or an inlet, yet unexplored by him, but that it is easier to sail many thousands of miles through cold and storm and cannibals, in a government ship, with five hundred men and boys to assist one, than it is to explore the private sea, the Atlantic and Pacific Ocean of one's being alone.

Although Thoreau wrote in these kinds of metaphors, he was simultaneously a precise and dedicated field naturalist. He spent every hour possible taking notes in the forests and fields, climbing mountains, rafting and hiking in all seasons, often at night, often in the worst weather. This life in the field probably contributed greatly to Thoreau's early death, at age forty-four, from influenza and tuberculosis.

Despite his early demise, however, Thoreau's contribution to natural history was significant. One of his last pieces of writing, "The Succession of Forest Trees," inspired by Darwin's *The Origin of Species*, was part of a longer projected work to be called *The Dispersion of Seeds*. During his life, Thoreau was elected a corresponding member of the Boston Society of Natural History and was appointed to Harvard's Committee for Examination in Natural History. At the time of his death, he was considered by most people to be, principally, a natural historian. Thoreau knew his own region so well that the children, it was said, "thought Mr.

Thoreau had made Concord." They were certain that "if anything happened in the deep woods which only came about once
in a hundred years, Henry Thoreau would be sure to be on the
spot at the time and know the whole story."

*   *   *

I REMEMBER hiking some years ago up Mauna Loa in search
of a small white flower that grows above seven thousand feet on
the slopes there. Called hinahina, a common Hawaiian name for
a number of local species, it has a five-petalled corolla and silvery
leaves. Having never seen this particular variety in the wild on the
island of Hawai'i, I looked intently for it as I hiked off the trail in
the cold, subalpine air, across old, red lava laced with straggling
kūkae-nēnē, 'a'ali'i, and pūkiawe. At last I spotted a single white
blossom and called to my companion. We hurried over and looked
intently at the flower for a long time, happy to have come upon
what to us was a small but rare find. At last we stood up, stretched
our legs, and looked around. To our surprise, we were standing in
a whole field of hinahina. Dumbfounded and embarrassed, we
went back to the trail; hinahina blossoms were everywhere, as if
suddenly they had become the most common flower on the mountain.

   Thoreau once wrote that objects are concealed from our
vision not so much because they are out of range, but because
they have never yet been fully in our eye and in our mind. "To see
the scarlet oak," he wrote, "the scarlet oak must, in a sense, be in
your eye when you go forth. We cannot see anything until we are
possessed with the idea of it, and then we can hardly see anything else."

   The early naturalists in the Pacific traveled at great risk to
see and collect the diverse wonders of the uncharted vastness.
Some brought back the very things they had expected to find,
"curiosities"—and little else. Others brought back simply every-

thing of a category that they could gather. The task for decades afterward—for those who sorted through the huge collections, and for those who ventured into the Pacific to find more—was to understand the diversity of life that lay before them. Though the plants and animals have today been given names and lie under glass in museums or are pressed in specimen books, a great many of the things that came into their possession have still not been truly seen or understood, and many have vanished from the wild.

How different are we from those early travelers? How little and how much do we really know about the natural world, not only about what is exotic and uncatalogued, but about what is local and underfoot? If nature were truly in our eyes and imaginations, as Thoreau suggests, we would finally know that we are possessed *by it,* instead of the other way around. We would comprehend the tragedy and error in the worldwide holocaust of species extinction that has been with us for decades, particularly in Hawai'i.

Literary natural history, at its best, attempts to awaken us: to "put nature in our eyes," so that, for the first time, we see it whole and all at once. At the same time, it attempts to have us be possessed by each of the parts—by even the smallest entities and creatures, and by their integrity and relation to the whole. Writing of this sort prepares the reader's imagination to see those plants, animals, and phenomena that are often impossible for most people to experience firsthand—those things that seem remote, exotic, and of no apparent personal value to us. Most amazingly, such writing prepares our eyes to see even those plants and creatures that are nearby, the ones underfoot, the ones we thought we knew.

Through some combination of all our cognitive resources—metaphor and cold measurement, poetry and taxonomy—through literary natural history, in short, we begin to understand the natural world perhaps for the first time, as both a part of it and self-consciously outside of it. This way of seeing is the revelation in all great nature writing: the revelation that natural history, in its fullest sense, is also human history, that the parts and the whole are not separable.

NOTES

1. For an overview of Pacific voyagers I have relied on many sources, but particularly on *The Explorers of the Pacific* by Geoffrey Badger, *The Exploration of the Pacific* by J. C. Beaglehole, and *French Explorers in the Pacific* by John Dunmore; for specific expeditions and persons I have relied especially on *The Flowering of the Pacific* by Brian Adams, *The Naturalists in Britain: A Social History* by David Elliston Allen, *Douglas of the Fir: A Biography of David Douglas* by A. G. Harvey, and *Magnificent Voyagers: The U.S. Exploring Expedition, 1838–1842* edited by Herman J. Viola and Carolyn Margolis.

2. See E. D. H. Johnson's *The Poetry of Earth.* Also, *The Golden Age of Plant Hunters* by Kenneth Lemmon and *Natural History and the American Mind* by William Martin Smallwood. More recent works include *A Species of Eternity* by Joseph Kastner, *Speaking for Nature* by Paul Brooks, and *Nature Writing and America* by Peter A. Fritzell.

3. E. Alison Kay has written an overview of the contributions to Hawaiian natural history of various explorers, residents, missionaries and scientists, in *A Natural History of the Hawaiian Islands: Selected Readings.*

4. In Hawai'i, the botanical names for pūkiawe (*Cyathodes douglasii* and *Styphelia douglasii,* now *S. tameiameiae*), hala (*Pandanus douglasii,* now *P. tectorius*), silversword (*Argyrophyton douglasii,* now *Argyroxiphium sandwicense*), and the pala fern (*Marattia douglasii*) all have included Douglas's name in tribute.

5. See Jean Greenwell, "Kaluakauka Revisited: The Death of David Douglas in Hawaii," *The Hawaii Journal of History* 22 (1988): 147–69.

6. Thoreau's first published book, appropriately, was about an exploration—but of a local waterway not an exotic one, down which he and his brother had leisurely floated in 1839. The title, *A Week on the Concord and Merrimack Rivers,* was surely meant to delight Thoreau's sense of self-mocking humor, so much did its modesty contrast with the titles of such popular and ambitious books of the day as *Adventures on the Columbia River* or *Observations and Reflections Made in the Course of a Journey through Rome, Italy, and Germany.*

ISLANDS FROM THE BLUE ABYSS

THE ISLANDS OF LIFE

GAVAN DAWS

Volcanic Origins

The only way to get to know a volcano, Thomas Jaggar believed, is to live with it.

He built his home on stilts, wedged into a crack in an immensity of dark volcanic rock on the southeast flank of the island of Hawai'i—latitude 19 degrees 5 minutes 47 seconds N, longitude 155 degrees 15 minutes 37 seconds W—at an altitude of four thousand feet, precisely so that he could go to bed at night and wake in the morning snug within the rim of the most continuously active volcano of the world.

After breakfast he would stride through the mountain mists to the cliff face of the crater of Kīlauea and clamber two hundred feet down a rope ladder, to stand with nothing between him and the firepit Halemaʻumaʻu. Here he was Thomas Augustus Jaggar, Jr., a human being of the early twentieth century, with his blood heat set by evolution at 98.6 degrees Fahrenheit, wearing the necktie of a serious volcano scientist, measuring the level of a perpetual lava lake that simmered and bubbled and fumed in his eyes.

Molten lava, pushing right up at him out of the earth's magma, eighteen hundred degrees and more at the surface. Primordial heat, searing the bare skin of his unbearded, unguarded face.

Jaggar loved to teeter on the very edge of personal physical scorching. He lived and breathed volcanoes. He sniffed his breakfast egg with its faint sulfurous smell and wondered if the egg of all life might be volcanic in origin, if evolution went back beyond the living embryo to the chemistry of volcanoes—sulfur, hydrogen, oxygen, carbon dioxide, ingredients of the egg and ingredients of the volcano.

He smelled out volcanoes wherever they were on earth. At Bogoslof in the Aleutians he saw hot lava tumbling into the ocean, the beaches aroar with sea lions, the steaming air above screaming with birds, life and deadly volcanism flourishing together. At St. Pierre in Martinique, molasses and Caribbean rum flowed like lava in the streets after Mount Pelée laid waste to the town in 1902, and Jaggar saw human beings dead by the hundreds, close up, a baby dead in an iron cradle, a big fellow dead on his back in a deep baker's oven—the flesh shriveled and drawn away from his joints by the heat—not of baking but of volcanism. In Japan he had himself rowed out in a little skiff to look down over a hot lava tongue licking the sea floor below. He trailed a thermometer in the boiling water. All about him floated dead fish, belly up, boiled. If the tiny boat should capsize, Jaggar—the pre-eminent American volcano scientist of his day, with three degrees from Harvard and a worldwide reputation, geology professor to the young Franklin Delano Roosevelt—would boil. He loved every moment of it.

In the furious world of volcanic eruptions Kīlauea was as gentle and generous as a volcano could be, active almost perpetually, giving out especially liquid lavas that often fountained spectacularly, making for wonderful viewing, but not normally going off with a deadly bang. People most times ran toward Kīlauea to watch, rather than away for their lives. And when the volcano was quiet tourists could saunter down into Halemaʻumaʻu with an egg in a pan and fry it on moving lava, and write home about this strange, entertaining breakfast, being sure before mailing their postal card to scorch its edges a toasty Halemaʻumaʻu brown.

Everything that made Kīlauea an ideal tourist attraction made it ideal for continuous scientific study—Jaggar's life passion. Early in the twentieth century, when he was climbing to the world peaks of his profession, only one permanent volcano observatory existed on the face of the earth, at Vesuvius. Jaggar argued that the United States should have its own observatory, and for the sake of the best science it should be located at Kīlauea. There, as nowhere else in the world, a volcano could be studied in all its phases—before, during, and after eruptions. And the resident observer—of course—should be no one but Thomas Jaggar. Jaggar was the primordial force behind the Hawaiian Volcano Observatory. He started work in 1912, in a little seismometer vault dug out of ash and pumice, rimside, five minutes from his house. He observed nonstop. He was forever designing new monitoring instruments (though none of them ever matched the fine tuning of his collie dog, Teddy, a domesticated sensing device who always knew before anyone else when Kīlauea was preparing to perform). In good times Jaggar could readily raise research money, public and private. In bad times he raised pigs to meet the payroll. Good times and bad, he published scientific papers continuously, like an intellectual lava flow from Kīlauea, an outwelling that pushed the world science of volcanology ever forward into the twentieth century.

Jaggar had a wife named Isabel. On his endless expeditions across newly cooled volcanic rock she looked after the food. She took dictation for his close-up eyewitness reports of eruptions. Thomas died before Isabel. She had his body cremated, respectably committed to controlled flame, and later, when she felt the

moment was right for her own private ceremony, she secretly
scattered his ashes in a greater fire—the perpetual fire of Jaggar's
life, Halemaʻumaʻu at Kīlauea.

ALWAYS think in millions of years, said Jaggar, and everything
is in motion to one who senses slow motion. Think of the Hawaiian archipelago in million-year motion.

The islands, all of them volcanic, were formed in turn by
upwellings from an eruptive hot spot below the ocean floor. Then
in turn they were rafted away with the slow, slow movement of
the huge Pacific Plate over the earth's mantle, seventy million
years of geological time travel, north and west across the Tropic of
Cancer, worn by wind and rain, sinking gradually under their
own weight as they went, oldest first, back beneath the surface of
the sea.

Today there are eight major islands and more than 120 smaller
islands, pinnacles, reefs, and shoals. The oldest and farthest to the
north and west have disappeared below the sea and are now
underwater seamounts. Kure and Midway are atolls with coral
reefs and highest points of no more than a few score feet. More
than fifteen hundred miles south and east of Kure, offshore of the
island of Hawaiʻi, a new island is forming. Still a half mile and
several thousand years of time yet below the ocean surface, it
already has a name: Lōʻihi.

Most recently emerged of the main islands is Hawaiʻi, often
called the Big Island. Shaped by the five volcanoes, it shows the
huge creative force of volcanism. Mauna Loa, still active, rises
more than 29,000 feet from the ocean floor, 13,677 feet from sea
level to summit. It is 10,000 cubic miles in bulk, meaning it is the
biggest single volcanic structure on earth—a hundred times bigger than Shasta or Fujiyama, indeed the biggest such feature in
the solar system anywhere between the sun and the planet Mars.

*   *   *

THE Hawaiian chain exists in the most profound oceanic isolation on the face of the globe, more than two thousand miles from the closest continental land mass.

Life had to come from far away, blowing in on the winds, floating in on ocean currents, rafting in on logs swept from the continents, touching down with migratory birds on their transoceanic flights.

In this sterile island world of volcanic rock and salt spray, plants established themselves only at the rate of perhaps one species in each hundred thousand years. No amphibian or land reptile successfully crossed the ocean to Hawai'i. No oak, no pine, no sequoia. No big game animal came from America or Asia, nor any beast of burden. In seventy million years only two mammals settled in: one for land, a hoary bat, solitary, nocturnal, reddish-gray and weighing less than an ounce; and one for sea, a monk seal of primitive habits.

The volcanic shapes of the islands were sculpted by wind and weather, and a varied physical foundation was laid down upon which an enormous range of life forms developed. A mountain peak on Kaua'i, Wai'ale'ale, is the wettest spot on earth (at least the wettest where anyone has maintained a rain gauge). Other, higher summits—Haleakalā on Maui, Mauna Kea and Mauna Loa on the Big Island—are alpine stone deserts. Within a few miles of each other on any of the main islands there may be tropical rain forest, lowlying drylands, sunstruck coastal dunes, and lightless lava tubes.

In these extravagantly varied habitats immigrant species adapted, and new species evolved, life forms never before seen on earth. One kind of drosophilid fly became eight hundred. Three hundred fifty kinds of immigrant insects evolved into over ten thousand native Hawaiian species. Twenty species of land snails became a thousand. Two hundred fifty flowering plants became eighteen hundred. The silversword colonized from bog to cinder desert. The 'ōhi'a lehua found ways to live almost everywhere, from new lava to ancient bog, and in the process took on an abundance of different forms. And the native Hawaiian honeycreepers changed so much as they adapted to the wide range of island habitats that they would have astonished Charles Darwin.

In the biological history of Hawai'i these are the big, sweeping developments, landmarks of worldwide significance. Other native creatures developed more modestly, but no less remarkably. Crickets by the shore, so adapted to salt spray that away from it they cannot survive. In the rain forest, carnivorous green caterpillars. At the extreme freezing height of a stone desert summit, the wēkiu bug, so finely adapted to cold that if you take it in your hand—blood heat 98.6 degrees Fahrenheit—its proteins cook.

All of this development and change occurred over millions of years. Plants and animals between them created soil, soil trapped moisture, moisture allowed more and more growth, until forests appeared which influenced climate. In all the different ecological zones of Hawai'i, particular groups of interrelated species clustered together. These groups developed into something that was more than the sum of their parts. They were interrelated, interactive, interdependent, promoting each other's survival. They became, in other words, natural communities.

And these elegant associations became numerous. In less than sixty-five hundred square miles of land mass, there can be identified more than one hundred fifty kinds of natural communities, each community a small island of life harbored within the larger islands of life that are the Hawaiian Islands.

Coasts & Sea Cliffs

One of the largest seabird colonies in the tropical world, for diversity and sheer numbers, is in the Hawaiian Islands.

During quiet times there you might not quite register this,

you might be aware of nothing more than the music of waves on coral sand and the sound of the albatrosses clashing their beaks as they dance, and you might well doze off.

Your eyes would be opened by the sooty terns. Suddenly one day they appear, by the scores of thousands, darkening the sky. Then they are on the ground, laying their eggs. After that, every day at dawn, they all go up in the air at once making a tremendous racket. No need for a morning alarm, just lie there and the sooty terns will go off. And at dusk off they go again.

The Hawaiian monk seal ignores this. It lolls all day on the beach—looking for shade, settling into moist sand, flippering to the water to cool off, shifting up the dunes at night to sleep out of reach of the waves. That is its routine, for months at a time.

The female Hawaiian green sea turtle has her own precise interest in sand temperature. She comes ashore in the dark of night, silently, to lay her eggs, setting them in the sand at a depth where heat and moisture are exactly right for hatching. By morning when the tern alarm goes off she has departed, leaving only her flipper tracks above the tide mark.

All this on a single Hawaiian island. But not within hundreds of miles of urbanized Honolulu. The green turtle egg does not tolerate human presence; just the heedless thump of five-toed feet on sand above can abort a hatching below. The monk seal wants to breed in privacy away from humans. And the sooty tern, the albatross, and the fourteen other breeding species of that immense seabird colony—all congregate on a tiny raised coral atoll, Laysan, highest point perhaps forty feet, latitude 25 degrees 42 minutes 41 seconds N, longitude 171 degrees 44 minutes 06 seconds W, part of the state of Hawai'i, but uninhabited and more than eight hundred sea miles northwest of Honolulu.

THE first men on Laysan in the nineteenth and early twentieth centuries were sealers, guano diggers, feather collectors—all takers. And then, with the idea of contributing, a man from Honolulu introduced rabbits. What he contributed was devastation. Within twenty years the rabbits ate virtually everything green on Laysan all the way down to the nubs, turning the atoll into a sand desert, just four of the twenty-five plant species surviving in small numbers and several bird species pushed to extinction by having their habitat gnawed out from under them.

A scientific expedition came in 1923 to get rid of the rabbits. One day the shooters spotted three birds, Laysan honeycreepers. The next day a sand storm blew up, gale force, and stung and buffeted all three birds to death—the last of their kind on earth, the only songbirds in the documented history of the world to go extinct within sight and sound of humankind, with the time of the end recorded to the hour.

Over the next few years the Laysan teal also came to the very brink of extinction. In all the world these birds lived only on Laysan, around a small lagoon, no more than a couple of square miles of habitat. They stepped among beach morning glory and sedge, puddled about potholes feeding on insects, and were never sufficiently shrewd about evading humans. The guano diggers slaughtered them, because they were there. By the 1920s, after those introduced rabbits had done their worst to Laysan's green growing things, there were many more teal skinned and stuffed in the world's museums than live ones left around their home lagoon. In 1930 a man from Honolulu found a last individual, a female fluttering about, perhaps decoying him away from her nest. He found the nest with its clutch of white eggs—and every last shell was punctured by the beak of a raiding curlew.

Yet the teal of Laysan survived. How? Well, by biological providence the female had enough semen in her oviduct to fertilize a second clutch of eggs. At least that is the story, and of course it is a wonderful tale of biological brinkmanship.

Did this small reproductive miracle actually occur? Or did the man from Honolulu simply fail to spot the male of the pair?

Or was there another female hiding silent and motionless on her nest in the bunch grass? The true answer has blown away on the Laysan wind.

At any rate, after the last rabbits were killed the island began greening again, bird habitat came back, and within another twenty years—happy ending—the teal was on its way to recovery.

These days Laysan is legally protected from unthinking intrusion by twentieth-century human beings. It is once more a tiny window opening upon the biodiversity of the past. The window is small and distant, but through it can be glimpsed an island of life.

ON ALL the eight Hawaiian Islands, where a million twentieth-century human beings live, there is no place like Laysan. Yet one spot that does offer a sense of what Hawaiian strand and coast were like before the time of our species is a stretch of sand dunes called Moʻomomi on the island of Molokaʻi.

Moʻomomi remains remote, uninhabited, a wild place. Walking there among great onshore riffles of wind-swept sand, you can easily find spots where the dunes have lithified—turned to sandy stone. And here erosion by wind and wave may bring to the present-day surface evidence of endemic native life forms long dead: shells of land snails, fossil bones of birds, an eagle, a giant flightless goose, a thick-billed crow, a long-legged, bird-eating owl.

Moʻomomi gives off a strong sense of uninterrupted connection with the old, the ancient, the slow motion of evolutionary time moving within the yet slower motion of geological time. No human beings live there. And that is precisely why, every so often, coming out of the northwest islands, there will appear at Moʻomomi a monk seal, looking to do nothing; or a female Hawaiian green sea turtle, to dig a perfectly conceived hole in the sand and lay her eggs by night; or a Laysan albatross, to cruise on the salty winds that blow forever over the dunes.

*   *   *

AMONG the coasts of the main islands, Moʻomomi represents extremity—the last strand, so to speak. Another kind of Hawaiian coastal extremity is found on northerly shores; soaring sea cliffs of fluted wet basalt, those of Molokaʻi rising as high as three thousand feet—the highest in the world.

And alive on a stark cliff face you may spot a single human being, at the end of a hundred feet of knotted one-half-inch nylon rope, hanging in the wind with a two-thousand-foot fall to the rocks below. This is Steve Perlman, doing extreme work, pollinating the rare, disappearing, endemic Hawaiian plant *Brighamia* with a paint brush.

In the old days forests grew right to the cliff edge, and perhaps the natural pollinator of *Brighamia*—a honeycreeper, a large moth, no one really knows—would come out of the forest and flutter down the wind to find its flower of choice. Now in many places the forests do not reach the cliffs, and anyway the pollinators are rare in the forests. So, late in the twentieth century, Steve Perlman has taken it upon himself to do their work.

From a kayak offshore he scans the cliffs through binoculars. He sights *Brighamia*, never more than a small population, perhaps only a single individual: he is willing to work one on one. He comes in on the surf to tackle the cliff climb, with altimeter, cutting knife, Japanese split-toed shoes that fit well to the rocks, recording notebook and pencil, seed-collecting bag, a single sandwich, two bottles of water for the thirstiness of the day's labor, a flashlight against having to stay late at work, and two lengths of rope, one to reach the *Brighamia* he has sighted, the other in case he sees something else exciting when he gets there— all the way out on the cliff face he would feel foolish coming up twenty feet short.

With his brush he collects pollen from the throat of the *Brighamia*, paints the stigma, and goes roping from plant to plant, cross-pollinating. Months later he returns, the same laborious roping way, to collect the seeds that have filled their capsules to bursting. Back in civilization he puts the seeds into cultivation, preserving *Brighamia* against a possible time in the future when wild habitat might be restored for them and their natural pollinator. A long-term holding operation. For other rare and endangered Hawaiian plants he does the same, wherever he finds them, up high in a drenched Hawaiian bog or hundreds of feet down some dryland gulch. In the islands of life this individual man has found his particular niche. The brush he uses is a regular painter's tool of trade, and he is an artist, a solo virtuoso of extreme habitat, one of a kind, *Homo sapiens, Explorator perlmanii maximus hawaiiensis*, willing to go to the extreme edge to bring native Hawaiian plants back from the brink.

Drylands

In the hot Hawaiian summer of 1854 the Frenchman Jules Remy went on an excursion to the northern and western parts of the island of Moloka'i, canoeing along the coasts past the valley of Pelekunu to the peninsula of Kalaupapa, climbing the cliff trail to Ho'olehua, taking a horse to Mo'omomi, to the beach at Kepuhi, then making his way back over the low West Moloka'i summit of Pu'u Nānā and down again to the south coast of Kaunakakai.

Remy did not enjoy himself much. He had to share his canoe with a seasick man, and ashore the man continued landsick. At Mo'omomi the wind blew stinging sand in Remy's eyes, and he did not venture in among the wild dunes. At Kepuhi there was only brackish water to drink and either this or something he ate upset his stomach, so that on the ride back across the island to Kaunakakai, through arid, dusty, uninviting territory, he felt poisoned all the way. He did not give the Moloka'i drylands high marks for picturesqueness.

Scientific value, though, was something else again. Remy was a naturalist, and on Molokaʻi, poisoned stomach or no, he botanized nonstop, gathering Hawaiian plant specimens, rejoicing when he found something rare, and noting every name in botanist's Latin: *Lobelia, Scaevola, Lysimachia, Euphorbia, Vaccinium, Phyllanthus, Cassytha, Sesbania, Dodonaea, Myoporum, Gnaphalium, Chenopodium, Lepidium....*

Traveling on horseback across Hawaiian terrain in mid-nineteenth century, Remy was well into the era of introduced livestock in the islands. He was able to fill his specimen bags and his notebooks and his naturalist's mind to overflowing. But in fact the dry landscape through which he rode was emptying out of native plant species almost literally beneath his horse's feet.

Remy's ride took him only a few days, no time at all in the annals of science. But by the chances of history he became the first Western scientist to do any systematic botanizing in the Molokaʻi drylands. And simultaneously he was the last to see with a scientist's eye any significant stand of dryland forest on West Molokaʻi.

Even at that, much of the forest was already gone before he got there. To reconstruct in his mind anything like a whole dryland natural community on Molokaʻi, Remy had to think back to forested land that he had seen earlier in his Hawaiian travels at Kaupō Gap on East Maui.

Later observers had to do even more extensive mental reconstruction, because on all the main islands ever more of the drylands were being transformed from their original condition. As late as 1860, the people of Kula on Maui got their water for drinking and farming from fog drip. But the forests of leeward Haleakalā were being cleared, and Kula became a much drier place. Offshore of Maui, the small island of Kahoʻolawe once produced its own cloud cover. But its forests were cleared and came to be seriously over-grazed by cattle and goats, wind and rain tore at exposed soil, and the whole island went virtually treeless, parched and barren.

These days, more than a century and a quarter after Remy's ride, the range of the drylands has been irreversibly diminished. For one thing, scores of thousands of acres have been cleared and planted in sugar cane and pineapple. Recovering an overall idea of the drylands is like the demanding task of reconstructing some vanished culture from the sparse evidence of pottery shards or slivers of fossil bone.

Still, a sharp observing eye can do a lot. Start on the leeward side of an island, always drier than the windward side, and at low altitudes very dry indeed. Look inland to the mountains and it may be raining high up, but not much of the rain gets this far down the leeward slopes. Summer is the driest time of all. Native annuals go brown and die, trees and shrubs jettison their leaves to save water, and plants that do keep their leaves stop growing to wait out the dry spell.

Then come back after the first rains of winter, when the drylands do get watered, and the color is green. Shrubs and trees quickly leaf out. Many plants are blooming. In Hawai'i native birds are often brighter than native blossoms, but up close all kinds of flowers can be seen.

Lift up your eyes to higher ground, often with more rock than soil showing, sparsely vegetated, and there on weathered lava flows or bouldery talus slopes you may see remaining pockets of native Hawaiian dry forest, especially where twists and turns in the terrain produce a northern exposure.

Higher again you can see mesic forest, moister, with a much greater variety of tree species and a denser, more tangled understory. Here you may pick out the distinctive stands of one of the classic native Hawaiian trees, the koa, with its gray-green rounded crown and its limbs sometimes covered with lichens subsisting off fog-borne moisture. And often enough, in among the trees, there

will be a population of native Hawaiian birds, red and green
honeycreepers and the fly-catching ʻelepaio.

Every piece filled in on the jigsaw puzzle of your mind shows
more and more of the drylands' past as one of former riches of
native plant and animal species. No single species of tree was
dominant in most dryland forests; there were diverse combina-
tions. More species of native birds used to exist in dry forest
than are found today in upland rain forests. For Hawaiian
biodiversity, acre for acre, these dry forests and shrublands offered
the most.

Finally, if you are willing to go the extra distance, walk the
extra mile, you can still see stretches of dryland much as they
once were; for example, in the upper reaches of the Waiʻanae
Mountains on Oʻahu, or on Lānaʻi, at Kānepuʻu, where an early
ranch manager put up fences against roaming cattle, salvaging a
unique forest of native persimmon, lama; and olive, olopua; spiced
with the rare Hawaiian gardenia, nāʻū. And on steep, rugged slopes
at Puʻu Kalī above Kīhei in Central Maui, the deciduous wiliwili
tree still flourishes in quantity, its swollen trunk decorated with
bright orange native lichen, its branches bursting forth in season
with light yellow or salmon blossoms.

In such places you can get some sense of what dry forests
meant in the biological history of the islands. They were the
hardy communities of trees and plants that extended organic life
to sterile leeward slopes. They made their gains slowly and with
effort, over long, long periods of time. Their gains made possible
more gains—soil built up, moisture retained, more seeds germinating, more trees growing, more moisture attracted—more trans-
formation of Hawaiian volcanic rock into islands of life.

ONE of the great recognized resources of the drylands in the
early nineteenth century was sandalwood. By the time of Jules
Remy's ride the big stands were just about all gone, cropped out

in only a few decades, to be sold on the Chinese market at Canton—at least the most highly fragrant species, the most commercially desirable. But sandalwood is rugged, a survivor, and several species held on, even on the island of O'ahu where the trade was most hectic. Today you can walk trails not all that far from Honolulu and find sandalwood growing sturdily.

Still tucked away in remote parts of the drylands are other potential resources for the twentieth and twenty-first centuries. Ma'o shrubland is found on dry red weathered clay, in places where it rains as little as ten to twenty inches a year. Ma'o is a shrub that grows two to six feet high, bringing forth bright yellow blossoms after the seasonal rains. It is a form of cotton, in the same genus as American commercial cotton. Ma'o by itself would not make a commercial crop. Its fibers are too short. But just because it evolved in a singular way, remote from the mainland, it has a striking usefulness to the commercial cotton industry, only recently realized.

The leaves of mainland long-fiber cotton exude a sweet nectar that attracts insects, and there are ants that "farm" these insects for the honeydew they produce. For cotton growers these infestations mean insect-ravaged plants, more use of pesticides, and higher costs. The Hawaiian ma'o developed in mid-Pacific isolation without ants and their associated insects, and its leaves produce no nectar. Put the attributes of the commercially desirable, long-fibered mainland cotton together with those of ma'o, which does not attract ants and other insects, and the combination amounts to a net gain for the industry. A hybrid has been developed and is available to mainland growers looking to cut down the use of pesticides and the costs that go with it.

Ma'o is found nowhere else in the world but Hawai'i. You can see it in any number of places, though mostly only as a scattering of plants among congregations of weeds. But here and there, beyond the point where dusty roads give out, or by the shores of remote bays like Keōmuku on Lānaʻi, maʻo grows in abundance, in association with native plants such as pili grass, ʻilima, and the nehe, a Hawaiian relative of the daisy.

Unnoticed or disregarded, maʻo would go the way of any number of other dryland plants, to endangerment, to extinction. Attended to and studied in all its Hawaiian particularity, maʻo carries a message, and the message is that maintaining diversity of species is by no means merely an exercise in the biology of nostalgia, but part of the ongoing life of the islands in their fruitful connections with the rest of the world.

Streams & Wetlands

If you ever managed to clamber to the very top of a mountain called Kaunuohua behind Pelekunu Valley on the north coast of Molokaʻi—and few human beings have done this—you would have scrambled up four thousand five hundred feet of the steepest imaginable slopes, and you would need a drink of water, badly.

If you knew where to look you would find a little natural hollow scooped out of the solid rock, no bigger than the hollow of a pair of hands, and in the hollow you would find cool, clear water. You would not be able to lower your face close enough to drink. The hollow is too small for that. But you could take the hollow stem of an uluhe fern and use it for a drinking straw. You could drink all you wanted, and so could your companions, and so could any who came after you, and you would never exhaust the water. The little secret flow is endlessly replenished from within the rock. The water of life.

Refreshed, you could stand and look down into Pelekunu, and there are very few sights in the world to match the vision of this great, green dreaming valley below you, with its silver stream coursing to a blue ocean.

The main islands of Hawaiʻi between them used to have 365

perennial streams, meaning that every day for a year you could have gone rockhopping along a different watercourse, each with the characteristic Hawaiian stream profile of riffles, rapids, falls, and plunge pools, always with the hypnotic sound of cascading water in your ears, up to the headwaters where ferns and mosses and lichens adorn the rock faces and everything is soaking wet, including you.

On the principle of leaving the best till last, Pelekunu stream and its tributaries in Pelekunu Valley might well qualify for the 365th day.

Pelekunu Stream is short, like all Hawaiian streams (the longest is the Wailuku River, at Hilo on the island of Hawai'i, only eighteen miles). And nearly all Hawaiian streams are prone to flash floods. You might be taking your ease in a delightful pool, doing nothing much, like a monk seal of humanity, in bright sunshine with no sign of rain anywhere that you can see, and you might or might not become gradually aware of leaves or flowers or the fruit of the mountain apple floating by you, something that was not happening before. Next thing, the water goes turbid and rises a foot, two feet, three, though the musical sound of the stream has seemingly not changed. Then suddenly out of nowhere comes a shocking flood, with a rush and a roar, huge, a colossal natural bulldozer mass-moving earth by water power, fierce enough to pick up not just little rocks but giant boulders and hurl them down, raking them over the stream bottom and flinging them against the stream walls, with a crashing roar that can be heard for miles, rolling thunder.

Pelekunu subjects you to all this at ultimate levels of intensity. If you work back into the high parts the stream channels become very narrow, the going gets hazardous, the valley walls rise a thousand feet above you, and there is evidence of landslides. Even in quiet times there is almost constant dribble of small rocks randomly falling. In a big storm big rocks will shear off the valley walls, and as they hurtle down they will take with them huge amounts of soil and vegetation into the watercourse, forming a vast slurry that jets downstream, slamming against the banks as it goes, ripping away more and more and more vegetation, until everything is dumped—thousands upon thousands of tons—at the river mouth.

In Pelekunu the valley and its streams are always making and remaking themselves, just as the active volcanoes of the Big Island do. At the crater of Kīlauea preparatory rumblings may beckon you to come closer to watch a majestic geological event. But in Pelekunu the rolling thunder of boulders breaking loose in a cyclonic storm should be attended to immediately as the most serious of announcements to get out, right now. Otherwise you yourself may become a part of the geological event, and be carried away by it, literally.

NOTHING can stop Pelekunu in flood. And even in normal times it always makes its way to the ocean. Elsewhere in the islands other streams come to the sea freely and directly in waterfalls over cliff faces. Others again reach the ocean only as intermittent trickles interrupted altogether in dry times. And there are stretches of coast where no streams at all reach the sea. In some regions of the island of Hawai'i the new volcanic rock is so porous, so permeable, that water is absorbed in great quantity almost instantaneously, and streams hardly get started. This can be seen on the southeastern and southwestern coasts, where not a stream mouth or estuary punctuates the coastline.

Stream life in the Hawaiian Islands has adapted itself to a wide variety of natural circumstances—from the shock of flash flood, to seasonal and annual variations in stream flow caused by drought, to the rigors of the dispersal of larvae between island streams. But major diversions of water to suit urban, agricultural, and industrial purposes can depopulate streams by disrupting the

flow of water to the sea. Many species need both the stream and
the sea to complete their life cycle.

A big storm in Pelekunu does fierce things to the valley's
main stream and its tributaries. Landslides may cause all aquatic
life to be wiped out, at least for the time being. But the storm
passes, and as the stream begins to carve a new channel through
the debris, life comes back: all kinds of freshwater snails, the
Hawaiian shrimp, 'ōpae, in plenty, native damselflies, craneflies,
and midges in amazing abundance, and high up, as far up as thirteen hundred feet, three species of Hawaiian goby fishes, 'o'opu,
schooling, as they are seen to do nowhere else in the islands.

The 'o'opu, the 'ōpae, and the hīhīwai snail spawn in the
stream, the eggs hatch, and the larvae float down, all the way to
the sea. Ocean currents sweep them away along the coasts, into
the community of marine plankton. They reappear at stream
mouths as tiny post-larvae, and then in the early phase of their
mature existence they fight their way upstream; up that steep difficult Hawaiian stream profile of pools and cascades, inch by inch,
the fishes thrusting with their tails and clinging with suction-cup
pelvic fins. Alongside them shrimps and snails are tenaciously
laddering up the waterfalls on ferns and mosses, up into the permanent fresh water where they will live all their adult lives.

ALL this life depends on the flow of streams, and the natural
flow of the streams depends on the intricate balance between the
falling of rain and the storage of rainfall. Up around the headwaters heavy vegetation cushions the fall of raindrops and allows
water to seep into the ground, to be stored behind natural dikes of
impermeable rock or to accumulate in perched aquifers above layers of dense lava. Up here springs and seeps can be the start of
streams. Lower down toward sea level, immensities of underground
fresh water ride on immensities of salt water, and can be tapped
by artesian wells. At the coast, fresh water discharges through

stream estuaries or else comes out as groundwater, forming undersea springs that well up as coldspots in the warmth of the salt shallows. And in a few places fresh water meets salt in alkaline pools, opening in coastal lava that is neither sea nor stream, a halfway world that harbors a unique fauna of adapted ocean species.

Parts of the Hawaiian Islands get heavier rainfall than many places in the world. But at the same time the demands placed on stream water and groundwater are heavy too, and late in the twentieth century this pressure is being felt by every species that depends upon water—and that means every species inhabiting the islands, from the goby and the ʻōpae and the damselfly to *Homo sapiens.* Perhaps more than any other single element, ready availability of water is becoming the limiting factor in the sustenance and the extension of life, all across the islands, in the streams and out of them.

Of all places in the islands, only Pelekunu has been recognized and given legal status as a nature preserve to protect an entire native stream system and its watershed. It is, so to speak, a motherlode stream for Hawaiʻi, and indeed for the whole Pacific region. What can be learned and experienced at Pelekunu has a value that can be traced along every stream in the Hawaiian Islands, and in other islands of life elsewhere in the great ocean.

Rain Forests

Where the trade winds blow in off the northern Pacific and encounter the mountains of Hawaiʻi, at elevations of two to five thousand feet, the air is forever moist. This is rain forest country.

From a distance the forest shows itself to the eye in colors that are unmistakable, a subtle blend of blue-brown-gray-green. In times of fog or mist or falling rain the light filters diffusely through overarching trees. In times of no cloud cover the sun comes sifting down to the forest floor in a shifting, dappled dazzle of wet silver-gold and green. Out of a carpet of the thickest, plushest moss, tree ferns grow to far above head height for a human, their trunks ten or even twenty feet tall, their fronds unfurling still higher. 'Ōhi'a lehua trees may rise to a hundred feet, and out of their branches sprout more ferns, herbs, and even other trees and shrubs. Natural diversity begets more natural diversity, things grow out of things that grow out of things, canopies above canopies, understories beneath understories. And when the dominant trees of the rain forest, the 'ōhi'a lehua, burst out in blossom, the 'apapane, a Hawaiian honeycreeper with crimson plumage, flies mile upon mile to feast upon the nectar, and the forest canopy is filled to bursting with vibrating life.

At such times—indeed at any time—the Hawaiian rain forest gives off a wilderness sense that everything is in precisely the right place and the right condition of existence, everything connected with everything else, exactly as it should be.

ABOUT all this the feral pig cares nothing. In the Hawaiian rain forest these days, the pig is just about everywhere. It has not yet set its cloven hoof upon the extreme heights of Oloku'i on Moloka'i, and it has not hoisted its powerful body up onto the remote plateaus of 'Eke on Maui or Nāmolokama on Kaua'i. But in almost every other rain forest area the pig is present, especially on the windward side of mountains on the main islands, all the way from Kaua'i to the Big Island, in fearsome numbers, perhaps as many as fifty thousand, meaning that for every twenty human beings in modern-day Hawai'i there is a feral pig.

In the rain forest this introduced animal rips up native mosses and chews on native tree ferns for the starch inside of the stems. It devours the three species of native Hawaiian orchids. It churns the earth to get at the roots of other native plants that it favors, and it snouts up earthworms and grubs and eats them. The feeding is excellent, and the breeding is wonderful: if this month you see a given number of feral pigs, in four months time you might see double the number. In short, in the pig's scheme of things, Hawaiian rain forest is nothing but a fabulously rich system for converting intact wilderness into rampant pig.

The pig likes introduced plants just as much as it likes native plants, and this is where things start to get desperately serious for the rain forest. Strawberry guava, which has been in the islands for decades, doing increasingly well for itself in a variety of habitats, has lodged in the rain forest. The pig enjoys it. A passionfruit vine from South America is a more recent introduction. Brought to Hawai'i as an ornamental, it has turned out to be superbly equipped to climb 'ōhi'a lehua trees, engulfing and suffocating them, and in the process wiping out understory. The pig has a big appetite for passionfruit. The pig eats and moves on, and guava seed and passionfruit seed move with it, journeying with the pig through the rain forest, traveling through pig gut and pig bowel, to be dispersed and fertilized in one movement.

Hawaiian rain forests are full of island species that have had life to themselves for a very long time. Against recently introduced plants such as strawberry guava and passionfruit vine, healthy rain forest might be able to hold its own. In contested terrain, on pig-disturbed ground, native species often cannot maintain their hold. Stricken, rain forest retreats before the invasion. And leading the invasion is the pig. Nothing stops the pig. To the Hawaiian rain forest, the pig is death.

It is death to the Hawaiian bog too. Every so often in rain forest you come unexpectedly upon a stretch of open country, the ground wet, the cover a low mat of hummocky sedges and grasses and curiously dwarfed trees and shrubs. Here heavy rainfall leaves the ground perpetually saturated. The bogs are islands of specialized growth within the rain forest. But to the feral pig a Hawaiian bog is just one more place to eat, offering something of a change of diet, earthworms and grubs again, but also scores of native lobelias and greenswords, showcase plants among the Hawaiian flora, some kinds of which are found in all the world only in these strange, secluded places. The pig snouts at the wet earth, churns the soil into muck with its hooves, and turns bog into piggery.

Everywhere the pig goes it loosens the spongy layers of moss that form the forest floor, producing slick mud, leaving wallows and little puddles of dirty standing water in which introduced mosquitoes can breed. This opens the way for yet another sickness to invade the rain forest, avian malaria, a killer of native birds.

And everywhere the pig goes, destroying the cover of the forest floor, it reduces the capacity of the rain forest to hold onto rain as it falls. One of the great, essential functions of these upland plant communities is to hold water in trust, so to speak, for the rest of the island terrain, capturing mist and fog, buffering torrential rainfall, absorbing water and releasing it gently to aquifers and streams, reducing immediate flow in wet seasons, maintaining it in dry.

The primal vision of the rain forest is of a great, green regulative sponge, a vegetative heart pumping clear water year round forever, the water of life.

If intricately related communities of plants are disrupted and replaced by stands of a single plant like strawberry guava or passionfruit vine, watershed is put seriously at risk. If this single plant should be wiped out, say by disease, then the earth would be bare, stripped of its cover. Then water would seek its own level unimpeded, uncontrolled. Erosion could spread and destroy the land. So the pig rampant in rain forest and bog creates disaster not only in its immediate surroundings but everywhere downstream as well.

Water flooding unchecked out of ravaged rain forest scours loosened soil and dumps it in the ocean, suffocating coral reefs which used to be rich habitat for fish. On its way it crosses what has become increasingly the domain of other feral animals that have gnawed and trampled their way through native landscapes: cattle, goats, and exotic breeds recently introduced as game for hunting—mouflon sheep, blacktail deer, and Axis deer. From the mountains to the sea, the words "feral ungulate" amount to a comprehensive curse on the Hawaiian landscape, and the imprint of a cloven hoof in disturbed and trampled soil is the mark of the beast.

DISRUPTION of habitat means loss of species. In the forest and bog country of Alaka'i on the island of Kaua'i there used to be a big population of a native bird called the 'ō'ō. They were described in 1891 as common, in 1903 as numerous, then by 1928 they were talked about as rare. By 1960 a survey could find only twelve of them, and by the 1980s they were down to two, and then to one—just like the Laysan teal, only this time the circumstance is truly terminally dire, because the one surviving Kaua'i 'ō'ō is a male, so that it is hard to envision a miracle of biological brinkmanship in the Alaka'i. Wildlife workers in the Alaka'i have spotted the last 'ō'ō in recent years, each time in much the same place, one small black bird, singing and building a nest each year, making all the right moves of its species to attract a mate. But there seems to be no mate to attract, and there probably can never be. The 'ō'ō was photographed not long ago, in silhouette, alone. Its solitary song was tape-recorded from up close and played back in the forest the next day. The 'ō'ō, this lone black bird, flew to the source of the song and found nothing but a single, wingless black machine, singing.

Summits

There is a colony of dark-rumped petrels that spends part of the year on the summit of Haleakalā. Before the dawn they launch themselves from their mountain home and glide thousands of feet down the wind to feed in the ocean. By night they make the arduous return flight: winging upward in the darkness, climbing through zone after zone of Hawaiian habitat—coast, strand, dry-land, rain forest, the headwaters of streams. They bank over scattered māmane, the last of the upland trees. Higher still, trees give out altogether, unable to tolerate dry winds and icy temperatures, and the petrels traverse terrain densely packed with low, compact, tough, slow-maturing shrubs growing amid hardy grasses and sedges. Finally, at eight to ten thousand feet, the petrels of Haleakalā touch down in their home territory.

This is unmistakably volcano country once more—rock, cinder, lichen. Here you are also above normal cloud cover, above the inversion layer, and the summits of Haleakalā on Maui and Mauna Loa and Mauna Kea on the Big Island appear to float on cloud banks—islands above islands.

Life at this altitude is hard. The extreme summits of Hawai'i are alpine stone deserts. The air is thin, the wind can blow blizzard-cold, and in some months of the year snow falls. At the highest of high altitudes, where even the soaring petrel rarely goes, life is ground down to mere flecks of biological being, tiny bugs with anti-freeze blood, some of them shaped to mimic their meager food supply, so that they can blow along with leaf litter and other plant debris into rock cracks to feed, safe out of the wind.

Life at the summit is not easy for human beings, either. The volcanologist Thomas Jaggar spent time at the extreme heights of the biggest volcanoes of the Big Island. But even he, Jaggar, an individual of world stature in a biological species of world stature, had to subsist at the top of Mauna Loa much like a wēkiu bug, in a rock crack roofed with iron sheeting. These days scientists are permanently and comfortably ensconced at high altitudes on the highest mountain of all, Mauna Kea. They are astronomers. They come from all over the world to this mid-Pacific summit because high-altitude Hawai'i is a place of remarkably clear air, the best for seeing into deep space, none better on earth.

Mauna Kea has huge telescopes funded at great expense by international scientific consortia, to look up and out, away from earth, to the planets and the stars. The astronomers do excellent work. Their scientific results are highly valuable to all humankind. No one would ever suggest otherwise.

It is just that in our time, late in the twentieth century—as conservation biologists are beginning to remark, with a certain irony—we have somehow come to know more about land surfaces light-years away in space than we know about the interior of rain forests on earth, including the rain forest of the island of Hawai'i, only a few thousand feet down the slopes of Mauna Kea from the giant telescopes.

ALWAYS think in millions of years, urged Thomas Jaggar, and everything is in motion to one who senses slow motion.

This might be all very well for geologists, or for the astronomers of Mauna Kea, who think professionally in light-years. But those who think biologically about the Hawaiian Islands these days do not have such luxuries of time, and they might well wish that the rate of motion were far slower.

Consider the silversword. One of the splendors of the summit of Haleakalā is this plant of such strong and distinctive form, its rosette of silvery leaves glinting in the sun. It has always been the signature plant, the emblem, of Haleakalā. Visitors liked to take home a leaf, or more than one, or more than several—something special from a unique Hawaiian place, like a scorched Hale-ma'uma'u postcard. And for the introduced goats on Maui, multiplying to tens of thousands on Haleakalā, silversword was truly excellent eating.

So picked at and picked over was the silversword that its future became doubtful. What began its rescue was the declaration of Haleakalā as a national park in 1913. Human beings were persuaded to be sparing of silversword leaves, and later on the goats were hunted and fenced out—down from tens of thousands to mere dozens.

But another enemy has crept into the park, unimpeded by fences and contemptuous of park rules and regulations. Undetected at first, the Argentine ant took up residence under rocks tenanted by ground-nesting, solitary native bees. Immediately, the introduced ants began eating the vulnerable larvae, and even the adult bees. For the silversword this was disastrous, because the bees are its essential pollinators.

These days it is possible to see silverswords in Haleakalā blooming by the hundreds, a wonderful sight. But because of the appetite of the Argentine ant, it is not possible to know whether abundant pollination is going to take place, whether enough seeds will be set to keep the population up at healthy levels. Native silversword remains hostage to introduced ant.

The only way to secure the survival of Haleakalā silversword is for human beings to develop—and soon—management and control programs with more power than the single-minded and intimidating program of the Argentine ant.

All these episodes in the life of the silversword—flourishing untroubled, then stripped by humans and devoured by goats, then recovering within the benign confines of a park, then threatened by the invasion of the Argentine ant, with the realization of a continued future in peril—all this has happened in the space of only eight decades, a mere eye-blink in the biological life of the islands.

THERE is an enigmatic saying that can be interpreted as a blessing or a curse: may you live in interesting times.

Certainly Hawai'i these days is an interesting place going through interesting times. Plant and animal species in great numbers have disappeared. But at the same time, species that have seemingly disappeared have been sighted again, sometimes after decades of presumed extinction. Perhaps even more surprisingly, in recent years a number of new species have been discovered, even on the densely populated main islands. And as recently as the last decade certain inconspicuous habitats have been recognized for what they are, home to whole communities of previously unobserved life forms: all the way from the alkaline pools, brackish enclosed ponds by the coast full of seaweeds and tiny shrimp that can turn the water red, to those strange lava tubes where little worlds of insects flourish in complete darkness.

Often—as with the po'ouli, a bird first sighted in rain forest on East Maui in 1973—the discovery that a species exists is simultaneously a discovery that the species is endangered. Interesting place, interesting times.

THE early chapters of the story of life in the Hawaiian Islands concerned an intricate set of life forms evolving in splendid isolation. The chapter we are living out today concerns the breakdown of that isolation, and what happens to life forms confronted with momentous challenges from powerful outside forces.

What is happening in Hawai'i is happening all over the world. Everywhere on earth humankind is creating new "islands" of all sorts, from the Amazon basin to the rain forests of Southeast Asia to Yellowstone National Park. Everywhere man, for his own purposes, has been surrounding natural environments, isolating them, and diminishing them. Everywhere the natural order of things has been rearranged to suit human purposes—cut up, divided, fenced, cropped, and cleared.

This makes for interesting times, and interesting times raise interesting questions. How do natural communities of plants and animals function when their surroundings are radically changed? How can native species be used to reclaim damaged landscapes and restore watersheds? How, for that matter, does rain forest flourish in poorly drained soils that have apparently toxic levels of iron, manganese, and aluminum? South American forests yield a plant poison, curare, which has been "civilized" to become an invaluable medical anesthetic. A plant from Madagascar, the rosy periwinkle, yields an anti-cancer agent that can bring years of extra life to many children with leukemia. How much more of vital use to humankind remains to be discovered? On the highest level, what is the global effect of human intervention on such a sweeping scale in natural environments? Fundamentally, how can humankind strike the right balance between exploitation and preservation in a world of limited resources?

These are questions that show up most urgently on islands, where in the nature of things limits on resources are readily apparent and outside pressures are felt immediately and strongly. And nowhere can such questions be more clearly addressed than in the Hawaiian Islands. The biological history of the archipelago has stamped this place on the world map as conveying the absolute essence of island life, in all its isolated splendor and its vulnerability to invasion.

Just as Thomas Jaggar envisioned Hawai'i as a world center of volcanology, just as the Mauna Kea astronomers see Hawai'i as a world center of their universal trade, so it is possible to see a future for Hawai'i as a creative world center of conservation biology, solving local problems in a way that can be of significant use elsewhere in the Pacific and in other world regions.

Interesting place, interesting times, and the most interesting moment of time is right now. To stand on a Hawaiian summit and look outward is to have a vision of the whole natural world in rapid-motion change. That vision carries with it an irresistible invitation, one that in the nature of things can never be repeated, to live a genuinely interesting life; to help save, reclaim, and perpetuate a flourishing island of life upon the greater island of life which is the planet Earth.

INTO THE ARCHIPELAGO

VICTORIA NELSON

WHO was I? A twenty-three-year-old with a graduate degree. What was I? (As the alchemist said, do not ask *who* but rather *what* a man is.) A bundle of raw affects and impulses unbounded by skin on the outside or shaped by any sort of bone or cartilage on the inside: a kind of sea creature, really. Why did such a jellyfish float to the middle of the Pacific? I had no reason. I had come to visit my friends, who had had no reason either. Like them, I knew why I was there a heartbeat or so after arriving.

What did I find in Hawai'i? *Wai* and *kai*—that is, fresh water and salt water.

I found many ways of being wet: *hōwai, kakale, kalekale, kele wai, ho'okakale, ukalekale, 'ōkalekale, hōkale, kele, kelekele, halahalawai, kēwai, holowai, wawai, 'ōhulu, palakē.* I found cool water (*wai hu'ihu'i*), sprinkling water (*wai kāpīpī*), tingling water (*wai konikoni*), misty water (*wai noenoe*), the brackish water where stream mouths hit the ocean, quite correctly called *wai kai.*

I found the mountain pool (*ki'o kawa*) and stream (*kahawai*). I found the waterfall, *wailele,* and the upside-down waterfall, *wai puhia* (these are common; the wind blows them back up).

Most of all I found the ocean, *moana,* in all its shapes: the calm, quiet sea (*kai malie, kai malino, kai malolo, kai hōʻoluʻolu, kai pu, kai wahine, kai kalamania, kaiolohia*), the strong sea (*kai koʻo, kai kane, kai nui, kai nuʻu, ʻokaikai*), the rough or raging sea (*kai pupule, kai puʻeone, kai akua*), the deep sea (*kai hohonu, kai ʻau, kai hōʻeʻe, kai lū heʻe*), the place where sea and land meet (*ʻae kai*), the sea almost surrounded by land (*kai hāloko*), the eight seas around the Hawaiian Islands (*nā kai ʻewalu*). Swimming underwater in the salt sea, *kai paʻakai,* I found the miracle of the offshore freshwater springs, unexpected eye-sweetening uprushings from the sea floor.

And with all these kinds of *wai* and *kai* I found as many variations on the color Blue: turquoise, cobalt, indigo, azure, cerulean, powder blue, sapphire, ultramarine, navy shading to lavender, gentian, mulberry, violet, purple. I found it in the sky, the ocean, the streams, set off by the colors Black (lava rock), White (wind-blown surf spray, *kai ehu*), and Green (trees, vines, plants of all kinds).

The Outer Islands, I found once I had got off Oʻahu, curiously resembled and disresembled each other. What struck me most in all the spots I came to know well was the superabundance of place names. Every rock, every turn of the bend, every rise and fall of the land, every surf break, every variation in the wind and rain had a name. Astonishing numbers of Hawaiian place names survived, even though countless more had been lost and those preserved on the maps were dropping away, too, as the intensely topographic sensibility subsided.

Hawaiian place names are, literally, poetry; their multilayered associations of topography, sexual innuendo, and mythic allusion dominate the chants and hula. Sayings also clustered around specific seas, rains, and winds attached to each island; in the very old days each place carried its own inimitable "halo of delight or sorrow," specific personal, historical, and mythic associations. The act of naming itself, as in the *Kumulipo*, held great power. Speaking the names, chanting them, established cognitive control of the surrounding environment. Old-time Hawaiian storytellers peppered their tales with long recitals of place names, both to authenticate the story as well as to allow listener and teller alike to participate in the joy of hearing an accumulation of well-loved names. Here is a simple example, a song that circles clockwise around the districts of the island of Hawai'i, translated by Samuel Elbert and Noelani Mahoe:

> Hilo, Hanakahi, rain rustling *lehua*.
> Puna, fragrant bowers, bowers fragrant with *hala*.
> Ka'ū, the wind, the dirt scattering wind.
> Kona, the sea, the streaked sea.
> Ka-wai-hae, the sea, the whispering sea.
> Wai-mea, the rain, the Kīpu'upu'u rain.
> Kohala, the wind, the 'Āpa'apa'a wind.
> Hāmākua, the cliff, the tropic birds flying cliffs.
> Tell the refrain, rain rustling *lehua*.

The main Hawaiian islands share place names among them—Kailua, Waimea, Mauna Loa. The similarity is pan-Polynesian in the same way that the New England states each have their Concords, Haverhills, and Readings, reflecting the origins of their Anglo-European settlers. 'Upolu, for example, is a name also found in Samoa, and in all the older Polynesian settlements "Hawaiki" (cognate with "Hawai'i") was the mythic homeland. The familiar Hawaiian place names "Kona" and "Ko'olau" mean "south" and "north," and thus their cognates "Tonga" and "Tokelau" designate the Pacific island groups lying farthest south and farthest north in the macrocosm of the known Polynesian world.

Adding to this sense of cloning and endless serial duplication, most of the main Hawaiian Islands, thanks to their volcanic formation, have analogous shapes. All have a windward and leeward side, the archipelago being oriented on the northeast-south-west axis. All but O'ahu, Lāna'i, and Ni'ihau have inaccessible northeastern wet valleys.

For all their maddening, dreamlike similarities, however, each island, and each spot on each island, has its own ineffable essence. During my time I had a proud boast: "Put me down in any valley on any island, and in half an hour I'll tell you where I am." Although nobody with a helicopter ever put me to the test, what if a person was to be airlifted, say, suitably blindfolded, into some anonymous dripping green Hawaiian jungle—how would the identification proceed?

Your first duty, naturally, would be to find the stream, which wouldn't take long in the average steep-sided Hawaiian gulch. Once you were at the stream and now possibly had a clear view of the walls of your valley, the next big clue would be the larger subliminal impression the island itself produced: Kaua'i, the oldest, where the mountains were a bit more worn down, their edges softened by the weathering of thousands of years, to Hawai'i, the newest and rawest.

Now, having guessed your island, you would need to determine if your valley lay on the leeward or windward side of a mountain range, and of which range: as a rule leeward is dry and windward wet, but most leeward valleys are wet at their heads. On all the islands the mountain walls are always far sheerer on the windward side, where the northeast trades and rains beat against them.

Your ultimate guide, however, would be the fact that all these deserted valleys, so alike with their waterfalls, streambanks, prehistoric house platforms, and overgrown taro terraces cloven by the roots of labyrinthine hau and guava forests, differ utterly in the way their features are combined. On one level they seem interchangeable. On another, deeper level they are not. For the individual identity of each valley grows out of a unique accumulation of thousands of specific natural features: the insanely sheer valley walls of the Big Island's North Kohala valleys. The hump of land blocking the mouth of Molokai's Wailau Valley that always kept you from mistaking it for the even huger Waipiʻo on the Big Island. The crook of Halawa's stream mouth. The rugged coastal cliffs where Kīpahulu Valley on Maui meets the sea next to the lava spillover of Kaupō Gap. The unmistakable way the windward Koʻolaus rear up, full of stern green menace, behind Kahana Valley on Oʻahu.

And the Hawaiians consecrated these details of the natural landscape in names, so that Halawa Valley was not simply Halawa but the sum of its expanding attributes, of— to take only the 1,200-meter stretch of land on each side of the mouth of Halawa stream—Manuwā, Kaʻio, Puaʻalaulau, Hakuheʻe, Keau-Hipuʻupuʻu, and Makaʻeleʻele; of its two heiau and innumerable smaller shrines, so that, focusing ever more sharply, a limited geographical area opens up a sense of infinite possibility: the continent of Hawaiʻi.

This continent of mine, the most geographically remote island group in the world, was actually an archipelago, a distinctive 2,000-mile-long undersea volcanic mountain chain that hooks far into the middle Pacific latitudes. After the inhabited eight islands of the Hawaiian universe—Hawaiʻi, Maui, Kahoʻolawe, Lānaʻi, Molokaʻi, Oʻahu, Kauaʻi, Niʻihau—came the dry Leeward Necker and Nihoa, seasonally inhabited by fishermen in prehistoric times, where Mad Jack Percival from Honolulu once hid out in the early nineteenth century, now a bird sanctuary reeking of guano. Hundreds more miles of water, then numerous bits and dots poked out of the Pacific: the French Frigate Shoals, the Garden Pinnacles, Midway, Laysan Island, Pearl and Hermes Atoll.

East, toward America, were more islands in the making. Off the southeast tip of the Big Island, the volcanological factory was busy manufacturing the next link in the island chain.

Naturally, this yet-to-surface Hawaiki already had a name: the Lō'ihi Seamount.

The pre-Contact Hawaiians understood the process by which undersea volcanoes had formed their islands, as a traditional gourd-beating (*pā-ipu*) hula demonstrates. Of this hula the translator, my friend Kenneth Davids, writes: "It is quite clear from this chant and from many other sources that the ancient Hawaiians knew the origin of their land: that volcanic eruption raised it from the ocean, and furthermore, that Kaua'i, the westernmost island of the Hawaiian chain, was the oldest geographically, and Hawai'i, the easternmost and still volcanically active island, the youngest. This knowledge of actual geologic history structures the Gourd-Beating Hula, which follows the geological drama of volcanic conception of the land, beginning with Kaua'i and moving eastward through O'ahu (the second oldest of the four major islands), Maui, and finally Hawai'i, the youngest. The language is, as usual, sexually charged."

The refrain, working from Kaua'i to Hawai'i, runs:

Where the sun comes up there's a pit:
Pele's hot pit.
Clouds hang down,
lightning shoots out,
shoots out down here,
shoots out up there,
crickle crackle
the stick goes in,
the stick comes out,
the first man yells:
who's digging there?
It's me, Pele,
who digs the pit and stokes the fire,
burning inside Kaua'i.

Whether you thought of Hawai'i as an archipelago or a continent, with that land's-end aura oozing from every little airstrip, green pali, and deserted beach, the Outer Islands still had a way of bringing you up short, making you realize you were, in some inscrutable but definite way, at the end of the line. In the very old days the Hawaiians thought so, too. The northwesternmost point of an island, they believed, was a place that funnelled the souls of dead people to their ultimate destination, the underworld. On Kaua'i, I knew, it was Polihale on the leeward side of the Nāpali coast. On O'ahu, says Martha Beckwith in her classic scholarly work *Hawaiian Mythology*, this *leina-a-'uhane*, or leaping place of the souls, was somewhere near Ka'ena Point, now a rugged, desolate place accessible only by jeep, frequented by fishermen and joyriding soldiers from Schofield Barracks. Originally, every district had its leaping-off place for souls, where a tree—like my hala tree?—acted as a path either toward or away from the underworld.

When I returned to California, I confronted, with a shock of recognition, that supreme American *leina-a-'uhane*, the Golden Gate: a symbolic westernmost spot of land, its bridge a convenient launching pad to the underworld, the only difference being that here the souls, though lost, were not yet dead when they leaped. The poet Lew Welch, hypnotized by these spots like so many others, vanished into the landscape just north of the Gate. In "The Song Mt. Tamalpais Sings" he had written:

> *This is the last place. There is nowhere else to go.*
> Human movements,
>   but for a few,
> are Westerly.
> Man follows the Sun.

When you got to the edge, did you jump off to baptism or death? This was the tightrope all Pacific young people, haole and Polynesian, walked.

* * *

LAPAKAHI, Christmas 1970: a two-week holiday-break clean-up dig at a dryland coastal habitation site was my introduction to the Big Island. Lapakahi, an ancient fishing village, was about a quarter of a mile south, down a short footpath, from Māhukona Beach Park in the North Kohala district. Māhukona was an abandoned harbor with an old concrete wharf where the burnt sugar-cane stalks harvested from the fields of North Kohala were formerly loaded on the Spreckels barges for processing down at the plant in Kawaihae, South Kohala. The Holo-Holo campers that the university's Anthro department had rented were set up in a grove of kiawe trees whose notorious two-inch thorns could penetrate the thickest zori devised by Japanese technology, and the night was periodically rent by the screams of the unwary en route to the camp toilets.

Every evening we jumped from the dock to wash off the Lapakahi dirt, and in this way my friend Joe Kennedy, one of the archaeology students, shortened his little finger a quarter inch by diving straight onto a lava rock. Underwater the little bay was like an aquarium gone mad; hundreds of thousands of vivid fish wheeled and turned, pressed their tiny mouths lightly against your body. Even from the dock you could make out huge masses of manini like slowly revolving yellow clouds—it seemed outrageous, somehow, to see these fish directly from our own medium of air, not water.

From the Māhukona wharf one Saturday morning we watched a winter storm surf hit the concrete bulwarks, sending cascades of seawater high in the air. Dancing around in the shower twenty feet back from the edge was a stupid thing to do; there was always a wave, not necessarily the seventh, twenty feet bigger than the rest. When one of these finally broke, the spray alone was powerful enough to knock me flat and drag me face down clear across the concrete. A foot or two from the sheer drop to the rocks, someone caught me by the ankle and hauled me back, shaken and bloody. Great Natural Forces do not tolerate child's play.

As further evidence of GNFs, the Big Island had lava fields, huge ones the size of cities. They were great fun to explore, providing you had a good destination. Bouncing in a four-wheel-drive jeep across the wasteland of the great Kona lava flow, mile after mile of shining frozen black cowpie, and suddenly over the rise came a flash of turquoise, a white crescent of sand, an old frame house with an outrigger beached nearby, under the coconut palms—a bit of the old days, nineteenth-century Hawai'i, once the old Magoon summer house, in my time a scuba-diving ranch but slated for development: Mahai'ula.

Our host, the current Magoon, remembered traveling to Mahai'ula as a little boy by motorized outrigger from Kailua-Kona. This Magoon's great-great-grandfather was that Chinese merchant of King Kalākaua's day considerably fictionalized by Jack London in his famous story "Chun Ah Chun": the eight Chinese-Hawaiian daughters married off and the lucky ur-Magoon, like all those other New England sailor adventurers who found themselves in the right place at the right time, soon to be the proud possessor of the *ahupua'a*—the traditional pie-shaped land unit stretching from mountains to seashore—of South Kona, much of it lava flow, much of it also green and verdant, all of it, eventually, valuable beyond imagining.

Something unbearably touching obtained in the atmosphere of Mahai'ula. In the living room, under fins, masks, and old *National Geographic*, squatted the huge battered mahogany dining table shipped over from Honolulu that King Kalākaua himself had once played poker on. Like the strange overlapping symmetry of the Nāpali valleys, this white frame house on the beach in the middle of the lava flow opened up a layered series of "times," lost worlds: pre-Statehood, prewar, pre-Territory, back to the genuine old days, when all haole tourists, in accordance with the nineteenth-century Romantic worship of Nature, made pilgrimages to Great Natural Forces. In Hawai'i that meant traveling to the Big Island, home of the live volcanoes. Witnessing an eruption from a prudent distance became the equivalent of viewing the tears of Christ on the shroud of Turin—the climax and crowning event of any supplicant's visit.

Denied the spectacle himself, Mark Twain was obliged to record in his notebooks the account of one Mrs. Henry MacFarlane, identified as the wife of a Honolulu liquor merchant. Let her eyes serve as his, and mine, too:

> 30 miles from the house—eruption began slowly at dusk—at 4 A.M. was shooting rocks and lava 400 feet high which would then descend in a grand shower of fire to the earth—crater overflowed & molten waves & billows went boiling and surging down mountain side just for the world like a sea-stream from 1 1/2 to mile & 1/2 wide and hundred feet deep perhaps—over cattle, houses & across streams to the sea, 63 miles distant (7 years ago) ran into sea 3 miles and boiled the fish for 20 miles around—vessels found scores boiled fish 20 miles off—natives cooked their food there. Every evening for 7 weeks she sat on verandah half the night gazing upon the splendid spectacle—the wonderful pyrotechnic display—the house windows were always of a bloody hue—read newspapers every night by no other light than was afforded by this mighty torch 30 miles away.

Except for a quick junket to the sulfurous rim of Halema'uma'u, plus sightings of the twin snow-covered peaks of Mauna Loa and Mauna Kea from my frequent vantage point atop their neighbor Haleakalā Crater across the channel on Maui, the most famous Great Natural Force in Hawai'i did not impinge heavily on my own consciousness. Evidence of the live volcanoes reached me in subtler ways: as an almost undetectable shaking

of the house in Honolulu like a cat walking across the roof, followed, a few days later, by a light rain of ash, Pompeii style. And
the detail of the boiled fish in Mrs. MacFarlane's description was
enough to put me off my single idle fantasy, vis-à-vis volcanoes—
namely, to rent scuba gear and see what flowing lava looked like
underwater.

For me the real Great Natural Forces were always valleys,
valleys, valleys. On the Big Island I found the same inaccessible
windward northern system as on Moloka'i and Kaua'i. This group,
consisting of the valleys Pololū, Honokānenui/Honokāneiki, and
Honopue, was linked by a formidable network of cobblestone
donkey paths used by workers maintaining the huge fluming
systems that watered the canefields of Kohala. The North Kohala
Ditch Trail, as it was called, came to a definitive stop at the far
rim of Honopue Valley, after which you encountered an impenetrable series of sheer gulches, then the lava flat known as Laupā-
hoehoe sticking out into the sea, and eventually the yawning
enormity of Waipi'o Valley, which could be reached by road
(barely) from the Hilo side of the island.

Our semiofficial status by virtue of the Lapakahi dig gained
us otherwise disreputable students, haole and local, permission
from the owners, complete with signed document, to hike the
North Kohala Ditch Trail. Off we trotted on the contour trail
cutting midway between the valley floor and the top of the thousand-foot cliffs to the head of Pololū. (At the mouth of this valley
several summers later archaeologist Tom Riley uncovered, then
reburied, the stone fish god that had stood as a sentinel at the
entrance.) Nights we spent in the ditch workers' tin-roof shacks
in the upland wilderness. In the neglected yards of these loneliest
of houses bumpy-skinned Mexican lemon shrubs grew; inside,
yellowed Tagalog comic books lay scattered under the sagging
iron bedsteads with their bare soiled mattresses.

Before we set out we were warned by a member of the

Solomon family up at the Parker Ranch in Kamuela that crossing the stream mouths of the North Kohala valleys was dangerous because of the big sharks lurking along this coastline. There was a test you could make—throwing ti leaves in the water. If the shark was hungry enough to snap at them, it wasn't a good idea to cross.

If the Big Island seemed to have more sharks and more fish off its coasts than any of the other islands, it also seemed to have more pigs in its mountains as well. All over the uplands you saw their traces: big rooted-up patches of eroded earth near the trails where they fed, lots of droppings. These feral pigs were a blend of the species the early Polynesians had brought, along with chickens and dogs, and the European pigs introduced by Cook, who had noted in his log for January 1778:

> No dependence can be placed, in the hogs taken on board at these islands, for they will neither thrive nor live on board a ship. This was one great inducement to my leaving of the English breed as the hogs we got at Otaheite, that were of the Spanish breed, thrived and fed on board the Ships as well as our own, at the very time that others were pining away and dying daily.

The hardy mutants resulting from this cross-breeding escaped domestication and ran wild in the uplands, where they flourish to this day.

Pig hunting is still a regularly practiced art in all the Hawaiian Islands, even on urban O'ahu. Fierce, battered pig dogs help hunters track down the enormous creatures and hold them at bay. Once a rather ghastly incident was reported in the O'ahu newspapers—it's wrong of me to laugh, I know—namely, a haole woman walking her little poodle on one of the ridge trails behind Honolulu encountered a pack of pig dogs struggling up from the valley below. Just the sight of the frou-frou little creature with the ribbon in its hair was enough to madden them; with no further ado, they tore it to bits. Their owners, emerging from the underbrush behind them and making a two-second inspection of the carnage, called out a hasty apology over their shoulders and quickly vanished down the side of the other valley.

The wild pigs had tusks like a fantasia of curlicues; they actually curved back, ingrown, into the jaw. A few times in burials I had uncovered separate pieces of bracelets made of these carefully matched tusks, the connecting sennit cord long since rotted away. But somehow it remains my impression that pig bones, like a lot of other land animal artifacts, were never as prized by Hawaiians as their magical *Kumulipo* counterparts from under the sea—whale tusks or shark's teeth, for instance.

Kama'pua'a, the pig god of the very old days, was known to have rooted lecherously into the land, leaving many gulches behind. "They call me Prick-eye the great, I've plowed up all the islands," boasts Kama'pua'a in a famous hula. Once this notorious "night-digger" (as he was celebrated in the *Kumulipo*) was lured by a goddess's vagina that left its imprint as Koko Head Crater behind Hanauma Bay.

My one face-to-face with a wild pig occurred on our North Kohala Ditch Trail hike. A large gap had opened between me and the person behind on this narrow contour trail, which fronted a cliff face on one side and dropped off steeply on the other into underbrush about twenty feet below. As I looked casually over my shoulder, I saw a large black dog galloping toward me on the trail, a sight that frightened me much more at first than I felt the next instant, when I realized it was a pig.

Trapped in my heavy backpack, I had nowhere to run. Mainly, I was trying to melt seamlessly—as literary critics like to say—into the side of the cliff when the charging pig reached a human's length from me. It was then I saw his eyes, realized he was just as spooked by me as I was by him. At the last possible second he veered away and plunged headlong over the sheer drop, landing with a thunderous crash in the bushes below. More thrashing, a few squeals, then silence. Pig-Pan had come and gone.

Our trip came to an abrupt stop about fifty feet down the cliff from the end of the trail above Honopue, where it was quickly determined—first man on the rope dangling in midair, the rest of us frantically digging in above, holding on to guava roots that were ripping out of the wet soil—that we would kill ourselves trying to get down that eroded valley wall.

Here at the end of our trail I ran into a variant of the story-behind-the-story theme of the Hawaiian natural landscape and its eerie serial duplications of cliffs overlapping cliffs, waterfalls pouring into waterfalls, like an M. C. Escher print. This was a valley above a valley, that is, a landlocked valley. In the very old days, these upland valleys that did not open directly onto the sea were said to be the birthplace of the highest nobility. King Kamehameha the Great, first ruler of Hawaiʻi, was supposed to have been born in a valley above Hālawa Valley, but even in an airplane over the three rugged East End valleys of Hālawa, Wailau, and Pelekunu I couldn't manage to locate this place.

Between Honopue Valley and the twin Honokānes (-nui and -iki, big and little, respectively) there was a toy version of a landlocked valley. A short distance up a culvert next to the trail you could climb up the side of a rockface, hook your head over the top, and peer into a tiny water-drenched secret valley, complete with its very own banana trees, passion fruit vines, and regulation waterfall. A chill fell over me at the terrible perfection of this miniature, a kind of Nature's designer showcase. Like one of those enclosed gardens of the medieval European and Islamic imaginations, a valley behind a valley is an allegorical spot that accumulates its power simply by being what it is. The Hawaiians correctly viewed this kind of valley as a supreme birthing spot, embodying as it did the pull backward, the regressive urge. In such a wet verdant flowing place you were back in the *Kumulipo* darkness, a murky uncertain symbiosis of plants, animals, and half-formed human thoughts. This little valley was a Great Natural Force.

A sudden premonition overcame me. If I pulled myself up and over the edge, if I walked into this valley, I would disappear. What a relief, it seemed at first, to turn away from the dawning of imperfect, troubled consciousness and merge gratefully with the perfection of original night! Then came the catch: Rapturously seduced by the natural world, letting yourself be swallowed whole, you discovered that, far from being reborn, you were going to be digested, excreted, and composted instead.

I climbed back down to the trail in an uneasy frame of mind. I had stumbled again on the real secret of these jumping-off places, the Outer Islands: Getting to them was no problem. The real trick was getting out of them.

THE PIG WAR

KENNETH BROWER

TWO miles into the tree-fern forest of ʻŌlaʻa Tract, Dan
Taylor pulled the jeep onto a grassy shoulder of the road. The
macadam ran on straight and narrow, bisecting the spring-green
wilderness of fronds. The secondary canopy here was continuous
and much more impressive than the first. It was as if some sparse
Serengeti had germinated atop Amazonian jungle. In the structure of their fronds, in the dark little dots of sori on the undersides, the hāpuʻu looked similar to any number of fern species on
the mainland, but they were much larger. The hāpuʻu canopy
formed twenty to thirty feet above the ground. Ahead the straight-
ness of the road wavered in the heat and the far fronds trembled,
as scenery might around a time machine building up steam. We
had left the twentieth century, the Big Island, and Hawaiʻi Volcanoes National Park. We had taken a chronological wrong turn, a
detour into the Paleozoic.

On the left-hand side of the road, behind the wire fence,
Taylor told me, was tree-fern forest from which feral pigs had
been eliminated. On the right was forest where pigs still rooted
and rambled. He led me into the right-hand forest first.

The light under the canopy was cool and green. The air was humid, the breeze stilled, the mood carboniferous. Overhead, the backlit fronds interdigitated with few gaps between, making a green tent of chlorophyll, but underfoot the forest floor was broken by black, muddy trails and turnpikes. Here and there the mud was firm enough to hold the impression of a cloven hoof.

Taylor picked one of these trails and proceeded down it. Daniel Taylor is a career man with the U.S. Park Service, a general in a war against the pigs. He is a fair-skinned, soft-spoken man of middle age and height, his features pleasantly weathered by a lifetime in the field. He came to Hawai'i Island in 1979, from a post in Glacier National Park. Before that he worked in the North Cascades, and before that in Yosemite and Sequoia. Today he wore his uniform slacks and a pair of lightweight boots. I was barefoot, and the black mud of the pig trail felt wonderful between my toes. In this matter, at least, I could empathize with the enemy.

"*Rubus ellipticus*, introduced raspberry," Taylor announced, fetching a vine and bending it toward me. He gave me a significant glance. Moving several steps on, we stopped before another vine. "*Passiflora mollisima*, passionflower. Banana-pōkā, in Hawaiian. It's South American, a minor constituent of the flora in Colombia, Bolivia, but here … it was introduced in 1952 by an imbecile. I can't remember his name. *Passiflora edulis* is the passionfruit humans generally eat, but pigs like *mollisima*. They love the fruit. They eat it, defecate, and spread the seeds. The vine goes up into the canopy and spreads." Overspreading the ferns, the vine stole the sunlight and took over the forest.

We walked a few dozen yards and then, beside a fallen tree-fern trunk, Taylor went down on one knee.

"See? This is a banana-pōkā seedling. A whole bunch of them—" The clump of seedlings made a perfect circle on the wet blackness at the side of the trail. "—eight, nine, ten, eleven …

eighteen," Taylor said, counting the legacy of that particular pig. Without rising, he leaned out to brush another circle of seedlings. The seedlings of this second clump were much smaller, having just broken the surface. "Here's another generation. Eight, nine, ten … There goes the forest."

We walked on, Taylor sensibly avoiding the muddiest places and I, barefoot, looking forward to them and squishing through the deepest parts.

"We're looking desperately for a biological control," Taylor said. "Right now a forester is working in Colombia and Bolivia, searching for one. But for the moment there's not a damn thing we can do. I think this forest is doomed."

We left the doomed forest and crossed to the other side of the road.

Inside the pigless forest the fronds overhead interdigitated flawlessly, leaving no breaks in the canopy. Where across the road the light had been cool and green, here it was cooler and greener. The going was slow, because pigs had not opened up avenues. Recumbent trunks and aerial roots were everywhere, and making progress into the forest was like trying to run a race over hurdles still stacked against the stadium wall.

At intervals among the trunks of the tree ferns were trunks of 'ōhi'a lehua, which ran up through the canopy to leaf somewhere out of sight above. Occasionally one of the 'ōhi'a stood on stilts.

The 'ōhi'a, a Polynesian myrtle, often begins life as an epiphyte on tree ferns, germinating on the fern stumps or high on the trunks, sometimes twenty feet or more above the ground. As a trunk-germinated 'ōhi'a tree grows, its roots begin to search for the ground, entwining their host. The tree fern, like a slender lifeguard who has rescued a desperate matron more vital than himself, begins to strangle. By the time the 'ōhi'a's frantic roots have found solid bottom, the fern has gasped its last, decayed, and disappeared, and the 'ōhi'a is left standing on stilts. The surrounding tree ferns hurry to fill in the void left by their fallen comrade—the tree fern's mission is to make a green heaven on earth—and soon the secondary canopy is complete again.

Taylor and I stopped and stood quiet for a moment, letting the silence of the forest sink in. It was a closer, deeper silence than the silence across the way. The effect of the green light was powerful and nearly instantaneous. It put a part of the brain to sleep, that region concerned with projects, ambitions, worry, war, death, taxes. It awakened another part, the region concerned with things less easy to name: listening, waiting, half-surmise.

"The key to this forest is the integrity of the tree-fern canopy," Taylor said, perhaps having decided that the green light had primed me sufficiently. "If you look twenty feet above your head, you can see that the tree-fern fronds interlock, forming a subcanopy. The woody canopy above is very open, broken, not contiguous. What really keeps the forest closed is that tree-fern subcanopy twenty feet or so above the ground.

"The canopy does a lot of things. It keeps the sunlight from penetrating directly to the forest floor, except in a very few places—and there for only a few minutes during the day. That keeps the temperatures down, keeps them more even, and maintains a more predictable environment for plants. The humidity is higher than in the forest across the street. The canopy breaks up the impact of raindrops. These big tropical raindrops don't impact the forest floor directly. What falls down here is a kind of mist. Atomized raindrops.

"When tree ferns fall down, as they naturally do, they try to grow like this one here." He pointed to the green python of a recumbent trunk lying at our feet. "You see how this main stem runs along the ground, then suddenly takes a right angle and grows up over there? Well, that's the way tree ferns regenerate. When pigs are present, and that tree-fern stem is lying on the ground, the pigs will come along and munch on it. They like to chew the starchy interior of the stem. It's a favorite food item with them.

"That chewing does a couple of things. It kills the tree fern, to begin with, so there goes the canopy. The pigs also leave a hollow behind when they've chewed on the stem, a trough in which water collects, and the water breeds mosquitoes. Mosquitoes are not native here, nor is the avian malaria that they carry. The native bird population doesn't tolerate the malaria very well. Introduced birds do better. We think one of the major causes, if not *the* major cause, of the decline of native forest birds is avian malaria. Pigs are implicated in that as well."

A GENERATION ago Hawaiian cowboys, riding by a certain burial site in the northern grasslands of the Big Island, were in the habit of reining in, dismounting, and urinating on the grave. Buried here was "Mongoose" Forbes. In the 1870s Forbes sold mongooses to the managers of Hawaii's sugar plantations, on the grounds that this import from Asia would eat rats. (Norway rats had jumped ship in Hawai'i and were raising Cain in the cane.) The disrespectful posthumous salute by the Hawaiian cowboys would have mystified Forbes. Like most of those men who have introduced alien animals to islands, Mongoose Forbes thought he was doing good.

Exotic wildlife wreaks plenty of havoc on the continents—starlings, sparrows, camels, and carp on our own, for example—but nowhere have exotics caused more devastation and disruption than in the simple, sheltered ecosystems of islands. Isolation from the rough-and-tumble of natural selection, mainland style, has allowed islands to develop a wonderful, often bizarre, flowering of forms. In Australia—a continent, actually, but so isolated that the island principle applies—marsupials filled all the mammal niches: marsupial bears, marsupial wolves, marsupial rhinoceroses. In the Galápagos Islands finches speciated to fill a wide range of avian niches, and giant lizards went to sea to play otter. Isolation makes islands into fine natural laboratories for scientists like Darwin, and islands have given rise to some elegant theories; but isolation also makes for vulnerability. In Australia the marsupials and the monotremes, the two most primitive mammalian orders, were living in a fool's paradise. On continents across the sea the placenta had been invented and had spread; evolution had passed Australia by and Australia never knew it. The marsupial wolf had a terrible shock when, for the first time, it saw a real canine face-to-face. For many insular species the first encounter with the outside world has been followed shortly by extinction.

The new arrivals have the power to alter the very landscape. Real rabbits, replacing the marsupial kind, accomplished that by desertifying vast stretches of Australia. The placental rabbit, with its enormous reproductive potential and its quicker wit, was a ninety-year plague on that island-continent. In one year, 1887, twenty-eight years into the plague, nearly twenty million rabbits were killed by the desperate inhabitants of New South Wales alone. Earlier the "European" rabbit, moving north from its native North Africa, had overrun Corsica, Sardinia, and the British Isles. Later it would overrun New Zealand and the San Juans, in Puget Sound. In 1903, during the Australian plague, some genius introduced the rabbit to Laysan Island, in Hawaii's leeward chain, and Laysan was promptly reduced to desert; of twenty-six native plants known in 1923 only four remained.

I didn't plan it this way, but my career has often deposited me on islands. The problem of exotic introductions to island environments is one that has grown on me. On Maui, across the channel from the Big Island, I have braked time and again for mongooses gliding across the road. My instincts were wrong—I should have accelerated. Some of those mongooses were hunting rats, as Mongoose Forbes had intended, but more were out after native birds and their eggs. (Hawaii's avifauna, thanks to pigs, cattle, mongooses, mosquitoes, and men, has suffered the highest extinction rate of any avifauna on this planet. In the past few centuries approximately forty percent of Hawaii's known native bird species have become extinct. On the current list of rare and endangered birds thirty of the sixty-seven species found in the United States were Hawaiian. The Hawaiian goose, the Hawaiian duck, the Hawaiian coot, hawk, thrush, stilt, and crow—among the others—are in imminent danger of joining the Hawaiian rail, last collected near the rain forest in 1864; the greater and lesser koa finches, not seen since 1896; the greater 'amakihi, not seen since early in this century; the kioea, the 'ula-'ai-hāwane, the mamo, the black mamo, and dozens of others that have passed into oblivion.)

In the Galápagos Islands I have tracked herds of feral goats that compete for forage with the giant tortoises for which that archipelago is named. From hotel windows in Britain I have drawn imaginary beads on the American gray squirrels that have overrun that island, displacing the smaller native red squirrels, barking and girdling thousands of good English hardwoods, and sorely testing the patience of the natives, that most animal-loving of peoples. In the Palau Archipelago of Micronesia, venturing out on dawn walks, I have passed armies of giant African snails headed the other way, crawling back to the bushes after their nightly depredations.

The giant African snail, *Achatina fulica,* grows nearly to the size of a football and can weigh more than a pound. Introduced from Madagascar, where it is native, to the smaller island of Mauritius, to the east, it quickly became a serious pest in cotton fields. In 1847 an English traveler, W. H. Benson, saw the snails on Mauritius and took a few along with him to India. (Mauritius, it happens, was home of the dodo, type specimen for extinct island animals everywhere. The gargantuan snail can be seen as the Dodo's Revenge.) Benson's snails multiplied prodigiously in India, as populations tend to do there. By 1900 the snail was in Ceylon, eating cocoa; next it was in Malaya, eating rubber trees. From its new centers of dispersal it made slow, slimy, but steady progress outward, eating melons, legumes, rice, rat poison—upon which it thrived—and the lime from any whitewashed walls and fences that stood in its way. It was introduced to the Micronesian Islands by the Japanese, who considered the snail a delicacy.

In the Palau Islands once, as an experiment, I tried feeding the huge African snails to the native estuarine crocodiles that were confined to cages on the lawn of the small biology laboratory where I worked and lived. The trouble with exotic arrivals on islands, I knew, is that few natural predators lie waiting for them. Nothing could be more naturally predatory, I thought, than a twelve-foot croc. The crocodiles rudely took the experimental snails from my hand through the heavy mesh. Crocodiles can be very fast when they want to be, and one small croc lacerated my finger against the cage before I realized its head had moved. Each crocodile, having taken the shell, invariably fumbled and dropped it. I think the crocodiles expected the whole arm, not just this calcerous thing the hand was holding. The reptile would then retrieve the snail, which clinked like a fifty-caliber shell casing against its teeth. Suddenly deft, the crocodile tossed and shifted the snail backward down its snaggly row of teeth toward the fulcrum at the corner of its jaw. It clamped down, cracked the shell, swallowed. After two or three snails, unfortunately, the dim reptilian brain came to realize it did not care for escargots, and each crocodile lost interest.

My crocodile results were typical. Those who have followed men like Mongoose Forbes and "Snail" Benson—as that short-sighted Englishman might have been called—and "Starling" Scheifflin and "Mynah" Hillebrand seldom have much luck undoing the deeds of those notorious tinkerers. In their unnatural contexts exotic pests seem to possess an unnatural vitality. Before coming to Hawai'i I had witnessed only one campaign—the program to control the coconut rhinoceros beetle in Micronesia—in which man seemed to be winning.

In Hawai'i Volcanoes National Park the most destructive of exotic pests is the pig. It is estimated that four thousand feral pigs live in the park, foraging 25 percent of its territory, or 60,000 acres. The damage they do is difficult to quantify—pigs have been loose in Hawai'i for centuries, and no pre-pig baseline data exist—but in 1968 the Park Service gave quantification a try, setting up an exclosure in the fern forest near Thurston Lava Tube. Pigs were fenced out from the exclosure's 900 square meters of 'ōhi'a trees and hāpu'u and *Sadleria* ferns. Thirteen years later, plots inside and outside the exclosure were sampled and compared. Where pigs had roamed freely, Park Service researchers found a more abundant cover of exotic grasses and herbs, a greater number of exotic plant species, more exposed soil, and more exposed roots. The exclosure experiment confirmed the intuitions of anyone who spends much time in the Hawaiian backcountry. The exclosure had become a small, ferny, atavistic island drifting back toward the flora of old Hawai'i. Around it, sharky with pigs, was a sea drifting the other way, toward pauperization, bastardization, and desert.

It seemed to me now, standing in the 'Ōla'a tree ferns with Dan Taylor, that the most cosmopolitan of the alien animals I had seen on islands was the pig. I remembered stumbling into the sandy bowls that feral pigs excavate in Galápagos beaches as they snout out the nests of sea turtles. I recalled the small deserts I had seen pigs make in the jungle around the stilted longhouses of Iban tribesmen on Borneo, and the feral-pig damage I had observed in the palmettos of the Sea Islands of Georgia. I decided that in the war against the pigs I would throw in on Taylor's side.

IN THE jeep again, Taylor made a U-turn, and we retreated from our detour into the Paleozoic of 'Ōla'a. We left the tree ferns behind, passed out of Kīlauea Volcano's rainy zone, and drove southward into the lava desert of the Chain of Craters Road. Zonation on islands is often radically abbreviated, and it was so here—a ten-minute drive brought us into entirely different country. If the 'Ōla'a ferns belonged to the Paleozoic, then this new terrain belonged to some Archeozoic age of vulcanism or to some dry and blasted age of our future. We passed through the small, black lithic sea of the 1969 lava flow, pushed up at regular intervals into small buttes. The buttes were tree molds. Inside each one were the remnants of an 'ōhi'a that the lava had flowed over. We passed the pit craters for which the road is named: Devil's Throat, Hi'iaka Crater, Puhimau Crater. The feral pig, versatile animal, lives in this country, too.

Taylor pulled the jeep off the road onto a cindery shoulder. On the eastern side of the pavement was Puhimau Crater. On the western side was a thermal area of whitened 'ōhi'a snags and steamy ground—a pit crater in the process of becoming, some vulcanologists believe. On the crater side was a pig fence. Taylor, climbing down from the jeep bent to tug at the lowermost wire.

"The bottom wire is real tight—they can't root under it," he said. "If they do start to root, we know it right away, because we walk the fence every two weeks on inspections. We pull trees off the wire and fix breaks. Pigs are fast but not particularly agile. They aren't good jumpers. The fence is only thirty-two inches high, but that's enough."

The fence ran to the edge of Puhimau Crater, incorporating that natural feature as part of the pig barrier, and then resumed on the other side. The pigs within this Puhimau Unit, fenced off from the rest of their kind, were under almost daily attack by Park Service hunters and dogs.

"Pigs were introduced two hundred years ago or more," Taylor said. "So a lot of people here think of pigs as native animals. They don't understand why we are trying to control them. The school system lets us down badly. The local schools don't teach Hawaiian natural history. We have a huge education effort at hand. We've got to manage the resource and educate people as to why. There's a lot of misunderstanding on why we manage the park as we do. We're tolerated by most people, understood by a few, disliked by some. Recreational pig hunters—the Hawaiians who hunt for meat—are the most hostile."

I considered for a moment the hypothesis that those hunters were right. Perhaps the native ecosystem was so shattered that any attempt at reconstruction was foolish. Better, maybe, to pretend that pigs and passionflowers were native, to let them achieve some new balance, and start managing from there.

"It's been two centuries now," I suggested. "Is there anything like a new equilibrium?"

Taylor shook his head. "The system has not begun to accommodate these organisms."

As we walked back to the jeep, Taylor nodded toward the roadside. "You see the lighter-colored green in there?" I did. Among the drab, desert green of scrub 'ōhi'a and pūkiawe were clumps of paler green. "Sandalwood," Taylor said.

I knew something of the story of sandalwood: discovered by Captain Cook in 1778; commercialized by Captain Kendrick in 1791; worth eight to ten dollars a *picul* in China, where the fragrant, close-grained heartwood was made into incense, carvings, and cabinetwork; nearly extinct by 1886, when the logging ceased. A *picul*, about 133 pounds, was the load that a Hawaiian was supposed to be able to carry from the woods. King Kamehameha financed his conquest of the Hawaiian Archipelago largely by the sale of sandalwood in Canton. I had written all this up once, but I had never seen the actual tree.

"Goats," Taylor explained. "There used to be a lot of them in here. Since we eliminated the goats here, the sandalwoods are just bouncing back."

The war against feral goats preceded the war against the pigs, and the rangers learned many of the rules of animal warfare in the earlier effort. The goat, *Capra hircus*, was probably introduced to Hawai'i Island by Captain Cook in 1778, in the vicinity of Kealakekua Bay, on the western shore, and it quickly spread over the entire island. In the 1920s control efforts began in Hawai'i Volcanoes National Park. Between 1927 and 1970, 70,000 goats were killed in the park by deputized hunters, rangers, foresters, Civilian Conservation Corps personnel under ranger supervision, and "goat-control companies" of professional hunters. In 1970 an aerial census showed about 15,000 goats left in the park— approximately the same number estimated to have been there when the goat-control efforts had begun, half a century before. The goat campaigns have been ragtag, intermittent, almost recreational, much like unsuccessful goat campaigns I had witnessed in the Galápagos. The campaigns in Hawai'i had also failed. The remarkable randiness and the high reproductive potential of *Capra hircus* had overcome every one of them.

After that 1970 census the Park Service declared war. Park planners devised a long-range strategy: goatproof boundary fences, internal drift fences, frequent drives, organized hunts, a vegetation-monitoring program to measure the success or failure of their efforts. Between 1971 and 1975, 12,976 goats were killed. *Capra hircus* became hard to find in the park. The citizen hunters participating in the program lost interest and dropped out, but Park Service riflemen continued, searching in helicopters—goat gunships—or on horseback, with dogs. Between 1976 and 1979, 1,596 more goats were killed. By 1980 goats had been fenced out of 90 percent of their former range and only about 200 remained in the park.

The surviving goats proved the hardest to eliminate, predictably, and the Park Service experimented with new methods to get rid of them. The last and perhaps cleverest was the old Judas-goat trick, updated. Radio collars were attached to captured goats, which were then released. Goats are not fond of solitude, and each Judas goat invariably joined up with a herd of its fellows. The rangers homed in on the beep of his signal. Today fewer than half a dozen goats hold out in the park.

Sitting in the jeep, Dan Taylor waved in the direction of Puhimau Crater. The Park Service had begun experimenting with radio collars on pigs, too, he said. Out there somewhere, in the Puhimau Unit, a sow was beeping. This was the first reference I heard to the animal called the Electric Pig.

BOBBY MATTOS, one of the park's six full-time hunters, sat at a desk writing up his report. Behind him a huge map of the park—a battle map, divided into hunting units—covered the wall. Mattos had just returned from a day's hunt in Puhimau Unit. He was sweaty and dirty, and his T-shirt was torn. The hunter is of Portuguese ancestry, lean, brown, and in his mid-twenties. His short beard had once been trimmed along the jawline, but the shaved part had since gone stubbly. He is handsome in a failed-bullfighter, Mexican-bandit sort of way. He looked rough—he was a professional cutter of throats—but his smile on greeting Taylor was shy. He told the boss that the dogs had bumped into the Electric Pig that day. They had missed her, once again, but later had caught a boar. He moved to the map, and his finger made a circle inside the Puhimau border.

"The dogs worked this area real good, but there were no hookups. So we went down the Sow Trail. It's a trail they always use from the bottom up. They got a main highway going up and down. Soon as we reached down, we started hitting some t'ick undergrowth, and the dogs started to go crazy. This is where they caught him. We couldn't see nothin'. Had to go crawling underneat' to go get him."

(The Sow Trail is named for a predecessor of the Electric Pig. This sow, like the Electric Pig, was one of six feral pigs trapped, fitted with radio collars, and released in the Puhimau Unit. The sow of Sow Trail was considerably less ingenious than the Electric Pig. Her invariable habit when flushed by the dogs was to run a beeline down what became known as the Sow Trail. The radio

man followed her flight with his antenna. He reported that she
would hide that night and most of the next day at the dry end of
the unit, and then the next evening would work her way back to
the wet end, where the foraging was good. This beeline sow was
no more. Of the six radio-collared pigs released in Puhimau, only
one, the Electric Pig, survived.)

"This one today, he put up a good fight," Mattos said, of
this afternoon's boar. "He probably said, 'Hey, you ain't gonna
take me.' He picked a good place to fight 'em, too—thick stuff,
dogs cannot move around. He gave Keoki some pokes, too. I got
a note down at the kennel, Keoki got one underneath the jaw, and
a couple of skins."

Bobby Mattos is a speaker of pidgin. When his ancestors
arrived from Madeira and the Azores to work in the cane, they
met immigrant workers from the Philippines, China, Puerto Rico,
Mexico, and Japan, and pidgin evolved among them as a *lingua
franca*, a *lingua sacchara*. Like most pidgin-speakers, Mattos can
turn the dialect up or down. In the field, hunting pigs, he turns it
up thick and strong. In the office he turns it down almost to
English, and Taylor can understand him.

"The pigs know what's going on, for sure," Mattos said, of
the embattled few in Puhimau Unit. "They're so afraid, you know?
They're running for their lives. This pig today, the tracker barked
him. Just one bark, and the pig was gone. I ooshed Pāʻele on
him, '*Go, go, go, go, go!*' He knew which direction that buggah
had run, and he found 'im again. We had Moʻo, too. Moʻo is a
grabber, too. But that pig was so aggressive, he couldn't get in.
Only Keoki got in."

Taylor turned to me. "Out of fifteen dogs, we have three
grabbers," he explained. "The grabbers are like infantrymen.
They're the ones that get hurt."

The tracker finds the pig, the grabbers grab it, and the help-
ers help, worrying its heels. The dogs' job is to surround and hold

the pig, cutting off its escape routes until the hunters come up.
The dogs sometimes kill small pigs on their own, and they rou-
tinely dispatch piglets, which the park's hunters call "rabbits."
This pig-hunting method—one or two men and a pack of dogs—
developed in the Paleolithic and is still the method Hawaii's sport
hunters use. Park Service strategists have given some thought to
new wrinkles. What would happen, they wonder, if they used a
single dog trained to bark at the pig and not attack; suppose it was
some small, unthreatening, yappy breed at which the pig would
laugh before resuming his rooting? The dog would flag the pig by
sound for the rifleman coming up behind. For now, however, the
park men are sticking with the Paleolithic method. Park Service
dogs are sometimes wounded, but the pack has yet to suffer a
fatality. Pigs run through human beings who stand in their way.
The humans go down like bowling pins, but the pigs are generally
in too much of a hurry to work them over on the ground. Men
hunting for pork are sometimes injured in Hawai'i, but none of
the Park Service hunters has been hurt.

"Keoki, he's kind of an old dog, isn't he?" Taylor asked
Mattos.

"Yeah. He's just a bull, too—pit bull."

"Pit bulls aren't good for this?" I asked.

"They're good," said Mattos, "but not too much brain, you
know?"

The hunter looked to the map on the wall. "Before this
program, wherever you go there's pig damage, no matter where
you look," he said. "Now all you see is green grass growing. Today
the only damage I seen was real hard to see. It was underneath the
uluhe ferns. They're not coming out anymore. They can stay
alive underneath the uluhe, but they're not gonna come out and
knock down hāpu'u, or nothin' like that."

The thick tangles of uluhe, the false staghorn fern, reminded
Bobby Mattos of the Electric Pig. "That sow, she sure knows what's
going on," he said. "She just knows where to run. Dogs cannot

pick up real good speed in the uluhe. They get all tangled up, whereas the pig will just put down her nose and—no problem. She's like a torpedo through there."

Pigs, built close to the ground, are made for crashing through brush, Dan Taylor explained. Dogs are rangier animals, and less canny. He asked if I had noticed the crack on Kīlauea. I had. Cracks ramify everywhere on the slopes of that volcano, a consequence of seismic shifts accompanying the mountain's vulcanism. Those cracks were often hidden by uluhe and other vegetation, Taylor said, and dogs sometimes fell into them. Pigs did not. Bobby Mattos nodded, and confessed that just last week the hunters had lost a dog in a crack. Dogs fell thirty feet sometimes, and the hunters had to go down after them with ropes and harnesses. It was slimy down there, Mattos added, making a face. "A pig knows the cracks, but the dogs don't know."

I could see how it was: The Electric Pig fleeing like a torpedo down her runways under the uluhe—captured again—the men cursing behind her, the dogs crashing through the fern tangles. Then the yelp as a tracker or a grabber felt the earth open up beneath, his barking suddenly frantic and distant, like the complaint of a fly trapped under a tumbler, the Electric Pig running on.

WE LEFT the watershed of Kīlauea volcano, the five dogs tied to the bed of the truck by short leashes. Ahead the smooth arc of Mauna Loa showed a pale red in the dawn light. Later in the morning a cap of cloud would form, cutting off the summit. Only early risers get to see the whole of the earth's greatest active volcano.

I could remember no mountain in my life that gave so poor a sense of scale. At this hour it looked more a mountain of sand than of lava. Mauna Loa might have been a near, lunate dune encroaching on the backside of this 'ōhi'a forest. It might have been a giant, pale-rose moon rising over the same 'ōhi'as.

The truth was somewhere in between. Mauna Loa contains 10,000 cubic miles of material. I once heard a park interpreter tell a Volcanoes Park audience that this one mountain contains more rock than the entire Sierra Nevada and Mount Shasta combined. Her facts were wrong but nicely suggestive. Mauna Loa is among the largest shield volcanoes in the solar system. Theia Mons, on Venus, is considerably larger, and Olympus Mons, on Mars, is even larger than Theia, but both those places are far away, and you can't get there by pickup truck.

Turning off the highway onto the Mauna Loa Strip Road, we left the 'ōhi'as behind and meandered up through koa forest. The turns were sharp, the surface cracked and potholed. The koa trunks, white in the early-morning light, reminded me of aspen back home. The truck flushed several coveys of California quail. They were exotics, but I was glad to see them. It was hard to feel indignant—I am an exotic from California myself.

This trip into the dry forest of Mauna Loa's lower slopes was a training hunt for the young dogs and for me. The pigs of Puhimau Unit, where the hunters had been concentrating their efforts lately, were so close to eradication—just three to six pigs left—that sometimes days passed without the dogs flushing a single one. Today the plan was to reacquaint the dogs and acquaint the writer.

Harry Pagan drove, checking the dogs occasionally in his rearview mirror. Pagan is Filipino–Puerto Rican, a dark-skinned man, stocky and quiet. At thirty-two, he is the oldest of the hunters.

"He seems to me the best of the lot," one of his Park Service superiors had told me. "He goes *through* the uluhe. He doesn't plan his hunt, or try to hunt *around* anything. He just goes where he thinks the pigs are going to be. He's a joy to hunt with. He's really good with a needle—good at sewing dogs up, getting them back to health once they get gored by pigs. Harry is unusual in that he hunts the 'Ōla'a Tract. Most hunters in the 'Ōla'a rain forest will look for signs right by the road. Harry will hike back for a couple of hours or more."

I had spoken with one female ranger who was convinced, having watched Pagan's calm intensity in the hunt, having seen his efficiency at killing pigs in hand-to-hoof combat, with a knife, that Pagan was a Vietnam combat veteran—had to be. He is not, but he does do weekend duty with the National Guard. He likes the military, and in conversation he often turns to soldiering for his metaphors. His partner today was Casey Baldwin, a young, blond Californian working seasonally as a hunter.

The dogs were Pā'ele, Gus, Hana, Shy, and Moku. Pā'ele was the tracker, the oldest and most experienced of the five. His name means "black" in Hawaiian, and he certainly was that. Gus looked to be part Airedale, and Hana looked vaguely like a collie. Shy was a short-haired, muscular mongrel with a snuffly, rasping way of breathing that came, Pagan said, from heartworm. Moku was a lean, raw-boned, ribby one-year-old that looked to be part black-and-tan. The park's kennel-keeper and dog-procurer had told me, earlier that morning, of the importance of finding dogs with the right "lines." I could not remember meeting a bunch of dogs with lines more sketchy and tangled. I suspected that these had been recruited from hangouts comparable to the ones where, in human society, the French recruit legionnaires.

Halfway to the end of the road Pagan pulled off and parked. We unbuckled the collars, and the freed dogs hit the roadside bushes, marking every shrub in sight. That accomplished, we entered the bush. One after another the dogs stopped, hunkered in the shamefaced way of dogs, and unloaded, lightening themselves for the job. For a time that odor was heavy upon us. Then all the dogs were running trim, and we smelled nothing other than the good desert pungence of the xeric vegetation on Mauna Loa's middle flanks. We wore long sleeves against the thorns, and baseball caps against the sun. We carried our lunch and water in day packs, and Casey Baldwin cradled the rifle, a lever action .30–.30.

A knife was best for pigs, Pagan told me as we walked. A knife was economical and less risky for the dogs. Sticking a pig wasn't as hard as it sounded—once you had a pig by the back legs, he was yours. In certain situations, though, you had to shoot. A .22 was too small for the job. I wondered aloud about other calibers. What about a 30.06? Both hunters laughed at me. Too big, they said: it would go right through the pig and hit the dogs.

"Oh, I hunt from ten years old," Pagan said, when I asked. "On my own, and with my uncle. At ten years old, I knew how to stick a pig—the whole works. My first experience, I was scared. We caught four pigs in one bunch. They make a big sound, let me tell you. Loud grunting. *Mean*! In those days there's so much pigs, man. I mean it was unreal. Now you really have to work for your pigs."

"And you still like it?"

He smiled and waggled his head weakly, ruefully—a man admitting to a powerful addiction. "Oh, I love it."

We were moving through open parkland broken here and there by pūkiawe thickets. Now and again Pagan would stop and intently watch Pāʻele, the tracker. It was as if he were reading in Pāʻele's behavior some transliteration of the olfactory messages the dog was picking up. We came to places where pigs had rooted. They had left furrows in the grass, the clods overturned, the undersides fine-bearded with rootlets. It was an old sign, and Pagan was not interested. The dogs coursed through the bush without barking, and the two hunters spoke very little.

"You don't give voice commands," I observed.

"We're not too much into obedience," Pagan answered. "The only thing is to get them to fight the pig, right now. It's in the dog. If he's going to be a hunter, he'll show signs of interest early.

Some are just natural. Some take longer than others. You got some cowards. You got some that just grab."

"They get hurt that way? Just grabbing?"

Pagan smiled and shook his head in sympathy for those dogs—yes, they got hurt that way. "Sows usually do the biting. I've seen dogs get their leg broken, just one bite. The boars use the tusk more. A tusk is what hurt Keoki the other day."

When we came to pūkiawe thickets, Pagan generally would lead us through the middles. I understood why—if hunters were afraid of bushwhack, if the centers of pūkiawe thickets remained inviolate, then pigs would never be eradicated from the national park—but fighting pūkiawe was hard work. The sun climbs quickly in the subtropics, and soon we were all sweating or lolling our tongues. As the heat rose, so did the odor of the dogs. This pack did not smell at all like domestic dogs. They smelled gamy and half-wild, like the feral animals they were hunting.

Moku, the rawboned one-year-old, was a frolicker in tall grass. Whenever we came to a vale of it, he set off bounding, sometimes causing a chain reaction among the others, who thought he was onto something. Harry Pagan would watch Moku's false alarms expressionlessly and then smile a small, skeptical smile. Moku, it seemed to me, had little future as a hunter.

Hana did not seem promising material either, and in this view Casey Baldwin concurred. "Hana's just a carpet," Baldwin complained. Hana malingered, as usual, hanging back with us human beings. "That dog was meant to be in the bathroom, to wipe your feet on." Harry Pagan, always the defender of young dogs, was more charitable. "He's still learning. Some take a while."

Pā'ele, the tracker, was all business. Shy, the dog with heartworm, was diligent enough, but after an hour or two in the sun his malady began to slow him. "He's good for just so long," Pagan said.

Our luck with pigs was poor, and Pagan apologized. The trouble was lunar, he said.

"When we got a big moon, the pigs they travel, they travel. They move all night and sleep during the day. Without no moon, the pigs they sleep at night. When the big moon, you see a whole lot of sign, and you keep following, following." The pigs were skinny up here in the dry forest of Mauna Loa, he said. Pigs liked it better in the 'Ola'a rain forest. They liked the cool, and the mud, and the hāpu'u, and 'Ola'a pigs tasted better. Pagan usually smoked his pig, or made it into sausage. He promised to take me to the 'Ola'a rain forest and show me some real pig hunting.

"You should have been here in July, when we were hunting in Nāpau," Pagan said. "If you were here in July, you'd need lots of notebooks. Forty-six pigs in twenty-one days. Camping out, drinking warm beer. No ice."

The Nāpau Unit, it happened, was where Kīlauea was currently erupting. Recently the volcano had been going off every thirteen days or so, sending up incandescent thousand-foot fountains of lava, building a new cone at the place designated "O-vent," turning the night sky red. Today, as we rested in Mauna Loa's shade, O-vent was due for its twenty-fifth eruption in the series. Two eruptions ago, in that time of phenomenal hunting luck and warm beer, the hunters had been out after pigs when the volcano began to rumble. They heard the roar, like a jet engine in an interminable takeoff. They looked up to see cinders everywhere coming down from the sky. The hunting was too good to break off. They killed eight more pigs before discretion won out and they retreated from the volcano.

Our rest over, we plunged into another thicket of pūkiawe. When we came out on the other side, Harry saw a farther pūkiawe thicket, and we plunged into that.

Pūkiawe, in the days of Hawaiian royalty, was the great equalizer. If a chief wished to lift his own kapu, temporarily suspending his untouchability in order to rub shoulders with commoners, he shut himself up in a smokehouse and cured himself over a smudge fire of pūkiawe. Bushwhacking through the pūkiawe now, sweaty and itchy, our pant legs burnished by the hides of sun-heated half-wild mongrels and slavered on by tongues, our shirts sappy and dirty and prickly with burrs, we had the common touch already. The pūkiawe wasn't necessary.

By eleven in the morning the dogs had begun to drag. Several times Baldwin, coming up behind Pāʻele, would shift his rifle, grab Pāʻele by the scruff, and pitch the tracker forward. No disrespect was intended. Pāʻele seemed grateful for these jet-assisted boosts onward into the fray.

We came to a stand of koas, and the dogs detoured inside to pant in the shade. At the edge of the grove were the remains of a pig killed on a previous hunt. A black, tusked head lay in the center of a dark and greasy circle on the grass. The smell was very high. I found the dead pig disquieting, like the pig that gave the title to *Lord of the Flies.* One of the dogs sniffed and prepared to roll in it. Pagan barked a guttural warning, and the dog drew back instantly. It pretended it had never really been interested in rolling, and trotted on into the shade.

When we reached the road again and the hunt was done, we had encountered no pigs. Pagan and I waited in the shade with the dogs while Baldwin walked down the road to fetch the truck. Moku sat between Pagan's legs and licked his face. The hunter accepted this for a while and then began to wrestle with Moku's jaws, holding them open while the dog squirmed. When Pagan released the jaws, Moku came back for more.

Pagan told me of a precocious puppy owned by a friend of his on the Kona coast, a puppy just ten months old and already covered with battle scars. A dog that aggressive was unusual. He spoke of Jim, one of the better trackers in the Park Service pack. As soon as Jim found a pig, he lost interest. He was a detective, not a warrior. While the other dogs cornered and fought the pig, Jim was off looking for another. "That was my dog," Pagan said. "I give him to the park. Too much noise, nighttime. Just want to go hunt." Harry spoke of hounds. Baying dogs were no good for this sort of work, he said. "You bring hounds here, no telling where the pig would stop. As long as he hears the hounds behind him, he's gonna keep running." Some sort of cross-hound was an interesting idea, Pagan thought. He spoke of the Electric Pig.

"That pig is so smart, you know? She has experience with people. On a transect one time, we saw her with three babies. On different hunts we managed to get all her babies. I think right now she doesn't have anything to look forward to. She doesn't have to worry about her babies. She can move out, she knows the terrain, she can hear the dogs. She won't stick around."

IN THE war against the pigs, as in most wars, the generals speak a different language from that of the troops.

"We achieved about fifty percent removal in mesic forest—medium-wetness forest, like on Mauna Loa Strip Road—in six months, which is better than you need to extinct the population in a three-year period, if our models and densities are about right," C. P. Stone told me.

Chuck Stone is the officer in charge of research for the pig-control program. Sitting at his desk, shelves of reports and bulletins and monographs behind him, he recited, off the top of his head, the figures on the enemy: The average age of the pigs caught was sixteen months, the average weight sixty-eight pounds. The oldest pig taken so far had been seven, and at that age its teeth were almost gone. Most of the pigs taken in Volcanoes Park were of the dark phenotype, but occasionally the hunters, or a trap, turned up a pig with Polynesian characteristics—the straight ears, the long snout, the woolly undercoat.

Stone had just returned from an emergency meeting in Kīpahulu Valley, on the island of Maui, where feral pigs were on an offensive into new territory. The Maui pigs were closer to domestic stock, with more red and brindled black-and-white in them.

In Volcanoes Park pigs, Stone said, the parasite load varied with the habitat. The pigs up in the mesic forest of Mauna Loa were generally quite clean. The pigs in the drier, more stressful Puhimau Unit were often loaded. Pigs could accommodate a lot of internal company, and some Puhimau pigs, when you opened them up, just crawled.

Stone told me that the first method tried against the pigs of Volcanoes Park had been box traps, which were all the rage against feral pigs in Australia and California. "We had really good luck with that," he said. "We took quite a few pigs fast, and we thought, 'Boy, we're really home free.' It only lasted a couple of weeks, and then the numbers of pigs caught started going down. We now think we were just creaming off some of the younger and more naive animals."

Since then, he said, the pig-fighters have tried snaring, with some success. They once tried netting, with no success at all. Stone has given some thought to poison but doubts that that measure would prove economical. A few radical pig-detesters on Hawai'i Island have contemplated introducing hog cholera and pseudo-rabies, but Stone has never favored such extreme measures. By far the best method to date, he said, has been hunters and dogs.

"The average success has been a pig every day's hunt. Lately we haven't been doing that well in areas where we have fewer pigs. With these last pigs we're going to have to get more inventive, as we did with goats."

My thoughts of late had turned Darwinian. I remembered the Electric Pig. "Has it ever crossed your mind that you might be producing a superpig out there?" I asked.

"Sure. That's what they've done with pheasants on the mainland, to a certain degree. All the pheasants that haven't flown before the gun are selected for, and you've got a lot more running pheasants. The same thing with some of the quail. And it's happened here, too, with our goat program. A lot of surviving goats in this park are the black ones, the ones that dive down into the cracks as soon as they hear the helicopter. We're going to get something like that with pigs."

"But the difference with pigs," I suggested, "is that the thing you're molding is intelligence. A pig is an unusually intelligent animal, no?"

"Sure. Psychological tests put them well ahead of dogs."

"You might be producing a pig that's able to handle any contingency?"

"Perhaps. What we're hoping, of course, is that by fencing areas, and doing a wipe-out in each area, we're preventing the pigs from passing those genes on."

AT 4:30 in the morning, a fragrant pre-dawn, the hunters assembled, joking sleepily and complaining, outside the pig-control office. Harry Pagan handed out headlamps and tested his walkie-talkie. We were headed for the Puhimau Unit in pursuit of the Electric Pig.

"You got rounds for the carbine?" Bobby Mattos asked.

"We got two clips over there," Pagan answered. "What a beautiful morning—to be in bed."

Pagan drove the Scout down to the kennel, and Bobby Mattos drove the pickup. The dogs were eager, whining and jumping up against the cages, the mesh thrashing in the darkness. Pagan, buckling Shy to his collar on the Scout, turned his face away as Shy tried to lick. He finished buckling by feel. I stood alongside Pat Finnegan, one of the hunters, and together we leashed dogs to the side panel of the truck. Finnegan was thinking about our quarry. "They think it's more important to get her out than the others," he said. "I don't know why. I'm tired of chasing her, really."

Pagan, Casey Baldwin, six dogs, and I began the hunt by walking to Puhimau Unit's southern fence. Bobby Mattos, Pat Finnegan, and their six dogs entered Puhimau from the other side and bushwhacked cross-country toward us. Andy Kikuta, the radio man, stationed himself on a dirt road that bordered the unit at right angles to our fenceline, and with a hand-held antenna he monitored the Electric Pig.

The dawn came on quickly, and we never really needed the headlamps. The steeply ascendant, sparsely foliated branches of the 'ōhi'a were lovely against the lightening sky. 'Ōhi'a branches beseech heaven in a way that has always made me think of Judith Anderson in *Medea*, and the old Hawaiians saw it more or less the same way—as a woman dancing the hula.

The light came up, color entered the world, and we could make out the scarlet of the 'ōhi'a blossoms. The blossoms made the only points of warm color in a landscape from the cool end of the spectrum, hot spots in a xerophytic vegetation of drab olives and greens. In the old days the flowers of the 'ōhi'a were sacred to Pele, the goddess of volcanoes. The reason, I would bet, is that each circle of long, scarlet stamens looks so much like lava fountaining. Each blossom is a little eruption.

Uluhe ferns grew everywhere, and the dogs floundered through. Sometimes the spring mats of ferns, like trampolines, refused to let the dogs down to earth; other times the mats let the dogs down hard.

"See the noise they make?" Pagan asked. He shook his head. "Pigs have tunnels underneath. Once a pig gets running in those tunnels, dogs can't stop him."

Mo'o, a pit bull with extraordinary vertical leap, was hunting in Pagan's pack today. This morning Mo'o was given to jumping the fence and hunting on the wrong side. Once, on impulse, from a dead standstill he cleared the thirty-two-inch fence with ease. Pagan looked back at me to see if I'd seen. "Mo'o is one of our acrobats," he said.

Mo'o is a grabber who has a long acquaintance with Pagan's sewing needle. He sometimes appears all slashed and bleeding from private wars of his own. Finding a pig by himself, he leaps in without bothering to bark for assistance. In Hawaiian, *mo'o* means "lizard, dragon," or "water spirit," or "young, as of pigs and dogs," or "brindled." Brindled dogs were favored as sacrifices to the water spirits. This was before pit bulls, of course, back in the days when Hawaii's dogs were vegetarian. It would have been impolitic to sacrifice a dog with the temperament of this particular Moʻo. Moʻo was brindled, all right, but sent on to the next world he would cheerfully have gone for the water spirits' throats.

At intervals Pagan would stop to confer by walkie-talkie with Andy Kikuta. He would inform Kikuta of our approximate position along the fence, and Kikuta would in turn give the Electric Pig's coordinates in relation to us. We were closing in on her, Pagan's dogs from one side, Bobby Mattos's dogs from the other.

Once, while speaking on the walkie-talkie, Pagan crouched and with an *épée* of swordgrass flicked leaf fragments from the twin clefts of a hoofprint. Until he cleaned it up, the print had been invisible to me. Another time, while listening to Kikuta give the new coordinates for the Electric Pig, Pagan pointed wordlessly to a spot low on the trunk of a small ʻōhiʻa, a place where the wood was debarked and worn smooth. A pig had rubbed itself there, Pagan whispered. Inside the smooth zone I saw the deep scratch of a tusk.

Pagan signed off and returned the walkie-talkie to his belt. We had the Electric Pig where we wanted her, he announced. We were driving her straight toward Bobby Mattos and his dogs.

Passing a seedling shrub, Pagan uprooted it. "ʻĀkia," he said. "They used this to make rope." Handing me one end, he invited me to pull and see how strong it was. It was strong indeed. I had read that the root and bark of ʻākia were poisonous, the hemlock of old Hawaiʻi. "This is to keep you alive," the Hawaiian who presented the bowl was supposed to have recited ironically. Rough humor, but welcome, perhaps, like that salutation Socrates himself offered before downing his last drink.

I thought of the Electric Pig. She was in at least as tough a spot as Socrates. I found myself wondering what would happen to a pig who took Hawaiian hemlock. Nothing, probably, considering the gastric prowess of pigs.

We were nearly to the dirt road. Kikuta and his radio antenna were just fifty yards away, through thick 'ōhi'a, and Bobby Mattos was closing in to our left. We heard Mattos's dogs jump the Electric Pig. Our own dogs vanished in that direction. We ran toward the sound ourselves, but after seventy yards or so the barking and crashing of brush was coming from too many quarters, and we stopped and waited. The walkie-talkie crackled, and Mattos came on to inform us that his dogs had failed to stop the pig.

We sat in the shade of the 'ōhi'a trees, temporarily defeated, waiting for the dogs to reassemble. After a time the brush parted and Kikuta emerged, carrying his antenna by the pistol grip. He gestured with the antenna toward the forest behind us. The pig had circled around that way, he said. He and Pagan exchanged fatalistic looks.

"That pig sending us to the cleaner, boy," Pagan said.

"And not so big, either," Kikuta said. "Sixty pounds."

"That size can run. She's got her plan all down already. 'If they hit me from the front, break this way one hundred yards, then cut left.'"

We heard a rustling from the brush. "One dog coming?" Pagan asked. "Yes," Kikuta answered.

Pagan listened hard. "Mo'o," he predicted, from the sound of the dog's breathing. Half a minute later Mo'o emerged from the brush.

Five minutes after Mo'o, Bobby Mattos emerged, sweat shining on his forehead, and right behind him was Pat Finnegan. Pagan took a look at Mattos's face.

"Bobby, Bobby, Bobby. No get mad. No get mad."

Mattos cursed the pig.

In the quest for the Electric Pig, Harry Pagan plays Starbuck to Bobby Mattos's Ahab.

Pat Finnegan joined the rest of us where we sat in the shade, but Mattos would not sit. "Ten meters, the bark, from me to you," Mattos told Pagan. The Electric Pig had been that close.

"I felt stupid," Finnegan said. "I was running toward the first bark when I heard the second bark way down there."

"Skid marks," said Mattos. He imitated, perfectly, the sound of a car squealing through a skid and then accelerating at the far end. "It looks like one place they try to grab her. Skid marks—bust-up, spin-around kind. What is this, my fifth time I hit her?"

The dogs Shy and Gus showed up, their tongues hanging, and they plopped in the shade. They had been hunting with Mattos's group today. "Can you tell us where the Electric Pig is?" Casey Baldwin asked. Neither dog seemed to have any idea.

The other dogs straggled in. Hana was among the first, and he immediately set to digging a hole for himself in the shade. Hana puts vastly more energy into making himself comfortable during rest stops than he puts into pig-hunting in the intervals between.

"As long as we take Hana, we always have fresh sign," Pagan said. "And *hana* in Hawaiian means 'work.'" He laughed at the irony. Baldwin, reaching out, made pig tracks with his knuckles in Hana's fresh black dirt. His tracks were good imitations. They would have fooled me, at least.

When the last of the dogs was accounted for, we returned to the hunt, working back in the direction we had come. Discarding any semblance of fair play, we began tracking the pig directly by radio. Andy Kikuta accompanied us, holding the antenna aloft to take a reading from time to time. The original purpose of the radio-collar—to study the behavior of pigs when flushed by dogs—had been forgotten. Casey Baldwin, whom I was following, grumbled a little. This was unsporting, he said. It made no sense to chase one pig this way, when five or six others still held out in the Puhimau Unit.

We were drawing close to the Electric Pig, and I had a strong

intuition that this time we would get her. My feelings were mixed;
I had developed considerable admiration for this pig. Suddenly
her radio signal ceased.

Kikuta cast about for it without success. This had never
happened before, and Kikuta looked puzzled. "It must be the
terrain," he said. "She must be down in a puka somewhere."

Climbing a small 'ōhi'a and getting no signal, he tried a taller tree. I lay on my back, folding my hands behind my head, and
watched him climb. Kikuta looked good up there, his legs scissor-
ing a crotch twenty feet high, with bright clouds moving above
him. He pointed the antenna in one direction, then another. We
listened for the beep. No sound came but the breeze in the crowns
of the 'ōhi'as. Perhaps this Einstein of pigs had figured a way
to avoid human radar entirely.

Harry Pagan, taking a plastic quart bottle from his pack,
raised it high and poured a thin stream for the dogs. Instantly
they convened under it. Today's hunt was over, I realized. This
tipping of the bottle was a gesture of concession to the Electric
Pig. She would live to root again, at least until tomorrow.

The dogs always behave for Pagan, and not one growled or
shoved in the slender waterfall from the bottle. They made a
pyramid of dusty hides and lapping tongues, and I thought,
oddly, of that statue of the Marines raising the flag on Iwo Jima.
This was dog sculpture. Pagan cocked his head to study the lines.
For an instant the stream would spatter off a dog's forehead, and
then that dog would reposition itself. Nothing was wasted; tongues
intercepted it all.

"And not a drop hits the ground," I said to Pagan.

He smiled in what I took to be agreement, though I was not
certain he was really listening. He emptied the first bottle and
started a second, smiling his secret smile of pure love for dogs.
Toward the end he remembered to save a swallow for himself.

KĪPAHULU: FROM CINDERS TO THE SEA

PETER MATTHIESSEN

In July 1969, under the sponsorship of Audubon, a trek was made into the rainy wilderness on the windward slopes of Haleakalā, the great volcano on the island of Maui, in Hawai'i: this region, the last great stronghold of Hawaii's surviving native birds, is a natural and desirable addition to the Haleakalā National Park. The three-man expedition, which began at the volcano's rim on July 22nd, and ended four days later at the sea, was led by Jack Lind, an Hawaiian naturalist who is manager of Maui's Kīpahulu Ranch, and also included Jack's son Terry. The following is an adaptation of notes taken on the trip.

A HIGH clear morning, after days of unseasonable rain. On the west rim of Haleakalā, at over 10,000 feet, we are well above the clouds, but clouds still cling to the windward slopes beyond the eastern wall of the volcano. The east wall rises in black jagged silhouette against the rolling whites, and at the base of the wall, ten miles away at Palikū, a glint of sun catches the roof of the ranger cabin where we will spend tonight.

Single file, we start a slow descent into the crater. In an air as clear and still as the air in the cool bell of a mountain flower, the pack mule, led by Terry, raises thin spirals of lunar dust, and its hooves ring crisp on the old cinders. The bowl of the crater is heaved up by furnace-red eruptions—mounds and cinder cones— and streaked by strange burns of white and orange, and gray lizard blues.

In the first fifteen hundred feet of the descent, there is no plant life, only the cold fire bed of twisted stones. Then small spurts of the heathlike *Styphelia* appear, and stray dandelions, like puffs of gold on the black cinders, and the first silversword, 'āhi-nahina: on the steep sides of the cinder cones, the silversword is often the only life, shining like snow patches in a clear March wind. The silversword is a rare composite with a base of sharp silver leaves; it may grow for twenty years before bringing forth its mighty inflorescence, a column of red-purple flowers that can be taller than a man. Having done as much, it dies. A number of silverswords were in full flower and here and there lay silver skeletons of others, dead in the previous year.

The west and north faces of the crater wall are bare as slag, but the low south wall is faced with a green wash of low brush and bracken fern; the bracken increases along our path as we drop to seven thousand feet. Here the crater floor levels off into a gradual decline toward the southeast, and fields of bracken, like a crop, rise from the black ash that flows in ancient rivers through the round red hills. The dandelions gather, and the first patches of endemic bunch grass, *Deschampsia*, but the ground cover is broken unaccountably by broad patches of desert emptiness, as if the crater here had not yet cooled. We reel across the emptiness like survivors, the dust of our passage rising like some lost signal into the ringing blue.

The blue is empty; there is no sign of a bird. On the wind from the high crags that march along the curling clouds comes the nag of feral goats; goats have run wild in the Sandwich Islands since the time of Captain Cook. In company with the wild pigs that came with the first Hawaiians, the goats are held accountable for much of the destruction of the steep native forest, and are shot on sight.

Eastward, down the slow incline of the crater, the *Styphelia* brush becomes mixed with the true heath, *Vaccinium*, and we pass mamanē, a pea tree valued for its dark hard wood, and the only sandalwood tree that has taken seed on the crater floor. Composites and a blue-flowered mint appear, and scattered small mushrooms, and some orange moss in the shadows of black rock.

The southeast corner of the crater rim has fallen, leaving an enormous breach, the Kaupō Gap. Here a torrent of dead lava rolls away into the sky, and clouds rise from below like somber mists from a great waterfall in the inferno. Above the clouds, far away on the far side of the channel, loom shadows of Mauna Kea and Mauna Loa, the volcanoes on the island of Hawai'i.

The Palikū Cabin lies in the shadow of the eastern wall, at an altitude of 6,400 feet. The wall is very steep, and at its rim, swirling clouds constantly threaten. At Palikū, the annual rainfall is 200 inches, over three times as much as it is in the open crater only three miles to the westward, and the cabin rests in a grove of native rue, with scattered mamanē, 'ōlapa, and 'ōhi'a lehua trees; the 'ōhi'a lehua, a myrtle, is the dominant tree of the mountain forests of Hawai'i. All these trees are rather stunted, and crusted over with lichens, mosses, shield ferns, and other epiphytes of wet terrains. South of the cabin, a rich pasture of *Deschampsia* flows off southward into the sky at the Kaupō Gap. Nēnē geese, once almost extinct, are raised here in a pen and encouraged to return to feeders in the pasture. Stripping my hot boots I walk down barefoot through the cool mountain meadows to have a look at them, and listen to their gentle calls to the wild birds beyond the pen. At mid-afternoon, the sun still holds the clouds at bay, and a three-quarter moon rises mysteriously out of a cleft in the mountain rim that we will climb tomorrow. Somewhere between my eye and its white ellipse is a hurtling silver thing in which the first men on the moon are coming home.

Toward twilight, as the crater cools, the clouds slip forward past Kuiki Peak, sending dank feelers down over the walls; the air cools rapidly, and we light a fire. In the night, the clouds settle into Haleakalā, the House of the Sun, shrouding Palikū in a dense weeping mist.

AFTER daylight, drinking coffee, we wait for the drizzle to ease. The mule will stay in the coral at Palikū Cabin; Larry Guth, the park ranger, will take it back tomorrow. From here we pack our equipment on our backs—a tent and fittings, sleeping bags, rifle, a machete, cameras and binoculars, a big tin container of dried food, a bottle of bourbon, and a change of clothes. All this is stuffed into three big burlap sacks and the sacks bound onto pack-boards with canvas shoulder straps.

At 7:30, the clouds still sink into the crater. In the mist, we cross the meadow and push through a thicket of Hawaiian raspberry to the foot of the escarpment; here a goat track ascends the cleft at what must be a 60-degree angle. The track is mostly hidden in waist-high ʻamaʻumaʻu ferns, bright red and green, and we are drenched from the beginning. The laborious climb up greased mud and roots and around loose rock abutments, thrown off-balance by the bulky packs, takes nearly an hour, from the crater floor to a low saddle on the rim under Kuiki Peak. The outside face of the narrow rim is the head of the Kīpahulu Valley, a great forested ravine several miles across that descends all the way to the sea; the Kīpahulu, which is our destination, is the last great stronghold of the *Drepanididae*, or Hawaiian honeycreepers; a family of birds even more remarkable than Darwin's finches, in the Galápagos, as an example of adaptive radiation.

This narrow sliver of the rim, only a few feet in width, was reached at just that moment when the sun rolled through the mist; as I cower here against the rocks, the crater is one thousand feet straight down on our right hand and the Kīpahulu a comparable distance straight down to the left. For a moment, both walls of the valley are visible, as well as the central escarpment that separates the valley floor into two levels; each level has its own wild river, the Palikea under the northeast wall and the Koukouai under the south.

Mist washes past us into Haleakalā, on a cold sea wind; this is the trade wind out of the northeast. The mist is touched by rainbows, and from below come stray calls of the nēnē. Around us, the black volcanic rocks sparkle with long tufts of silver lichens, and crimson *Vaccinium* berries glisten in wet crannies. Apparently, the pass is used by birds of the high forest on both sides: a flight of 'apapane, set free from the drenched foliage by the sun, dance through the pass and drop away into the canopy of cloud forest at the head of the Kīpahulu. Swirling mist, black crags, glistening trees, wind, sun, and rainbows: the setting for the first drepanids I have ever seen could not be improved upon. Moments later a green 'amakihi spun upward to a point of sun on a lichened branch tip, then folded its wings and fell into the forest like a stone. A note of red in the shining morning leaves of an 'ōhi'a tree that overhung the precipice was a male 'apapane; it followed the rest into the green below. The pleasure I feel in seeing these drepanids has little to do with the knowledge that over half of Hawaii's native land birds are extinct, or nearly so (the island of Maui appears to have lost less species than the other islands, and the Kīpahulu Valley is the wildest region of Maui); it comes from the wild light and the dancing birds and the two silent valleys.

Clouds come and vanish. We climb into our packs again and clamber up the hogback rim toward Kuiki Peak, where the south wall of the Kīpahulu begins its long descent into the sea. I pay close attention to footholds and handholds, and a very good look at the subvascular flora is obtained. Two lichens of this wild high place are unlike any I have seen. One crusts the bark of the dwarf 'ōhi'as that serve as handholds on the flank of Kuiki; it looks precisely like a sea-brown algae speckled with gold-green dots, like fern spores. The other is leafy, silver-white with a vivid black border given it by its black underside. Cladonia lichen is everywhere, and sphagnum.

Erosion by wind and rain and goat has reduced the crest of Kuiki to a barren volcanic rubble. On the far slope of the peak, stray goat shadows in the mists, and Terry sheds his pack and drops down behind the rocks, clutching his rifle.

Now it is midmorning, and we wait for the weather of the day before—early mist and rain followed by clearing along the rim—but our hopes are vanishing. The crest of Kuiki is as isolated as a sea rock in the blowing cloud and rain. We huddle in soaked clothes behind an outcropping, waiting for Terry, who is waiting in turn for the clouds to pass so that he may kill his goat. The Linds, who are mountain goats themselves, do not believe in rain gear, and I am badly equipped because I am traveling light; I wear a borrowed jacket that no longer resists water. It is hard to believe that one could be cold in Maui in July, but I am shivering like a stunned fish.

In two hours, Terry returns, as silently as he went. He is a very tall, strong boy who is cheerful but says little; in this, he is like his father, who is round-backed and steady as a barrel. Jack squats stolidly in the wet murk, nursing his canned heat; we gulp bouillon and crackers but find no warmth in them, and set off along the valley rim, in slow descent.

The descent from Kuiki to the sea is described after the fact; the rain and mud made it too difficult to take notes as I went along. That night I scribbled blind notes in the dark—to save weight, we carried

no light of any kind—and the following night I did the same, and
made what I could of these scrawlings in the days that followed.

WE HAD agreed to go down the south ridge of the Kīpahulu
rather than descend the valley floor, which was buried in clouds;
also, an expedition guided by Lind had come up the valley two
years before, whereas nobody had ever traveled the south ridge,
which presented us with an opportunity for exploration. We picked
our way along its rim, in a thick mist. From the head of the valley
almost to the foot, the rim remains about one thousand feet above
the valley floor, and the fall is nearly vertical all the way. Now and
then the clouds would thin to give a dim glimpse of the mountainside, but we depended for our bearings on the edge of the
precipice. Not that there was much chance of straying from the
ridge unless one fell from it, since its far side was only a few hundred yards to the south, falling away into the Kaupō Gap.

Soon rocks gave way to alpine tundra, and we crossed a crystal mountain pool inset in a young stream, softened by mist. The
tundra was inhabited by the dark twisted trunks of solitary ʻōhiʻa
trees: the flowing clouds, thinning and thickening, gave the place
an eerie transience, as if we were passing from one world into
another. Jack Lind, who had never seen this corner of the mountain, was enchanted; he kept stopping to peer about him, shaking
his head. "I'll come up here and stay for weeks," he said, "if I can
get Terry to come with me." Originally we had planned to make
our high camp in the grassland, but the poor weather drove us off
the mountaintop. We had come down perhaps a thousand feet,
and imagined we might make that point on the south rim, at
3,800 feet, to which the Linds had slashed an upward trail in the
past year.

At first, the going was merely uneven; we could not always
go where only goats had gone before. Still, the goat trails down
along the rim, honed to the most efficient routes by time, served

us very well, and by mid-afternoon another thousand feet of the descent—or so we estimated—had been accomplished. Furthermore, we had seen the first crested honeycreeper, which came to feed in the flowers of giant saxifrage. But it was just here that our doubts and troubles began. Due to the clouds, we had had only glimpses into the abyss, and once, when the mists lifted, Lind glared in surprise at what he could see of the steep ridge just opposite; it looked too close to be the central escarpment of the Kīpahulu, and Jack, looking haunted, was momentarily convinced that in the mist we had wandered southward onto the ridge of another valley. But Terry and I, from our recollection of the maps, did our best to convince him and ourselves that this was not possible; we pitched ahead.

Just after the alpine grassland had been replaced by dense scrub forest, Jack had remarked that the valley itself was harder going than this ridge; now he changed his mind. The forest had become so tangled that even the goats had been turned back; for the rest of this day and all the next, the machete was in use full time. A break in the mist revealed that this south rim, at about six thousand feet, leveled out in a narrow peninsula of thick forest. We would be here tonight and a good part of tomorrow before a real descent could be resumed.

We chopped our way ahead. The forest was mostly 'ōhi'a, interspersed with aralia, saxifrage, and rue; many of the 'ōhi'a trees were prostrate, with dense ranks of vertical branches, like prison bars, and others had grown prop roots, to accommodate themselves to the wet terrain. The soft ground, hidden by rank ferns, was root-ridden and rotten in the gloom of a canopy that, in this weather, cut off all the light; it was a troll forest, squat and dank, all drippings and creepers and hanging shapes, picturesque in a weird way and quite impenetrable. Furthermore, the ridge had narrowed, falling away sharply on both sides, and presented a very small choice of route. Toward twilight Jack said, "We better find a place to camp," but we never came upon a clearing. Finally we settled for a spot where the fallen trees had not yet been replaced by live ones, and hacked out a less than level place that was just big enough for the small two-man tent. Fronds from the tree ferns made an acceptable substitute for air mattresses. While Jack and Terry pitched the tent, I set up a wind shelter for canned heat—a wood fire in this soggy place was not a possibility—and squeezed a potful of fresh rain from the mosses that carpeted the trees, then filtered it by pouring it through a neckerchief. Dissatisfied, Jack ran it through a yellowed T-shirt that he peeled from his own wet back to serve this purpose, but the water remained the color of bitter chocolate, so we put it on to boil without further ado. Some of the cruder elements surfaced in the pot in the form of a scum that could be scraped away, and such matter as remained gave body to the dehydrated soup, and did nothing to harm the flavor. Jack cooked the soup to a kind of lava in which thick bubbles bloomed and burst, and we ate it standing in the raining darkness. Then one by one, our dinner done, we hunched under the fly of the little tent and dragged off pants and boots in one amorphous mass and left them out there in the rain; we squirmed into dry clothes and got into our sleeping bags, warm for the first time since midmorning, and tried as best we could to make room for the others. Jack is broad and I am tall, and Terry has more big bones than either of us, and all three have strong shoulders; poor Terry, squashed in between, evolved a trick of locking his shoulders the way a bird on a limb locks its feet when it falls asleep, so that no amount of quick shifting or devious elbow work could shift him an inch. On the contrary, even in sleep he spread so rapidly into any vacuum that, turning back after lying on my side, I would find myself cockeyed, hung up on that implacable shoulder, my nose pressed into the wet canvas of the tent in which, Jack claimed, three people could make do in a pinch.

All night it rained, and it was raining in the morning. Since dry clothes would be soaked in minutes, there was no choice but to reach out into the cold mountain mud for the rags of yesterday and wring them out as best we could—they were slippery with mud—and drag them on over bare quaking skin. By the time the wet pants were on, the rain was already pouring down my back, and I was shaking: I remember thinking, I'll never get warm again today, and I was right. There was no slow torture about it, as there had been the day before: we were racked with cold right from the start. Jack Lind was wearing the solitary rain jacket that we had between us, and perhaps because no one else had one, he wore it wide open, so as to derive the least possible benefit.

It seemed to take hours to drag the pathetic little camp back into the muddy sacks and lash the sacks onto the packboards. By 8:00 we were underway, but our progress was too slow to speed the blood. Only the lead man, swinging the machete, had a chance to warm himself, and his advantage was offset by the cascades of cold water that the slightest touch brought down from every branch. Each time we dragged ourselves over a fallen tree, the spongy moss soaked us all over again. More than once we were belly-down in mud, bumping along under the hairy trunks, the limbs catching at our load, but already we were too begrimed to mind the mud; the enemy was cold. By noon, no one suggested that we stop to eat: in the blowing rain and mist that swept up out of the valley, it was not bearable to stand still long enough to fumble nourishment out of the shapeless packs.

Now and then during the morning came glimpses of small fleeing birds, mostly 'amakihi and Maui creepers, and one 'i'iwi, and a crested honeycreeper (the day before we had seen three honeycreepers, which are orange-streaked black birds with a curious "crest" at the base of the upper bill; these 'akohekohe are now restricted to Maui, and even here they were considered very rare, though they are not uncommon in the Kīpahulu). But in the dark dull light, the colors of the birds were lost; but for Jack Lind, I would not have known what I was looking at.

Here in the cloud forest, the epiphytes had taken over, not only the mosses and the ferns, but iris and mistletoe and plants such as *Styphelia* and the tree ferns and the *Astelia* lily, which had been entirely terrestrial at higher altitudes: apparently the ground in the lower forest is too wet for them. The aralia, rue, and saxifrage families all occur here as small trees, and also several varieties of giant lobelia. On the end of the twelve-foot stem of one lobelia was a lovely lavender inflorescence—the only nonchlorophyllous color that emerged from the green monochromes of mountain forest. The woody lobelias of Hawai'i are one of the most striking features of a unique flora, and there are at least twelve species in the Kīpahulu alone. This strange valley should be protected if only for the fact that nearly ninety percent of its higher plants are native, a situation which is unique in the islands. "Within three miles," wrote Dr. Charles Lamoureux, the botanist with the 1967 Nature Conservancy expedition, "one can find communities ranging from tropical rain forest to a subalpine zone with frequent frosts.... Since most of the Hawaiian species of plants are endemic, these communities are like no others, and Kipahulu in this sense offers an opportunity [for research] not available elsewhere on this planet."

But I remember best how little I noticed; one needed one's full attention to deal with the constant obstacles, and anyway, there was simply too much rain. Falling repeatedly, or catching the feet on hidden roots, or jamming a leg into mossed-over holes between the rotting carcasses of fallen trees, or nicked by a deflection of one's own careless frustrated machete, I was very conscious of how helpless a man would be with any disabling injury. I said as much to Jack, who merely grunted, shaking his head: he didn't want to think about it. A stretcher could not be carried through this tangle, which was also inaccessible to a helicopter. In consequence, one paid close attention to the footing, and dealt with the obstacles right before one's face; there was no margin for accident, much less error.

In the early afternoon, we came upon an old machete cut, though the trail had been grown over. We were off the level ridge now and descending steeply. Not long after this, Terry shot a great bristly brindle sow, long-snouted and high-backed; the old Polynesian pig lay wide-eyed in a blood pool in the broad mud wallow of her own making. Jack slashed some meat off her tough ham, and we went on again. Glancing backward in the rain, I caught the eye of this wild-eyed old pig-of-the-mountains.

THE trail was beginning to emerge, and we made progress. At just after four in the afternoon, we came out on a grassy point of the south ridge where Lind had cached some stores. Here the sun shone, and the mist lifted briefly to reveal the blue Pacific, 3,800 feet below. We sank down in the wet grass and had a drink. I was foot-sore and stiff-legged as a zombie, and Jack wore an expression of stunned surprise, as if a friend had kicked him in the stomach. "Now I know why nobody ever came down that south ridge before," he said. "You have to be crazy." In eight hours of violent hacking and falling and crawling and climbing down this godforsaken ridge, we had descended at most 2,000 feet, and covered a distance of less than two miles.

At 3,800 feet, in the new sun, the air was warm. Lying in the dank grass, we finished the bourbon, staring in silence at the sparkling wet blossoms of the 'ōhi'a trees and the white crescent of surf on the black shore of eastern Maui. From the valley below rose the thunder of the Koukouai Stream, now a mountain torrent. Far below, where the valley nears the sea, lies a string of paradisical waterfalls and pools known as the "Seven Sacred Pools"; although the remnants of an ancient Hawaiian temple lie nearby, the pools have only been sanctified in recent years, as part of an attempt to lure tourists to the remote, rainy, and immensely beautiful coast of eastern Maui.

Terry went to fetch water and Jack and I put up the tent.

While the light lasted, Jack, lying on one elbow like a Roman, cooked up a great batch of soup and rice and dehydrated beef stroganoff, while I fried strips of the wild pig that Terry was carving from the ham. This was our first real meal since the supper at Palikū Cabin, two nights before.

The sun was still shining when we lay down in the tent, and we were much too tired to cut fern fronds. Jack Lind was snoring before my head touched the ground.

By morning it was raining once again, and once again we climbed into cold clothes, but the air was much warmer at this altitude. Jack and I broke camp, and Terry went on ahead. There was a discernible trail from this point onward, but now we were assailed by tropic downpours. The trail was slick, and at times it slithered along ridges so narrow and precarious that I was tempted to sink onto my knees and crawl, but my knees were so sore from clambering over the dead trees of the day before that I kept my eyes glued to the ground instead. Descending steep rain-slick ridges with a bulky pack is tricky work, and even sure-footed Jack Lind had his feet go out from under him repeatedly; since he always landed on the food tin strapped to his back, he made a gloomy booming sound each time he fell. As for myself, I was flat on my back so often that I had ample time to contemplate the changing scenery. The 'ōhi'a forest had been replaced by lovely great koa acacia trees, some of them six feet in diameter; further down, the koa became mixed with tropical species like candlenut and guava. Climbing pandanus was rampant in the trees, and ti plants and Hilo grass filled the open places; the day before, there were no open places that had not been under water. We had eaten nothing fresh in several days, and as we went along I nibbled greedily at thimbleberries—a rather dull wild raspberry— and the new fiddlenecks of the pahole fern, and an alginous cup fungus from the wet tree limbs that Hawaiians consider a great delicacy; near the lower reaches of the montane forest there were guavas.

As we descended, the rain-charged Kīpahulu rivers became louder and more ominous; a noise like the ocean on a reef rose from the mists below our feet. The drepanids were left behind at three thousand feet; those species endemic to the lower slopes had been extirpated long ago by new invaders of the island ecology, from bird parasites to man. (The introduced mongoose, which is frequently blamed for the destruction of the *Drepanididae*, did not come until the late nineteenth century, long after the worst damage had been done.) The small bat which is the only land mammal native to the islands has also declined seriously in recent years, and so have the lovely tree snails; the snails have apparently been killed off by cannibal snails introduced to combat still another snail introduced earlier from Africa. In consequence, the forest of the lower mountain is inhabited almost exclusively by imported creatures such as the pig, mongoose, cat, and common rat. Still, it is very beautiful, and once in a while, one could actually take a step without watching where one put one's feet. The air was soft, and the sea glinted in the distant sunlight, and the song of the Pekin nightingale, which had the trees almost to itself, brought the silent mountainside to life.

At one thousand feet, we came out into the high pastures of the Kīpahulu Ranch. Terry had left a Land Rover for us on the farm track down the hill, and we went pitching down to it. With the end in sight, my feet immediately became so sore that I could hardly walk; the first thing we did was strip off our shoes. From head to toe we were smeared with mud (quite literally; I didn't get the mud out of my toenails for two weeks) and I felt bruised all over. Standing there in the shining sun, only minutes away from a drink and a hot bath, I did my best not to giggle foolishly out of sheer relief. Jack glared at me balefully. "I'm glad we did it," he said finally, "because it's never been done before." He managed a grin. "And as far as I'm concerned, it'll never be done again."

FIRE IN THE NIGHT

JAMES D. HOUSTON

AMONG geologists and volcano buffs there is a little rite of passage, whereby you stick your hand-axe into moving lava and bring away a gob of the molten stuff. In order to do this you have to be where the lava is flowing and hot, then you have to get your body in close enough to the heat to reach down toward the edge of the flow, and it usually means you have to walk or stand for at least a few seconds on some pretty thin crust.

My chance came one night last year, on the Big Island of Hawai'i, when I hiked out along the southern shoreline toward the spilling end of a lava tube. I was traveling in the company of Jack Lockwood, a specialist in Volcanic Hazards with the U.S. Geological Survey. He is a trim and wiry fellow, with wild hair and a devilish grin, a man from New England who has found that island, its craters and its lava fields, to be his natural habitat. He loves it there, he loves the look of the ropy pāhoehoe, the many shapes it takes. He will stop the car to study the way today's flow has poured over yesterday's, making a drapery of knobs and drips. He will remark upon the metallic sheen in the late sun, and then point out that newer lava can be crumbled with your shoe, while the stuff that came through yesterday has already hardened under a rainfall and thus is firmer.

We parked where the yellow line of the coast road disappeared under a ten-foot wall of new rock. We got out the packs, the gloves, the canteens, the flashlights, the hard-hats. Jack's hat was custom-made, with his name in raised letters on the metal. His hard-toe boots were scuffed ragged with threads of rock-torn leather. I was going to wear running shoes for this expedition, until he told me no. "Where we're going," he said, "the soles could peel right off."

Hunkered on the asphalt, lacing up the high-top boots I'd borrowed, I could already feel it shimmering toward us. Minutes later we were hiking through furnace heat, over lava that had rolled across there just a few hours earlier. Through cracks and fissures you could see the molten underlayer showing, three or four inches below the dark surface.

"You can actually walk on it fifteen or twenty minutes after it starts to harden," Jack said, "as long as you have an inch of surface underfoot."

Soon the red slits were everywhere, and we were crossing what appeared to be several acres of recent flow. Jack plunged ahead with great purpose, with long firm strides, planting each foot and leaning forward as he walked, as if there were a path to be followed and we were on it—though of course there was no path, no prior footprints, no markers of any kind to guide us across terrain that had not been there that morning.

"Jack," I said, "have you ever stepped into a soft spot? I mean, got burned, fallen through?"

He shook his head vigorously. "Nope."

"How do you know where to step?"

He stopped and looked at me with his mischievous eyes, his beard and his squint reminding me of a young John Houston.

"You just pick your way and pay attention as you go. It's partly experience and partly faith."

"Faith?"

"You have to put your trust in Pele. Tell her that you come out here with respect, and she will take care of you."

As he plunged on, I wanted to trust in Pele, the goddess of fire, who is said to make her home in a crater about fifteen miles from where we were walking. We had already talked about her, while driving down Chain of Craters Road, and I knew he meant what he'd just said. But I have to confess that at the moment I was putting my full trust in Lockwood, placing my feet where he placed his, stepping in his steps as we strode and leaped from rock to rock.

Eventually the heat subsided, and we were hiking over cooler terrain, though none of it was very old. "Everything you see has flowed in the last six months," he said. Two-and-a-half miles of the coast road had recently been covered, as well as the old settlement of Kamoamoa, near where we'd parked. Inland we could see some of what remained of Royal Gardens, a subdivision laid out in the early 1970s, laid out right across a slope of the East Rift Zone. In the Royal Gardens grid, cross-streets had been named for tropical flowers—Gardenia, Pikake—while the broader main streets sounded noble—Kamehameha, Prince. Now the access road was blocked in both directions. From our vantage point it looked as if great vats of black paint had been dumped over the highest ridge, to pour down the slope through the trees, to cover boulevards and lawns.

Our destination—the spilling tube—was marked by a steam plume rising high against the evening sky. When we left the car it was white and feathery at the top, two miles down the coast. After the sun set and the light began to dim, the plume turned pink and red. Spatter thrown up from the collision of lava and surf had formed a littoral cone now outlined against the steam. As we approached, tiny figures could be seen standing at the edge of this cone, like cut-outs against the fiery backdrop.

On one side of the cone, flat spreads of lava were oozing toward the cliff. On the other side, an orange gusher was arcing some thirty feet above the water, while a mound slowly rose beneath it. Beyond that tube, another spill obscured by steam sent lava straight into the water at about sea level. Red and black floating gobs spewed out from the steam or sometimes flew into the air, breaking into fiery debris that was gradually building the littoral cone.

These fires lit the billowing plume from below. As it churned away toward the west, it sent a pinkish glow back down onto the marbled surf, which made me think of the Royal Hawaiian Hotel, where they spend a lot of money on light bulbs and filters trying to tint the offshore waters a Waikiki pink that can never come close to Pele's cosmetic kit.

A video cameraman was there, perched at the cliff edge, filming the build-up on the mound below the arching orange tube. His tripod legs were spindly black against the glow. Nearby a couple of dozen people stood gazing at the spectacle, staffers from Volcano Observatory and the University of Hawaii. They were out there in numbers, Jack told me later, because this was a rare night. Spills like this were usually closer to the surf, and the lava would pour until the mound built up from below to seal off its opening. But this littoral cone was unstable, and part of it had fallen away and beheaded the end of the tube, so that lava was spilling free from high up the cliff, making a liquid column of endlessly sizzling orange.

If you could take your eyes off its mesmerizing arc and turn inland, you could see another glow in the night. It hung above the nearest ridge, light from the lake called Kūpaianaha, the source of the lava moving around us. It was a new lake, inside a new shield cone. From there the lava snaked seaward via a channel that looped wide to the east, then back toward where we stood. You could see evidence of its twisting, subterranean path about halfway down the mountain, where tiny fires seemed to be burning, four or five eyes of flame against the black.

We lingered for an hour, maybe more, chatting, bearing witness, sharing our wonder with the others lucky enough to be out there on such a night, at the cutting edge of destruction and creation. We were about to start back when Lockwood said this was probably as good a time as any for me to add my name to the "one thousandth of one percent of the human population who have stuck their axe in hot lava." And with that we began to prowl around a couple of oozing streams, to see how close we could get.

I watched him step out onto some hot stuff that had barely stopped moving, and saw the surface give under his boot. With a grin he jumped back. "That's probably a little too soft."

We moved around to the far side, forty feet away, and approached the fiery mush from another angle. With axe in hand he hopped across the one-inch crust and dug into the front edge of a narrow strip, but it was already cooling and a little too thick to lift. He could only pull it up an inch or so, the front lip already in that halfway zone between liquid and solid stone.

He was pulling so hard he lost his footing and half-fell toward the crust. His gloved hand reached out to take the fall, and for a moment his crouching body was silhouetted against the molten stream, while behind him the red and orange steam plume surged like a backdrop curtain for his dance. He came rolling and hopping toward me with a wild grin and a rascal eye.

"That's a little too viscous. It's surprising. It's cooler than it looks."

So we moved on, heading back the way we'd come, under a black sky with its infinity of stars, our flashlight beams bobbing across the rocks, while the plume grew smaller behind us.

We dropped down to a new beach of dark volcanic sand,

then climbed out of the sand onto that day's fresh lava, where the red slits once again glowed all around us. As we picked our way, in the furnace heat, we came upon a flow that had not been there when we crossed the first time.

"Pele is being good to you," said Jack, grinning, his beard red-tinted underneath. He handed me his axe. "This is perfect. Just keep your back to the heat, and move in quickly."

Which is what I did. The stream was maybe twenty feet wide, seething, creeping toward the sea. I back-pedaled up next to it, reaching with the flat chisel-end of the metal blade, dipped and scooped into the burning lip. It was smoother than wet cement, thicker than honey, thicker than three-finger poi. Maybe the consistency of glazing compound, or the wet clay potters use. For the first mini-second it felt that way. As I dug in and pulled, it was already harder. It clung to the flow, but I tugged and finally came away with a chunk the size of a tennis ball, which held to the blade as I leaped back away from the heat.

Jack was excited. "Throw it down here, quickly!"

I plopped it between us, on a black slab.

"Now press your heel in hard!"

I pressed my boot heel into the glob, flattening it with a boot print. When the rubber began to smoke, I pulled my foot away.

"Now," he said, with a happy grin, "we'll put this on my shovel blade and carry it to the car while it cools, and this will be your souvenir."

By the time we reached the asphalt road the heat had given way to balmy coastal air off the water. The slits and fissures and plumes and flows were all behind us, and that was the end of our expedition.

But it was not the end of my relationship with that flattened piece of rock. I lived with it for another week, trying to decide what to do. It was mine, I suppose, because I had marked it with my boot. Now it was smooth, as shiny as black glass, and if I lived on that island I'd probably have it sitting on my desk. But I did not feel right about bringing this trophy back home. I kept thinking about the tug of the lava as I pulled the axe away. Through the handle I had felt its texture, its consistency, and something else that haunted me. A reluctance. A protest. As if live flesh were being torn from a body.

Maybe this was what the Hawaiians meant when they said all the rocks there belong to Pele and should not leave the island. Maybe the unwritten law that said be respectful of the rocks was another way of honoring that old yearning in the stone. Maybe Pele was another word for the living stuff of earth, and maybe I had finally understood something, through my hands, something I had heard about and read about and talked about and even tried to write about.

Before I left the island I drove down to the south shore again. Sighting from the new black sand beach, I think I got pretty close to where we'd been. I dropped the chunk of lava down into a jagged crevice and asked it to forgive me for any liberties I might have taken, and I thanked Pele for letting me carry this rock around for a while. Then I drove to the airport and checked in my rental car and caught my plane.

I don't tell people about this, by the way. Not here on the mainland. You come back to California and tell someone you have been talking to rocks, they give you a certain kind of look. I'll mention it to Jack Lockwood, of course, the next time I see him. It's easier to talk about when you're in the islands. You meet a lot of people over there who claim to be on speaking terms with rocks. When you're in or near volcano country, it's easier to remember that they too have life, that each rock was once a moving thing, as red as blood and making eyes of fire in the night.

COOLING THE LAVA

JOHN McPHEE

IN 1911, when the Hawaiian Volcano Research Association was founded, it adopted the motto "*Ne plus haustae aut obrutae urbes*": "No more swallowed-up or buried cities." Field artillery was contemplated as a means of living up to the commitment, also high explosives tied to the ends of sticks. When lava extends as a river, its upper reaches crust over, forming tubes that insulate the orange-hot liquid racing within. In 1935, Keystone bombers of the United States Army Air Corps bombed a lava tube on Mauna Loa. The source vent was high on the mountain at nearly nine thousand feet, but the advancing front, far below, was threatening the port of Hilo. The tube, blown apart, became effectively clogged with debris, and lava spilled to one side, yet the result was inconclusive, because the mountain stopped erupting. In April of 1942, with Hawai'i blacked out and Japanese carriers at large on the ocean, Mauna Loa erupted again. The lava river flowed so fast it included standing waves. Once again, the direction of flow was toward Hilo. The eruption was a military secret. People spoke of it in whispers, lest it serve as a beacon to the Japanese. This time, the planes were B-18s—Bolo bombers. Their target was a natural levee hardened at the edge of an open flow. The bombs breached it. The lava spilled sideways. It ran alongside the original stream and rejoined it a short distance below.

It should be mentioned that these historic efforts to do battle with lava in Hawaiʻi were few in number, futile in nature, and not conceived by Hawaiians. They were products to some extent of mainland-educated scientific minds and to a much greater extent of West Point—educated military minds. Hawaiians had lived with eruptions throughout Hawaiian history, and their primary way of dealing with the problem was through votive offerings. To this day, one sees strewn flowers at the edge of active craters, flowers in vases, offerings of tobacco, of food, and, most of all, of gin. The offerings are there to placate an irritable deity whose dark humors are expressed as earthquakes and whose rage takes form as molten fire. Pele. Among the forces of the earth, she is as powerful as any but her sister the sea. Hawaiians have been as susceptible to science as everyone else, but their passive acceptance of the errant moods of Pele remains intact even if their belief in her does not. In what is now approaching two centuries of recorded data, their Long Mountain—their Mauna Loa—has erupted, on the average, every three and a half years, and in that short time has poured out four billion cubic yards of lava: enough to pave Iceland. Mauna Loa has coated and recoated itself so often that it has never had time to erode. Whatever the rain may have taken away has quickly been replaced. The long mountain is fifty miles long. Viewed from the edge of the ocean, it is an astonishing trompe-l'oeil, because it is so smoothly constructed that it appears in two dimensions and presents a deceptive depth of field. It looks like a low friendly hill, a singing dune, at worst a bald Scottish brae. You think, I'll run up there and have a look around before lunch. The long mountain is as high as the Alps. If it were dissected by streams—given promontories and reentrants, serrated by canyons, invaded by shadows—it might look something like the Alps. As is, it's just a massive shield, composed of chilled magma, looking the way the Alps would look if a dentist could repair them.

The big island of which Mauna Loa is a part consists of five volcanoes, which appeared at different times and grew close beside one another. Slightly higher and somewhat older than Mauna Loa is Mauna Kea the White Mountain, 13,796 feet. The youngest Hawaiian mountain that is visible above water is Kīlauea, one of the two or three most active volcanoes in the world. Kīlauea was in a state of continuous eruption for the entire nineteenth century. Its present altitude is about four thousand feet. Its summit crater, an irregular oval, is two miles one way and two and a half the other. In addition to the flowers and the food and tobacco and assorted measures of gin, there stands on the rim a small compound of buildings that are in themselves a votive offering. They are the United State Geological Survey's Hawaiian Volcano Observatory, the highest part of which is a glassed-in room that closely resembles an airport control tower, and from which—with respect to lava—no control of any sort is contemplated, attempted, or exerted. Thomas L. Wright, Scientist-in-Charge, who has seen Styx itself come out from under his office—seen an Amazon of new, flowing rock—says he can envision no rational alternative to "letting nature take its course." When I called on him at the observatory one spring day, he remarked that "the Hawaiian heritage is to be fatalistic," and went on to say, "They accept the renewal of land by volcanic eruption. There's no feasible way of dealing with large, continuing flows. Political issues have aligned the state and county in a fatalistic mode. The consequences of diverting lava from one place onto another would be unacceptable. To me the idea of putting explosives on the upper reaches of a volcano—of putting artificial things into a natural environment—is abhorrent."

Eleven thousand feet up the north slope of Mauna Loa the

National Oceanic and Atmospheric Administration has housed
an expensive collection of instruments in a few small buildings
that could easily be lost in new rock. In 1986, NOAA built a large
barrier above the compound, in the shape of the Greek letter
lambda—λ—with legs a couple of thousand feet long, to divide
any lava coming from above and make the scientific station a kīpuka, an island in a river of lava. Barriers had been proposed in
Hawai'i before—in various configurations to protect Hilo—but
this is the first time in the United States that large defenses have
ever been set up to protect property from volcanic eruptions. The
NOAA barriers are in a high remote place, and when lava does
come against them it is not going to carom into someone's kitch-
en. Near Hilo, though, on the low slopes of Kīlauea, that sort of
thing could happen. As on Heimaey [in Iceland, a small island on
which in 1973 an extraordinary battle was waged against a lava
flow that threatened to destroy the harbor town], lava deflected
from one route could wipe out houses on another. And this is not
Iceland, the home of the fair; this is the United States, the home
of the lawyer. When Mauna Loa erupted in 1984, the state was
asked if, in dire emergency, an attempt would be made to save
Hilo. The answer was no. The Department of Land and Natural
Resources regarded such a struggle as futile in the first place, and,
moreover, could not imagine any way to deal with the legal consequences of lava diversion. The Hawaii County Civil Defense Agency's standing instruction to firefighters is to try to prevent lava
from causing runaway fires but to make no attempt to stop or
divert it. Hawaiian firemen spend a good deal of time tracking
hot lava through people's yards. Say an ooze-out from the main
flow is threatening to raze the house of Louis Pau. The Fire
Department turns its hoses on the lava in an attempt to keep the
house from catching fire. This is a situation of some nuance. You
can't pour water on lava without in some way affecting the movement of other lava. In the words of Pall Zophoniasson [town en-

gineer of Heimaey], "If you stop the lava here, it moves there." That would seem to be the message from the Battle of Heimaey.

The juxtaposition of Mauna Kea and Mauna Loa has created something that an explosives-maker would call a shaped charge. In the crease where the mountains touch are many rivers of frozen lava and one of flowing water. The crease is a natural conduit, a natural slot; and its lower end is Hilo. This is the second-largest city and second-largest port in two thousand miles. An article published in 1958 in *Pacific Science* described Hilo's situation in terms that soon echoed in Vestmannaeyjar [the island group that includes Heimaey]: "The loss of Hilo harbor would be disastrous to the present economy of much of the island of Hawai'i, for there is no other harbor in that part of the island capable of handling the cargo that moves through the port of Hilo." Hilo's beautiful harbor, like the one on Heimaey, consists entirely of cold lava. The eruptions of 1852, 1855, 1942, and 1984 all started at the summit of Mauna Loa and all stopped within a dozen miles of Hilo. In 1855, the lava was five miles away; in 1984, only four. As Tom Wright said, "Hilo was looking right at it." Mauna Loa was capable of sending forth as much as twenty-five million cubic yards per hour. In 1881, a flow entered what is now a part of Hilo, and came within a mile of Hilo Bay. Diversion barriers were proposed, but were so controversial they were never built.

In 1973, the story of Vestmannaeyjar traveled around the Pacific Basin like a message writ in smoke. Inspired by the triumph in Iceland, the U.S. Army Corps of Engineers considered building a dam high up the crease between the huge volcanoes. The dam would create a reservoir, the source of water for the chilling of future lava. Confronted with these developments, Harry Kim, director of the Hawaii County Civil Defense Agency, pondered what to do. The next time Hilo was looking right at it, people would be mentioning Vestmannaeyjar. "I knew there would be questions posed with regard to this technique, questions I could not answer," Harry Kim told me. "So I invited someone to come from Iceland—anyone at all."

The person who went to Hawai'i was Patton. When Auckland asked similar questions, Thorleifur Einarsson went to New Zealand. But Patton himself—Sveinn Eiriksson—flew to Hilo and conferred with Harry Kim. This was the first summit conference in the history of fighting lava. Unfortunately, there is no transcript. Sveinn Eiriksson has since died, of a heart attack, and Harry Kim is careful to say that Eiriksson—whom he found "enlightening"—cautioned him not to be influenced by the publicity that attended the Icelandic situation. Harry is an intense man, serious and dedicated, slim to the point of being weightless. Deep is his love of the terrain, before and after it is altered. When he said to me that Eiriksson had told him that nothing much had really been accomplished in Iceland, I was about as startled as I would have been to learn that Eiriksson's American namesake had let it drop that nothing much had been accomplished in the Battle of the Bulge. The dubieties of Harry Kim seemed to me to be as astute as they were pragmatic. When lava starts filling Hilo Harbor, someone is going to be expected to rally forces and stop it—stop it in the way that Patton did in Iceland—and someone's name is Harry Kim. "They did not stop the flow," he said. "They worked on a small lobe, not the main flow. If we were going to attempt anything like that, it would have to be cost-effective. I would not spend a million dollars to save five houses. And government has to be careful. We must not destroy one home to save another. Morally, we should not do it—even if you give me legal protection."

I asked him what he thought of the Corps of Engineers' proposed reservoir and dam.

"Ridiculous," he said. "A discredit to what was tried in Iceland."

It has been asserted in scientific circles that Mauna Loa will

inevitably destroy Hilo. This has given Harry Kim a visceral an-
tipathy toward some, if not all, volcanologists. He thinks that
their alarming predictions have needlessly frightened the people.
He said, "The town was in a state of great agitation when '84
came." The numerals referred to a time when only three and a
half million cubic yards of molten material was pouring from
Mauna Loa per hour. "I think for the most part the panic was
controlled," he went on. "But certain individuals create a mentality. The mentality says, 'We *must* do something.' If Madame Pele
could not be stopped by the Pacific Ocean, how dare mankind
attempt to stop her with pumps?"

WHEN '84 came and a bright-orange river poured for three weeks
from Mauna Loa, an eruption of much greater duration was
simultaneously taking place on Kilauea. As on Mauna Loa, the
lava was emerging from a mountain flank, and not from the summit crater. The Kilauea eruption, which began in January 1983,
was to continue for years. It began half a dozen miles from the
Kalapana coast. Crossing roads, eating through villages and sub-
divisions, consuming great acreages of forest, it has several times
entered the ocean. There have been times of crisis when it was
consuming a house every thirty minutes, between quiet times when
the lava stream, making a ruddy borealis against the night sky,
just crackles along slowly on top of earlier flows. In a subdivision
called Royal Gardens, a family whose house was lost had the lava
field surveyed and—in the manner of the pastor's monument at
Kirkjubaer—had a new house built on the new rock, above the
old site. Nearby, I noticed a house that had been spared when the
lava stream divided, flowing past it on both sides. The owners
were still in residence. One result of the present flows from Kilauea
has been the wholesale devastation of numerous marijuaneries—
or homesteads, as they are called—established by agriculturists
from the mainland. Marijuana has been described as Hawaii's foremost cash crop.

If, for the first time, you were to touch down in a jet at Keāhole Airport, west of Mauna Kea, you would not be altogether irrational if you were to look out the window and decide that a distressingly imaginable navigational error had brought you to Iceland. The terrain surrounding Keāhole and the terrain surrounding Keflavik are much the same: rivers of lava frozen in time. Vegetation has scarcely reached them. At Keflavik, the jagged 'a'ā has a green blush of moss; at Keāhole, the apalhraun is black, without a hint of life. The Hawaiian flow is younger. In 1801, it came down off Hualālai, a lesser volcano eight thousand feet high, and poured into the sea. There on the leeward side of the island, where rainfall is ten inches a year, the lava has remained essentially unchanged. Resorts have been sculpted in it like movie sets, landscaped with imported soils. The bunkers of designer golf courses are not concave and full of sand but—lovely in the green surrounding turf—solid black islands of undisturbed basalt. Use your wedge on that. Your hands sting for a year. If a long approach shot lands on one of those, it bounces to Tahiti.

Flows of many ages cover the Big Island like wax that has grown on a bottle. But the action at the moment is all in the southeast, in the evening shadow of Mauna Loa, where Kīlauea is. At the Hawaiian Volcano Observatory, a waiver was presented to me early one morning by Christina Heliker, a volcanologist. In Vestmannaeyjar, I had walked a good bit on rock so young that its interior was still in liquid form, while steam, in a reversal of the artesian process, was running uphill within the volcano and dancing away from the rim. Evocative as that was—as palpably as it told its story—a recent flow is not a live eruption. Heimaey had been quiet for something under fifteen years. Kīlauea since 1983 had not been quiet for fifteen minutes. The waiver was in the first person, the prose of a ghostwriter who had studied law. Over my signature I mentioned "unusual hazards to persons and property," and went on to say, "I freely choose to encounter such hazards on my own initiative, risk, and responsibility," and "I do hereby, for myself, my heirs, executors, and administrators, remise, release, and forever discharge the Government of the United States, its officers, and its agents from all claims, demands, actions or causes of action, on account of my death." After signing, I got into a fire-resistant flightsuit, property of the same government, and a pair of what I hoped would prove to be heat-resistant boots, property of myself. Heliker's boots were new, and she thought them a little tight. She said, "Once they melt a little, maybe they'll fit."

We waited on a tarmac helipad with Ronald Hanatani, who is a native of Hawai'i, and is therefore, like an Icelander, a birthright volcanologist. Heliker is a convinced volcanologist. In 1980, she was working somewhere in the Pacific Northwest on a minor conundrum in glaciology when Mt. St. Helens exploded. Young, mobile, adventurous, she just packed her gear and went there to ask what she could do. "Once you get red-rock fever, you are never the same again," she remarked now. As if that were a cue, the chopper came over the trees.

We flew to Camp 8—a makeshift platform tent resting on a kīpuka in a newly frozen river of black-and-silver lava. It was not all hard, by any means. Below its surface were arterial tubes in which the unceasing flow was descending in the direction of the ocean, which was eight miles from the source vent, in the mountain's eastern rift zone. For a year or more, the magma coming up from the interior of Kīlauea had been emerging in a lava lake—a new crater some hundreds of feet across. The outlet of the lava lake was the mouth of the main-trunk tube, and it was larger than the Lincoln Tunnel. The main tube and its distributaries traced sinuous patterns under the lava field, their integrity—here and again—imperfect. Bits of roof had fallen into the tubes. These skylights, as they are called, were windows into the inferno, which is exactly what was there. From a panoramic altitude, they were

bright specklings of white-orange in the silvery-black surface of
the stream. If the helicopter hovered close enough, you could see
Cerberus. While we hovered above one skylight, Heliker said, "I
wouldn't want to stand on the edge of that." And she added,
"This whole field was forest a short time ago." The field was as
wide as the Mississippi River in New Orleans. It narrowed with
distance from the lava lake. Camp 8, a mile downstream, was
literally the eighth base of its kind. In the course of the long eruption, Camp 1 had gone under the lava. So had Camps 2, 3, 4, 5,
and 6. Camp 8 was on a small knob, covered with ʻōhiʻa trees and
fern forest, in the middle of the flow. The knob was the summit
of a cinder-and-spatter cone from an earlier eruptive story, now
all but lost in the new lava, which stood a hundred and fifty feet
higher than the previous surface. Another kīpuka, not far away,
was so new that the trees at its edges were still burning.

Hanatani shot a laser at established reflectors, to see if
Kīlauea was locally expanding—swelling with increased magma.
Calling off numbers, he said that the first reflector was "roughly"
1,505.718 meters away. He and Heliker also used a theodolite to
measure the angle between Camp 8 and the rim of the lava lake,
and when they had finished that part of the work we pulled on
gloves and walked up there. The gloves were to prevent cuts when
you slipped and fell on this newly minted terrain. It was a surface
known as shelly pāhoehoe ("pah-hoy-hoy"). Very different from
jagged ʻaʻā, pāhoehoe is the other general texture of newly solidified lava. They are the results of varying gas content and viscosity,
and their appearance is consistent wherever lava flows. In a mag-
nified way, the version we were walking on might have been pea-
nut brittle. You weren't sure what would happen to your next
step. The rock would break, and you would crash through—dropping six inches, a foot—and you put out your hands to brace
yourself. The rock, being essentially glass, was very sharp. It was
also hot, particularly where a tube lay below and molten lava was
running there. We came to a skylight and inched toward it. Steam

swirled above it but did not close off the view—of the racing orange currents of an incandescent river. By an order of magnitude, this was the most arresting sight I had ever seen in nature. The time spent gazing into it could not be measured.

Gradually, I began to think. Out of curiosity, I asked Christina if we were looking down into the near side of the tube or were standing over the middle and looking at the far side of the tube.

"The far side," she said.

If my legs still had knees in them, I was unaware of it.

A few minutes later, continuing uphill, I crashed through the pāhoehoe and fell about a foot, hammering a tibia against an edge of glass. The blow was sharp enough to draw blood, I discovered later, and the resulting limp lasted two months, but I don't remember feeling pain. I attribute this less to terror than to pure excitement. We were nearing the lava lake.

On any given day, the elevation of the lake will vary depending on the efficiency of the tube system that drains it. On this day, the crater walls—which were sheer—were forty feet high. The lake was just what the word says: liquid. It appeared to be covered with elephant hide. There was an overlaying scum produced by contact between the lava and the air. This gray surface was continuously moving, heaving, tearing. It would rip apart from one side of the lake to the other, sending forth a red-orange wave. Lava would dive beneath lava. Or one patch of it would slide past another. Or one acre would separate from another and move in an opposite direction—opening a rift of brilliant red. Perhaps not by simple coincidence, the lake's stiffened surface was imitating plate tectonics. It is sometimes said that the way plate motions function is the way a thick soup will behave in a saucepan as it simmers. Scums form on the surface, and, driven from below by the convecting soup, they move. They slide under one another, they slide past one another, they diverge—like the Eurasian, Persian, Pacific, North American, Arabian, Bismarck, Fiji, China,

Philippine, Solomon, Turkish, Adriatic, African, Aegean, Australian, Antarctic, Carribean, Cocos, Nazca, and Juan de Fuca plates. In the Archean Eon, before there was land, soft-shelled continents are thought to have slid about as scums, experiencing comparable tectonics. This is what was going on in the lava lake. The plates of elephant hide were passing one another on transform faults and coming together in triple junctions, like the plates that make the surface of the whole earth. In the lake, the plate boundaries blazed with volcanic fire. The air was acrid. After Mark Twain was at Kīlauea, he said, correctly, "The smell of sulfur is strong, but not unpleasant to a sinner." The heat was so intense you could lean on it.

Behind us, about fifteen feet back from the edge, was a crack about ten inches wide that ran on as far as we could see and was parallel to the rim. When we first stepped across it, I had remembered Christina Heliker at Camp 8 expressing irritation with the air traffic that often congests around the lake. She said, "The fixed-wing aircraft are limited to five hundred feet. Helicopters are not supposed to fly low enough to cause a safety hazard. They fly ten feet off the ground. They're out of Hilo control, so they police themselves—and they don't. Three or four helicopter tours and a fixed-wing plane may all be going for the site at once. They're an accident waiting to happen. They hover near the lake. If they have news media on board, they're trying to get pictures of geologists near the lake. The place is deafening. Hearing is important to the geologists, and we have complained to the F.A.A. You'd want to hear the crack if your piece of the rim were about to cave into the lake. With so many aircraft, that could be difficult. Sometimes, the smell of jet fuel is as strong as at an airport. The rim is unstable. Frequently, you get collapses with no warning. If you're near the rim and you hear a cracking sound, you want to jump back. But you would not hear it if a helicopter was hovering overhead."

While we were there, we saw only one tourist helicopter. It hung around like a dragonfly. Then it left.

I wish not to exaggerate the danger, which, for the most part, was more apparent than real. It should be noted that in Hawai'i in the twentieth century only one person has been killed by a volcanic eruption. Lava in Hawai'i is rarely explosive. You can be quite near it and know what it will do. When the bombs were falling on Heimaey, the people below were just flush with luck. Workers up on the lava were known for a time as "the suicide squad." They gagged on sulfur and suffered burns, but no one died.

On a transceiver, Heliker called our helicopter. A few hundred feet from the lava lake, we stamped out a crude helipad in the shelly pāhoehoe. We flew downslope and landed near the toe of the lava stream. On that day, it was four or five miles from the lake to the place where the lava came out of its tubes and flowed red and black in the open. The bright-red channels, perhaps twenty feet wide, were configured like a braided river. The color was ruddier and duller than it had been in the skylights near the source, the lava somewhat cooler, and viscous. The flow stood up ten or fifteen feet, and moved slowly—chiming, crackling—with an occasional heavy thud as a partly hardened blob tumbled to one side and broke. Bulges would develop, then break, laterally spilling red-hot lobes. If the skylights in the tubes had been portholes of the underworld, and the lake the earth primeval, this association with the flowing rock was a good deal more intimate, and, thereby, even more stunning. We were next to it—to hot red tongues like tidal pools, to a mass of jagged fins moving downhill like sails. Ron Hanatani, shielding his face with a canvas bag, dipped a hammer into the lava and pulled forth a dripping coagulation that he set on the ground. Blackening on the outside, red on the inside, it slowly cooled. I asked if I could borrow the bag and the hammer. Holding the bag in front of my face, I dipped the hammer into the stream, and discovered that the liquid lava had the elastic texture of egg-white chocolate mousse. When I set it down, none of it stuck to the hammer, the temperature of the steel being so different from the temperature of the lava. Meanwhile, the canvas bag had turned brown at the edges and was giving off smoke. My own temperature felt abnormally high, but perhaps not so much from the radiant heat as from a critical case of red-rock fever.

I waited for my new rock to cool, with intent to take it home, where rock samples lie around in abundance and typically have ages of five hundred million years, fifty million years, five million years. The age of this one was five minutes. While it grew older and colder, I walked around the toe of the lava stream, in part to have a look at the actual front and in part to indulge the utmost desire to pee. About fifteen feet from the toe, I stood at parade rest, and—pissa a hraunid—faced the crackling, crunching, pooling, spilling, steadily advancing lava. Until that moment, I had no idea how hot the surface was on which I was standing—the hard pāhoehoe of an earlier flow. The water, falling, instantly turned to vapor, and barely had time to hiss.

ICELAND and Hawai'i in a sense are twins. They are geophysical hot spots, the two most productive in the world. According to the theory that at present describes them, they are places where heat of very deep origin has found a surface outlet. Radioactivity in the deep rock creates so much heat that it must find a way out, and some think it originates as deep as the core. Traveling upward in plumes of, say, two thousand miles, it eventually encounters the thin surface plates, and may help explain why they move. In any case, when the heat reaches the underside of a plate it punches through, and, as the plate moves, punches through again, and soon again, like the needle of a sewing machine penetrating moving cloth. The plates average sixty miles thick. Beneath them, the

narrow plumes of rising heat essentially remain in place, like the
navigational stars. While the Pacific lithosphere slides overhead,
the Hawaiian heat source stays where it is, making islands. There
are five thousand miles of Hawaiian islands, older and older to the
northwest, reaching to the trench just east of Kamchatka. Almost
all of them have long since had their brief time in the air, and have
been returned by erosion and seafloor subsistence into the fathoms from which they arose. The northernmost part of this chain
is named for Japanese emperors, and the oldest emperor is about
to dive into the trench. While the Pacific Plate moves north-north-
west, the fixed hot spot, as it manifests itself on the surface, appears to move south-southeast. In the state of Hawai'i, the oldest
major islands are Ni'ihau and Kaua'i, which, as peaks of volcanoes, have been out in the air for five million years. Kauai's amazing beauty—its huge canyons, its fjordlike coastal valleys—derives
from the fact that it has been inactive long enough to erode. As
successive lavas and intruded magmas, the islands build up from
the ocean's abyssal plains to surprising volumes and heights. Mauna
Kea and Mauna Loa, from seafloor to summit, are by far the highest mountains on earth. Their base is a hundred miles wide, and
they are thirty-three thousand feet high. Kīlauea continues to build.
The Pacific Plate continues to move. As Kīlauea goes off the top
of the plume, something new will rise. In fact, it is already rising,
twenty miles offshore—a new Hawaiian island, twelve thousand
feet high at this writing, and three thousand feet below the present
level of the ocean.

THE BURNING ISLAND

PAMELA FRIERSON

Kīlauea, Desert and Rift

Ka'ū, hiehie i ka makani.
Ka'ū, regal in the gales.
—*Hawaiian saying*

The southwest rift zone of Kīlauea extends to the sea (and beneath it). It makes a long and wild, torn and riven western border to what is, to me, the heart of volcano country—the Ka'ū desert. Like the red stone deserts of Arizona, or the sculpted badlands of the Mojave, this is a land of deep mineral expanse, of the awesome silence of stone. But the Ka'ū desert is not the ancient, monolithic world of the continental desert. This is volcano desert, a land so fully in Pele's embrace that few now venture into it except those who honor solitude and silence. It is a place to meditate not on eternity, but on change.

The Ka'ū desert is a hot and dry region, but not by virtue of climate only. Rainfall is sparse, on this leeward slope of the mountain, but it is volcanism that determines the complex character of the Kaʻū desert: successions of lava flows have made the land a tapestry of change. Expanses of stone that seem as lifeless as the moon give way suddenly to pockets of older land hosting native dryland forest; an absolute silence yields to the sound of wind in leaves and the drone of insects.

It is a world at once more gentle and more extreme than the continental desert. The Kaʻū desert is quieter and emptier—few creatures live here. The land has not had eons of time to evolve its own community to match the myriad tough denizens of continental deserts, with all their wonderfully peculiar adaptations to desert survival. Like the Hawaiian rain forest, there is nothing poisonous, horny, thorny, or spiky here—leaving the land, even in its stony harshness, vulnerable and open. Since early in this century, feral goats have wreaked havoc among the fragile plants of the Kaʻū desert, which may disappear before they can evolve the thorns to defend themselves.

In its isolation, the Kaʻū desert cradles remnants of the past. Along the coast, in places where no lava has reached for generations, are the ruins of villages. Inland there are trails paved with stepping-stones across the roughest lava, lava-tube caves with petroglyphs carved into the walls, rock quarries, and burial mounds. No one knows much about the archeology of the inlands, since only the coast has been extensively surveyed.

Archeologist Laura Carter and I were spending a day with geologist Tina Neal exploring and mapping an area of the southwest rift. We were about half a mile inland, a point from which we could contemplate the great sweep of volcanic desert to the east. The Kaʻū desert, which covers a good portion of the south flank of Kīlauea, is some of the newest land on earth—most of it is covered by lava flows less than 1,500 years old, though a few pockets of land may have rested undisturbed for more than 10,000 years. Undisturbed by lava, that is; what marks this land most are its great fault scarps—the precipitous cliffs that give it the contour of a Titan's staircase. Each fault scarp represents a point where a great section of land has slumped or slid downhill. If one descended in a bathyscaph offshore, one could follow similar giant steps down Kīlauea's steep, submerged flanks to the ocean bottom.

On all sides but the farthest extension of its east rift zone and this, the vulnerable south flank, Kīlauea rests against the massive bulk of Mauna Loa. Lō'ihi, the undersea volcano growing twenty miles to the south, may provide some buttressing for the tip of Kīlauea's southwest rift zone. But the entire south flank, built up of loose, porous lava, is unsupported. Scientists debate whether the slumping is caused by magma intruding into the rift zone, forcing the land outward, or whether the land moves from its own gravitational pull down the volcano's steep slopes. They are also puzzled as to whether these huge scarps (the Hilina Pali, for example, which extends all across the south flank to the east rift zone of Kīlauea, is over 1,000 feet high in some parts) developed from a few catastrophic slumps or a long series of smaller displacements. Answers to these questions may be crucial to gauging the probability of future cataclysm in this region.

There have been two "slumps" on Kīlauea's south flank in historic time (that is, from the early 1800s when the first data about Hawaiian volcanoes were recorded by Western observers), and both were potent reminders of human vulnerability in such a landscape. In 1868, what remained of the once-proud Hawaiian fishing village culture of the southlands, already decimated by Western disease, was virtually obliterated by the *tsunami* (tidal wave) unleashed by an enormous land movement that seems to have involved the south flanks of both Kīlauea and Mauna Loa. Just over a hundred years later, in 1975, a large section of Kīlauea broke along the Hilina Pali fault system and slid seaward, with disastrous consequences for a group of campers on the coast.

Like the catastrophic event of 1975, the 1868 slump was

accompanied by an eruption, but it is impossible to determine a causal sequence. The summit caldera of Kīlauea had been actively erupting for much of the first half of the nineteenth century, and at the beginning of 1868 it was steaming heavily and pouring lava from several cones within the caldera. On the morning of March 27, passengers on a whale ship off the west coast of the island observed "a dense cloud of smoke rise from the top of Mauna Loa, in one massive pillar, to the height of several miles, lighted up brilliantly by the glare from the crater Moku'āweoweo."[1]

The next day the earthquakes began. By the beginning of April, they were coming at a frequency of more than one hundred a day. In the Ka'ū area it was impossible to walk across the ground at times; it rolled like an ocean swell beneath the feet. Missionary families in the region moved out of their houses and into tents, and held services out under the trees. They were wise to do so: on April 2 a shock came that knocked down nearly every stone wall in Ka'ū and destroyed the church at Wai'ōhinu. A missionary wrote of that day,

> First the earth swayed to and fro, north and south, then east and west, round and round, then up and down ... the trees thrashing about as if torn by a mighty wind. It was impossible to stand, we had to sit on the ground, bracing with hands and feet to keep from rolling over. In the midst we saw burst from the pali [cliff] [a mud slide] which rushed down its headlong course and across the plain below swallowing up everything in its way, trees, houses, cattle, horses, goats, men.[2]

The giant mud slide triggered by the earthquake traveled "three miles in not more than three minutes time." A village of "31 natives" was buried alive. From the coast of Ka'ū to the summit of Kīlauea, the earth opened up in cracks and fissures. Geologists now estimate that land along the southern coast slumped as much as six feet. The earthquake, or the subsidence, or both, triggered a tsunami. The waters receded, then rushed back in, sweeping away the fishing villages that dotted the southern coast, with the height of the wave, according to one account, "equal to that of the coconut trees that grew near those houses."[3] A passenger on a ship sailing offshore reported later, "The sea stands some six feet deep where houses once stood." Before the end of the same day, small eruptions had broken out on Kīlauea's southwest rift zone and inside the volcano's summit caldera.

It was not over yet. The earthquakes continued, though none approached in intensity the great jolt of April 2. On April 7, lava erupted at the 2,000-foot level on Mauna Loa's southwest rift, just a few miles above the present-day Kahuku Ranch. A witness claimed that "here (at Kahuku) the lava burst forth, April 7th, through an enormous fissure of nearly three miles in length ... the great fissure having been formed, in all probability, on April 2nd, the final breaking through of the lava seems to have begun almost without noise."[4] In a little over two hours, the lava flowed nine miles to the ocean. The eruption lasted for five days, covering the devastated region with a pall of dark smoke. "A terrible roar was heard . . . while the fire was flowing," reported a Hawaiian resident. "The natives and the whites were excited, thinking that their last hour had come, for such was the explanation of the learned whites."[5]

Had the fishing villages remained along the Ka'ū-Puna coast, the disaster that struck in November 1975 would have claimed many more lives than it did, for it came virtually without warning. The only hint had been an increase in seismic activity beneath the south flank of Kīlauea during the early part of that month. On Thanksgiving weekend, thirty-four people—fishermen, a group from Sierra Club, and Boy Scout Troop 77—were camped at the idyllic little cove at Halapē, an oasis of coconut groves and white sand beach in the heart of the Ka'ū desert. Once you arrive under the rustling palms at Halapē, you can forget the

torn and riven country you have walked through to get there;
you can pitch your tent on the soft sand and slip into dreams of
paradise.

These campers, if they dreamed such dreams, jolted awake
to a living hell. A minor shock woke a couple of campers at 3:36
A.M.; a father reassured his anxious young son that there was nothing to worry about. At 4:48, an earthquake with a magnitude of
7.2 struck, with an epicenter several miles to the east. The shaking
went on, it seemed, forever. The campers, crawling from their
tents, were thrown to the ground. Rocks came tumbling from the
cliff just inland from the beach, and some campers fled toward
the shore to escape them. It was the wrong direction to run. The
first wave struck thirty seconds after the earthquake subsided; the
second, much larger, swept everything in its path as far as 300 feet
inland. Incredibly, only two people were killed, one battered against
the rocks, the other disappearing out to sea.

About half an hour after the main shock, seismographs
recorded harmonic tremors under Kīlauea. At 5:32 A.M., a long
fissure opened in the floor of the summit caldera, spouting a
continuous curtain of fire.

Scientists later determined that the south flank coastline had
subsided as much as ten feet. The summit of Kīlauea itself sank
six feet, and the entire south flank of the volcano was "displaced
seaward" by several yards. Just as pressure buildup along the San
Andreas fault guarantees that earthquakes will occur in that part
of California, it is inevitable that such displacements will continue to happen along the south flank of Kīlauea. What geologists
can't predict thus far is either their frequency or magnitude.

IF THE south flank of Kīlauea, encompassing the Kaʻū desert,
begins to seem as precarious as a house of cards, a few days of
walking along the southwest rift zone can deconstruct permanently
any remaining notions of *terra firma*. At the top end of the rift

zone, the land is heaped with great dunes of volcanic cinder blown down from summit eruptions. Thin sheets of volcanic mud, remnants of the explosive 1790 summit eruption, can still be found in pockets where the wind has uncovered it. The 1790 explosion was "phreatomagmatic"—or "steam induced"—and it turned a normally "gentle" volcano into a killer. Lava in the summit caldera apparently sank deep into the mountain as a result of a great draining of lava out low on the east rift zone. The subsiding magma encountered a table of groundwater. The resulting steam-powered explosion blanketed the top of the rift zone with choking fumes and a rain of volcanic mud, ash, and cinder.

This was, in both oral and recorded history, Kīlauea's most violent eruption—and it came at a most significant moment in Hawaiian history. The army of Keoua, the hereditary chief of Ka'ū, was returning from the Hilo area to Ka'ū after battling Kamehameha's allies (Keoua was the last holdout against Kamehameha's hegemony).[6] Keoua's army, traveling (as was the custom) with women, children, and domestic animals, stopped to make offerings to Pele at the summit caldera. They were greeted with rumbles and small explosions that began to increase in ferocity. Keoua divided the army into three groups, sending each ahead on the trail to Ka'ū at two-hour intervals. The third group, reaching a point six miles southwest of the summit, found the group that had preceded them lying on the ground, looking, at a distance, as though they were resting. They were, in fact, dead, with only a few pigs as survivors of what must have been a cloud of poisonous gas on the heels of a huge explosion.

For these people who worshiped Pele both as god and ancestor, to have the volcano goddess show such anger must have been profoundly demoralizing. Perhaps this explains why, in the next year, Keoua allowed himself to be trapped by Kamehameha. The latter had spent the last year at Kawaihae on the Kona coast, overseeing the building of an enormous war temple.

When the heiau was finished, Kamehameha invited Keoua to come to the dedication. Keoua made preparations that indicate he knew he might be traveling to his death, choosing old friends to ride with him as "companions of death" in his huge double-hulled canoe. One of Kamehameha's men slew Keoua with a spear as he stepped ashore under the shadow of the huge temple, and his body was offered as its first sacrifice. That day in 1791 marked the beginning of the end of proud independence for the peoples of Puna and Kaʻū.

In the upper regions of Kīlauea's southwest rift zone, one still comes across footprints, in the solidified mud from that explosion, that may have been made by Keoua's retreating army. Much of this area, however, was covered by an enormous, lengthy eruption in 1920 that built its own small shield, given the name Mauna Iki ("little mountain"). The glossy pāhoehoe fields of Mauna Iki cover a tremendous area. Below them, one enters a region marked on maps as "the highly fractured zone." It is here that the true temper of the rift zone reveals itself.

FOR the last month or so, Tina Neal had been mapping land around the lower part of what is called "the Great Crack," a huge continuous fissure that extends for nearly fifteen miles down the spine of the rift zone. The Great Crack is testament to the paradoxical nature of stone, its simultaneous elastic and brittle properties. Under slow pressure, it can bend and move with surprising plasticity, like ice in a glacier, but at some crucial point pressure or movement will shatter and rend rock apart. There was an incident, famous in local history, when, during the 1960 eruption of the east rift, the ground opened in numerous fissures. Some sprang back together again. An unlucky cow fell into one of these before it closed up—a photo from the time shows one leg of the beast protruding from a very narrow crack.

The Great Crack is the result of repeated fracturing caused by the pressure of magma moving into the southwest rift zone. At the point where we were standing, the crack was perhaps twenty feet wide and forty deep, and we looked into the tops of a dense grove of kukui trees that had populated the bottom, where rainwater probably accumulated. They were the only trees in a land that is mostly barren lava, for a large portion of the lower rift zone was covered in an 1823 eruption. This rapid, very fluid flow issued, apparently with little warning, out of a six-mile section of the Great Crack. Since the bottom of the fissure is only half a mile from shore, the lava must have reached the sea very quickly. The Reverend William Ellis, passing through this area soon after, reported that "the people ... told us that no longer than five moons ago Pele ... had issued from a subterranean cavern, and over flowed the lowland.... The inundation was sudden and violent, burnt one canoe, and carried four more into the sea."[7]

The fast-moving 1823 flow drained quickly toward the sea, leaving in some areas a thin sheet of cooling lava only a few inches thick, coating the landscape in a kind of volcanic shellac, draping features rather than obliterating them. Empty, cylindrical "tree molds" reveal where forest once stood. Through the glossy surface protrude archeological features made up of older, weathered rock—remains that Laura Carter, if she works her way painstakingly across the Kaʻū desert from Wahaʻula, may get around to cataloguing in the year 2040. But some of the traces of the past Tina Neal had reported stumbling on in this raw, remote landscape had piqued Carter's curiosity, and so she too had decided to accompany Tina Neal for a day, to match her knowledge of culture with Neal's knowledge of nature.

Neal herself was filling in the last details of what eventually would be the definitive map of the southwest rift, an area previously explored mainly by aerial photography. Her systematic rock sampling would provide a chemical history of the rift zone. She was chronicling the extent of flows and identifying cracks and faults, along with checking for evidence of lava "intrusions"— lava activity that never quite made it to the surface. For a volca-

nologist all this information feeds one underlying, elusive goal—
to be able to predict the future.

Tina Neal was wearing one of those field vests that is all
pockets, stuffed with pens, notes, magnifying glass. Her rock
hammer hung from a loop. She took notes and samples, but spent
most of her time staring at the landscape. Watching her, I imagined she was the first haole to give this landscape her full attention
for such an extended amount of time. There was something priestly
in her wandering and pondering—I thought of the ancient
Chinese geomancers whose job was to determine the *feng-shui*—
the cosmic energy or lines of power in a landscape. The Chinese
believed that every place had such patterns, and that humans must
consult the wisdom of a place in order to determine how to live in
harmony with it. Many of the riots against the Christian missionaries in nineteenth-century China came about because the missionaries built their structures without even considering the
feng-shui of the land.

Tina was now at the tail end of 1,000 miles of walking, mostly
alone, in the lands of Kīlauea's southwest rift zone. She was
delighted when I told her about *feng-shui*, and my image of her as
a modern geomancer. "Something has happened to me out here,"
she said, "that I'm still trying to fit in with my training as a scientist. Spending time near Puʻu ʻŌʻō, monitoring the action, was
exciting, but what has really shaken me is the stronger sense of
presence I've felt here, in this lonely, desolate place."[8] She paused
for a long moment, scanning the empty landscape in a way that
seemed almost expectant. I followed her gaze down to where, a
few miles distant, bare lava fields, a quilt of matte and shiny grays
and blacks, gave way to the blank blue of the sea. "I guess I'm still
uncomfortable, as a scientist, saying these things," she said finally.
"But it's like having a sense of something very powerful, yet not
knowing how to acknowledge it. I finally came up with my own
little ritual—a kind of prayer or greeting to the land, or the spirit
of the land."

We detoured to show Laura Carter some of the archeological sites that Tina Neal had stumbled on. Most impressive were a couple of small platforms on a pocket of high ground surrounded by 1823 lava flow. They are carefully covered with a flat surface of slabs of older lava, which Neal has identified as rock from a vent, two miles upland, that erupted about two thousand years ago. Carter is puzzled and fascinated by these features—they resemble the burial platforms that Hawaiians began making in historic times, but their foundations are partly covered by an older flow—one that Neal has dated as around 500 years old. "Put that on my list for excavations," said Carter. "Maybe I'll get to it before Pele decides to visit this area again."

We followed the 1823 flow down to the sea, then walked the coast west to Pālima Point. The coastal area is dotted with the remains of temporary shelters, walls, fishing shrines. The sea cliffs are high here—30 to 50 feet—and the sea dashes against them. According to Tina Neal, the lava flows that drape over the cliff edge like thick frosting are 400 to 750 years old. The rocks that make up the sea cliff are about twice that age. What did they cover—a small, beautiful cove, perhaps, where the first voyagers touched land? Layers of lava; pages in a volcanic book of time.

The bulb-shaped head of a rare green sea turtle broke the surface of the water, and I wondered if an ancient instinct had made it search this stretch of coast for a nesting place that is no longer there. A few terns wheeled in the updraft from the cliffs. From this spot, in every direction, the land appears huge and empty. To the west, the coastline stretches, wild and magnificent, to the very tip of Ka Lae, or South Point, where sand dunes cover the oldest settlement thus far found. To tourists, it is better known as the "southernmost point of the United States." It projects horizontally, like the snout of a needlefish, into a gray-blue haze of sea and sky.

Pālima Point lies three miles outside the National Park

boundary, on land owned partly by the state and partly by private parties. For years the park had planned to acquire another section of this land, incorporating the coastal portion of the southwest rift zone and extending park boundaries westward to within a mile of Pālima Point. But funds were perpetually scarce and there seemed to be no hurry—no one dreamed that any economic use would be found for this stretch of wild lava coast, just as no one twenty years ago could have imagined the huge resorts hacked out of the lava plains of Kona.

The park has come to realize, a bit too late, that no land, however wild, is immune from speculation any more. For the last two years, state and private monies have been pumped into feasibility studies for a commercial "spaceport"—a satellite-launching facility—on the Big Island's sparsely populated Ka'ū coast. The search has been narrowed to two choices, and one is Pālima Point. The spaceport, which would launch commercial and possibly military payloads, would require a safety zone with a three-mile radius (extending to the current boundary of the National Park), which would mean that lands and offshore waters would be closed to the public during launching periods. The rocket pads and other launching facilities would be highly visible for many miles. Noise at time of launch is estimated at 115 decibels for a distance of up to three miles from the launching site. As one feasibility study states, this sound would be "approximately six decibels higher than would be experienced by a person seated near the stage at a rock music concert."[9]

What concerns Tina Neal, besides what she terms the "inap-propriateness" of such a facility adjacent to a national park, is the geologic risk. Part of the land is actually on the southwest rift zone; on all of it, ground cracks and relatively recent lava flows reveal the inherent instability of land in the heart of volcano coun-try. "Space launch facilities should be sited to minimize risk associated with earth displacements, lava flows, and gas and tephra [ash, cinder, and solidified bits of lava] emissions," the feasibility study suggests.[10] How much "minimizing" can humans do on the unstable flank of a very active volcano?

STANDING here on that magnificent wild coast, I thought about the hubris of those who come from outside, who seek to place quantifiable measures on this land, who think that humans can (and should) always find a way to control nature. That hubris has included volcanologists: I was reminded of Thomas Jaggar's motto, *Ne plus haustae aut obrutae urbes*, "No more buried cities." Thomas Augustus Jaggar founded Hawaiian Volcano Observatory in 1912. Like most scientists of his time, he firmly believed that science was primarily a tool to aid humanity in gaining control over nature.

But something has shifted in the view of some of the volcanologists I have met here, those who have come to love the wild power of the land. When I mentioned Jaggar's bombing war on the Mauna Loa lava flows of 1935 and 1942 to Jaggar's present-day successor, observatory scientist-in-charge Tom Wright, he shook his head in distaste. "Not only do I believe bombing ultimately futile," he said, "but I find abhorrent the idea of destroying a pristine lava flow." Tina Neal feels the same. It is as though loyalty has shifted from human-scape to landscape. As though, in touching this land long enough, deeply enough, these Westerners had become, in a sense, Hawaiian.

Sacred Darkness

> Pele is my goddess,
> a chiefess of sacred darkness
> and of light
> > —*fragment of a chant recited at dawn and*
> > *dusk by Mary Kawena Pukui's grandmother*

Enter not prayerless the house of Pele.
—*from a chant translated by Emerson in* Pele
and Hiiaka

At its highest point, the scarp of the Hilina Pali plummets 1,200 feet to a broad lava plain. To the east, the plain declines gently and then sweeps up again, like a nearly cresting wave, to the back of Puʻu Kapukapu. Puʻu Kapukapu is what geologists call a *horst*—a piece of land left high and dry as fault systems all around it allowed its surrounding terrain to sink downward. To either side of Kapukapu, the land slopes more gently to the coast. Out of sight, in the shadow of the horst's seaward cliffs, is Halapē, the once-idyllic cove and stand of coconut trees, much of the land now submerged, the broken remnants of trees immersed in water at high tide. But the beach there is slowly filling in again, and small new palms have sprouted, hiding the scars of the land shattered by the 1975 earthquake under their green fronds.

From here at the top of the Pali, one can see more than forty miles of coast. To the southeast, basalt seacliffs emerge again beyond the shadow of Puʻu Kapukapu, and curve into points and shallow bays until they vanish in a volcanic haze. To the southwest, the land bends outward and disappears into the horizon at the distant point of Ka Lae. The rain clouds that have shrouded Kīlauea for the last two weeks are breaking up just to the northwest, and a rainbow arches from them, falling over the edge of the Pali. Thunder and rain season, the inseminating rain of Lono.

There are four of us here at the top of Hilina Pali, eyeing the first steep switchback of the trail down. Archeologist Laura Carter and Fay-Lyn Jardine, a tall, graceful backcountry park ranger of Hawaiian-Portuguese blood. And Tamar Elias, an athlete and Jill-of-all-trades, currently employed changing the recording papers on the seismographs at the observatory.

We are headed into the midst of the lava plain below us to

find two lava-tube caves containing petroglyphs and cultural remains. The caves were discovered in the 1970s. No archeologist has visited them since, and Laura wants to see how they are faring, and to leave a sign in one of them reminding hikers that might stumble on the site to leave the remains undisturbed.

The trail down the Pali makes a dozen turns down the rocky face, over stretches of rubbly ʻaʻā. Halfway down, Fay-Lyn points out the place where a Park Service packhorse named Battle Star got off the trail and tumbled "ass-over-teakettle" fifty feet down to the next switchback, emerging, miraculously, with just a few scrapes, but a strong aversion to packing.

At the bottom of the Pali, we take an altimeter reading, then fan out across the rough country to look for the caves. Waist-high grass masks jagged flows of ʻaʻā, in between billowy mounds of pāhoehoe; the land dips and sways like a choppy sea. The "cave" opening is actually the fallen roof of a lava tube, so its entry will be from a depression in the ground; in this country, one could walk within ten yards of it and not see it.

But I come across it just as I think we may have walked too far. The collapsed roof of the lava tube has created a pit thirty feet or so wide, and a low opening yawns at the north end. It is like a thousand such "caves" in the layered lava of this country, but the pile of stones at the entrance is arranged into a low wall. I climb down to the wall, and find that its top is laid with water-worn stones, here, three to four miles inland. In front of the wall, an area of the rocky pit has been leveled and thin, flat stones upended in a square to form a hearth.

The petroglyphs cluster so thickly at the entrance that at first I don't perceive them. Then my eyes register the darker, incised rock on the mottled, vitreous surface of the cave's inner walls, and human figures startle me, crowding forward from the darkness.

The shapes are cut or pecked into the thin, glazed coating left by the molten river that once flowed through the lava tube.

Perhaps because this surface is easier to work, these petroglyphs are richer in detail than others I have seen: many of the human figures have fingers and toes; some have spiky hair or headdresses. There is a hawk-headed man with bird feet and an arrow-shaped penis. Turtles, dogs, and chickens. And three life-sized incised feet, the broad shovel-shape of Hawaiian feet, good for walking on lava.

The archeologists who explored the cave a decade ago uncovered more petroglyphs under rubble and midden. Charcoal in the midden furnished a date of plus or minus 300 years. No historic artifacts (such as nails) were found in this cave, and none of the petroglyphs are of European motifs (horses, for instance), suggesting that use of this site ceased before Western settlement. These caves may have provided seasonal water and shelter, as a large number of water gourds found in a nearby cave would seem to indicate; crops may have been grown nearby at times in the year, and water carried down to fishing villages on the coast. But these figures spilling from the darkness hint at other uses than water and shelter, at other powers felt or honored here.

Perhaps the hawk-headed figures are a key to the mana of this particular place, for, though not unknown elsewhere, such petroglyphs are rare, and there are several here. But what secrets the cave holds it does not readily reveal. The figures thin out and then stop some twenty feet into the cave. Forty feet farther, the cave narrows down to a space one could crawl through, painfully, with some padded clothes. My flashlight is not strong enough to penetrate the night beyond.

We return to the caved-in pit and open sky to eat our lunches, next to the hearth with its surrounding midden of 'opihi (limpet) shells, evidence of meals eaten here long ago. Then we explore the south entrance to the lava tube, crawling over the fallen rocks that narrow the opening. A few petroglyphs cluster at the entrance, but the glazed walls farther in are empty of figures.

The lava tube appears to continue on into a pitch blackness. Laura and Fay-Lyn and Tamar turn back to the entrance, determining to go search for the other cave mentioned in the archeological report, the one that contained fragments of many water gourds.

I linger behind, deciding on impulse to do something I've never done alone before, to follow that dark passage.

Left to myself, I reconsider. Beyond the reach of my light, the tube opening is a dense, black maw. I have one flashlight, no spare batteries. But if I watch carefully to make sure the tube does not branch anywhere, I could feel my way back out if I had to. I have long since lost all but a reflex anxiety, in the country, about predatory animals or snakes. The only large animals that frequent the lava tubes are feral goats, who shelter in them, and in sickness or old age may crawl into their recesses to die.

Indeed, fifty feet in, at the furthest reach of the light from the entrance, a goat skull and bones are scattered across the floor, white remnants of a natural death, but I can't stifle an inner shiver that makes me read them as sentinel or warning to the dark passage beyond. Some deep-seated reflex in me links darkness with death, but it has come to seem less like a primal response and more like a cultural legacy. I am reminded once more of H. Rider Haggard's nightmare journey, in his novel *She*, into the caverns of earth somewhere in darkest Africa. There his hero found a savage tribe inhabiting vast catacombs, ruled by a strangely immortal female given over to a cult of death. A fantastical story, but compelling, as it must have been to Haggard himself, who wrote it, it is said, in six weeks, as though it poured in some great stream from the unconscious.

Haggard's images are crude, as dreamscapes often are, but disturbingly familiar, as though they tap a deep vein in the Western mind where the shadow side of the natural world has been replaced by an inner darkness. The darkness, loosed from its moorings in the natural cycles of birth and death, no longer something we can reach or touch, or make our peace with, terrifies us from within, elicits rage and fear toward all that is alien or wild or "other," all that reminds us of the tenuousness of human control.

Armed only, as in Haggard's dreamscape, with a sense of the darkness as unholy, one would find in this landscape only a mirror of inner terrors. But other visions rise from the land, and are given voice in Hawaiian myth: images, prolific in this volcanic world, of the deep-rooted, creative powers of darkness:

An incandescent river pours through a black labyrinth, streams briefly into the light at the edge of a seacliff, cools to steaming black at the edge of an ocean wave, shatters from the pressure of its still-molten heart, and is flung back on shore as tiny grains of glistening jet. "Born was the island, it grew, it sprouted, it flourished, lengthened, rooted deeply, budded." From the black maws of the lava of last year, tiny ferns sprout like lambent green flames. As the legends of the land tell, the mouths of darkness, like the wombs of women, are the channels through which flows "*Pō nui hoʻolakolako*," "The great night that supplies."

I walk into the black tunnel of the lava tube. The walls curve gently to the right, ridged horizontally like striations of muscles, marking the levels of the molten lava as it diminished and narrowed. The tube must once have been filled to the brim with a fiery river; as it drained, it cascaded and pooled, creating intricate, molded patterns on the floor. When the molten rock subsided, the residue on the ceiling hardened into smooth, conical drips, teat-shaped, like some vast statuary of a many-breasted mother goddess.

For a few hundred paces, the smooth musculature of the cave makes walking easy, but then the ceiling narrows to a crawl-space. I shut off the light and lean against the laminated wall.

Absolute night surrounds me, warm, moist, palpable—the pressure of amniotic fluid, or of the eyelid on the eye. It is a nonhuman presence so overwhelming that it threatens to dissolve the fragile boundaries of self. Nothing in it seems benign or disposed toward humans. Nor indisposed. Simply there, a vast mystery behind every element of this landscape. I switch the flashlight back on quickly. "*Enter not prayerless the house of Pele.*" Some great current seems to flow from the inner recesses, propelling me back toward the entrance.

And into an astoundingly noisy outer world, where the darkness fractures into a million forms. The wind is hissing through grass, and for the first time I hear in its lower register the base note of waves pounding the coast. I glance at the crowd of human figures at the north mouth of the lava tube. Midway between the light and the darkness, arms akimbo, some point up, some pointing down, guarding the passage, or pointing the way.

NOTES

1. As quoted in William T. Brigham, *The Volcanoes of Kilauea and Mauna Loa* (Honolulu: Bishop Museum, 1909), p. 479.

2. F. S. Lyman as quoted by Brigham, *The Volcanoes of Kilauea and Mauna Loa*, p. 102.

3. *Pacific Commercial Advertiser*, 1868, as quoted by Harry O. Wood, "On the Earthquakes of 1868 in Hawaii," *Bulletin of the Seismological Society of America* 4, no. 4 (December 1914), p. 106.

4. Dr. William Hillebrand, as quoted by Wood, "On the Earthquakes of 1868," p. 210.

5. As quoted in E. S. C. Handy and Elizabeth Green Handy, *Native Planters of Old Hawaii* (Honolulu: Bishop Museum Press, 1972), p. 567.

6. Kamehameha was a chief of Hawai'i Island who succeeded in bringing all the islands under his rule, becoming the first "king" of the archipelago.

7. Harold T. Stearns, "The 1823 lava flow from Kilauea volcano, Hawaii," *Journal of Geology* 34, no. 4 (May–June 1926), p. 340.

8. Pu'u 'Ō'ō is a large volcanic cone formed during the eruption of Kilauea's east rift zone that began in 1983 and still continues.

9. As quoted in Arthur D. Little, Inc., *Evaluation of the Potential for Space-related Activities in the State of Hawaii* (Honolulu: Little, 1987), pp. iv—26.

10. Little, pp. iv—9.

THE LIVING OCEAN

A CITY PERSON
ENCOUNTERING NATURE

MAXINE HONG KINGSTON

A CITY person encountering nature hardly recognizes it, has no patience for its cycles, and disregards animals and plants unless they roar and exfoliate in spectacular aberrations. Preferring the city myself, I can better discern natural phenomena when books point them out; I also need to verify what I think I've seen, even though charts of phyla and species are orderly whereas nature is wild, unruly.

Last summer, my friend and I spent three days together at a beach cottage. She got up early every morning to see what "critters" the ocean washed up. The only remarkable things I'd seen at that beach in years were Portuguese man-o-war and a flightless bird, big like a pelican; the closer I waded toward it, the farther out to sea the bird bobbed.

We found flecks of whitish gelatin, each about a quarter of an inch in diameter. The wet sand was otherwise clean and flat. The crabs had not yet dug their holes. We picked up the blobs on our fingertips and put them in a saucer of sea water along with seaweeds and some branches of coral.

One of the things quivered, then it bulged, unfolded, and flipped over or inside out. It stretched and turned over like a human being getting out of bed. It opened and opened to twice its original size. Two arms and two legs flexed, and feathery wings flared, webbing the arms and legs to the body, which tapered to a graceful tail. Its ankles had tiny wings on them—like Mercury. Its back muscles were articulated like a comic book superhero's— blue and silver metallic leotards outlined with black racing stripes. It's a spaceman, I thought. A tiny spaceman in a spacesuit.

I felt my mind go wild. A little spaceship had dropped a spaceman onto our planet. The other blob went through its gyrations and also metamorphosed into a spaceman. I felt as if I were having the flying dream where I watch two perfect beings wheel in the sky.

The two critters glided about, touched the saucer's edges. Suddenly, the first one contorted itself, turned over, made a bulge like an octopus head, then flipped back, streamlined again. A hole in its side like a porthole or a vent opened and shut. The motions happened so fast, we were not certain we had seen them until both creatures had repeated them many times.

I had seen similar quickenings: dry strawberry vines and dead trout revive in water. Leaves and fins unfurl; colors return.

We went outside to catch more, and our eyes accustomed, found a baby critter. So there were more than a pair of these in the universe. So they grew. The baby had apparently been in the sun too long, though, and did not revive.

The next morning, bored that the critters were not performing more tricks, we blew on them to get them moving. By accident, their eyes or mouths faced, and suckled together. There was a churning. They wrapped their arms, legs, wings around one another.

Not knowing whether they were killing each other or mating, we tried unsuccessfully to part them. Guts, like two worms, came out of the portholes. Intestines, I thought; they're going to die. But the two excrescences braided together like DNA strands, then whipped apart, turned pale, and smokily receded into the holes. The critters parted, flipped, and floated away from each other.

After a long time, both of them fitted their armpits between the coral branches; we assumed that they were depositing eggs.

When we checked the clock, four hours had gone by. We'd both thought it had only been about twenty minutes.

That afternoon, the creatures seemed less distinct, their sharp lines blurring. I rubbed my eyes; the feathers were indeed melting. The beings were disintegrating in the water. I threw the coral as far out as I could into the ocean.

Later, back in town, we showed our biologist friend our sketches, I burbling about visitors from outer space, and he said they were nudibranchs. This was our friend who as a kid had vowed that he would study Nature, but in college, he specialized in marine biology, and in graduate school, he studied shrimps. He was now doing research on one species of shrimp that he had discovered on one reef off O'ahu.

A new climate helps me to see nature. Here are some sights upon moving to Hawai'i:

Seven black ants, led by an orange one, dismembered a fly.

I peeled sunburn off my nose, and later recognized it as the flake of something an ant was marching away with.

A mushroom grew in a damp corner of the living room.

Giant philodendrons tear apart the cars abandoned in the jungle. Tendrils crawl out of the hoods; they climb the shafts of the steam shovels that had dug the highway. Roofs and trunks break open, turn red, orange, brown, and sag into the dirt.

Needing to reach explanations of such strangeness, we bought an English magazine, *The Countryman*, which reports "The Wild Life and Tame" news.

"STAMPED TO DEATH—A hitherto peaceful herd of about fifty cows, being fetched in from pasture, suddenly began to rush around, and bellow in a most alarming manner. The source of their interest was a crippled gull, which did its best to escape; but the cows, snorting and bellowing, trampled it to death. They then quieted down and left the field normally.

—Charles Brudett, Hants."

Also: "BIG EYE, Spring, 1967—When I was living in the Karoo, a man brought me a five-foot cobra which he had just killed. It had been unusually sluggish and the tail of another snake protruded from its mouth. This proved to be a boomslang, also poisonous but back-fanged; it was 1-1/2 inches longer than the cobra and its head-end had been partly digested.

—J.S. Taylor, Fife."

I took some students to the zoo after reading Blake's "Tiger, Tiger Burning Bright," Stevens's "Thirteen Ways of Looking at a Blackbird," and Lorenz's *King Solomon's Ring*. They saw the monkeys catch a pigeon and tear it apart. I kept reminding them that that was extraordinary. "Watch an animal going about its regular habits," I said, but then they saw an alligator shut its jaws on a low-flying pigeon. I remembered that I don't see ordinary stuff either.

I've watched ants make off with a used Band-Aid. I've watched a single termite bore through a book, a circle clean through. I saw a pigeon vomit milk, and didn't know whether it was sick, or whether its babies had died and the milk sacs in its throat were engorged. I have a friend who was pregnant at the same time as her mare, and, just exactly like the Chinese superstition that only one of the babies would live, the horse gave birth to a foal in two pieces.

When he was about four, we took our son crabbing for the "crabs with no eyes," as he called them. They did have eyes, but they were on stalks. The crabs fingered the bait as if with hands;

very delicately they touched it, turned it, swung it. One grabbed hold of the line, and we pulled it up. But our son, a Cancer, said, "Let's name him Linda." We put Linda back in the river and went home.

A Sea Worry

This summer our son body-surfs. He says it's his "job" and rises each morning at 5:30 to catch the bus to Sandy Beach. I hope that by September he will have had enough of the ocean. Tall waves throw surfers against the shallow bottom. Undertows have snatched them away. Sharks prowl Sandy's. Joseph told me that once he got out of the water because he saw an enormous shark. "Did you tell the lifeguard?" I asked. "No." "Why not?" "I didn't want to spoil the surfing." The ocean pulls at the boys, who turn into surfing addicts. At sunset you can see surfers waiting for the last golden wave.

"Why do you go surfing so often?" I ask my students.

"It feels so good," they say. "Inside the tube. I can't describe it. There are no words for it."

"You can describe it," I scold, and I am very angry. "Everything can be described. Find the words for it, you lazy boy. Why don't you stay home and read?" I am afraid that the boys give themselves up to the ocean's mindlessness.

When the waves are up, surfers all over Hawai'i don't do their homework. They cut school. They know how the surf is breaking at any moment because every fifteen minutes the reports come over the radio; in fact, one of my former students is the surf reporter.

Some boys leave for mainland colleges, and write their parents heart-rending letters. They beg to come home for Thanksgiving. "If I can just touch the ocean," they write from Missouri and Kansas, "I'll last for the rest of the semester." Some come home for Christmas and don't go back.

Even when the assignment is about something else, the students write about surfing. They try to describe what it is to be inside the wave as it curls over them, making a tube or "chamber" or "green room" or "pipeline" or "time warp." They write about the silence, the peace, "no hassles," the feeling of being reborn as they shoot out the end. They've written about the voice of God, the "commandments" they hear. In the margins, they draw the perfect wave. Their writing is full of clichés. "The endless summer," they say. "Unreal."

Surfing is like a religion. Among the martyrs are George Helm, Kimo Mitchell, and Eddie Aikau. Helm and Mitchell were lost at sea riding their surfboards from Kaho'olawe, where they had gone to protest the Navy's bombing of that island. Eddie Aikau was a champion surfer and lifeguard. A storm had capsized the *Hōkūle'a*, the ship that traced the route that the Polynesian ancestors sailed from Tahiti, and Eddie Aikau had set out on his board to get help.

Since the ocean captivates our son, we decided to go with him to see Sandy's.

We got up before dawn, picked up his friend, Marty, and drove out of Honolulu. Almost all the traffic was going in the opposite direction, the freeway coned to make more lanes into the city. We came to a place where raw mountains rose on our left and the sea fell on our right, smashing against the cliffs. The strip of cliff pulverized into sand is Sandy's. "Dangerous Current Exist," said the ungrammatical sign.

Earll and I sat on the shore with our blankets and thermos of coffee. Joseph and Marty put on their fins and stood at the edge of the sea for a moment, touching the water with their fingers and crossing their hearts before going in. There were fifteen boys out there, all about the same age, fourteen to twenty, all with the same kind of lean, V-shaped build, most of them with black hair that made their wet heads look like sea lions. It was hard to tell whether our kid was one of those who popped up after a big wave. A few had surfboards, which are against the rules at a body-surfing beach, but the lifeguard wasn't on duty that early.

As they watched for the next wave, the boys turned toward the ocean. They gazed slightly upward; I thought of altar boys before a great god. When a good wave arrived, they turned, faced shore, and came shooting in, some taking the wave to the right and some to the left, their bodies fish-like, one arm out in front, the hand and fingers pointed before them, like a swordfish's beak. A few held credit card trays, and some slid in on trays from McDonald's.

"That is no country for middle-aged women," I said. We had on bathing suits underneath our clothes in case we felt moved to participate. There were no older men either.

Even from the shore, we could see inside the tubes. Sometimes, when they came at an angle, we saw into them a long way. When the wave dug into the sand, it formed a brown tube or a gold one. The magic ones, though, were made out of just water, green and turquoise rooms, translucent walls and ceilings. I saw one that was powder-blue, perfect, thin; the sun filled it with sky blue and water light. The best thing, the kids say, is when you are in the middle of the tube, and there is water all around you but you're dry.

The waves came in sets; the boys passed up the smaller ones. Inside a big one, you could see their bodies hanging upright, knees bent, duckfeet fins paddling, bodies dangling there in the wave.

Once in a while, we heard a boy yell, "Aa-whoo!" "Poon-tah!" "Aaroo!" And then we noticed how rare human voice was here; the surfers did not talk, but silently, silently rode the waves.

Since Joseph and Marty were considerate of us, they stopped after two hours, and we took them out for breakfast. We kept asking them how it felt, so that they would not lose language.

"Like a stairwell in an apartment building," said Joseph, which I liked immensely. He hasn't been in very many apartment buildings, so had to reach a bit to get the simile. "I saw somebody I knew coming toward me in the tube, and I shouted, 'Jeff. Hey, Jeff,' and my voice echoed like a stairwell in an apartment building. Jeff and I came straight at each other—mirror tube."

"Are there ever girls out there?" Earll asked.

"There's a few women who come at about eleven," said Marty.

"How old are they?"

"About twenty."

"Why do you cross your heart with water?"

"So the ocean doesn't kill us."

I described the powder-blue tube I had seen. "That part of Sandy's is called Chambers," they said.

I have gotten some surfing magazines, the ones kids steal from the school library, to see if the professionals try to describe the tube. Bradford Baker writes:

... Round and pregnant in Emptiness
  I slide,
    laughing,
into the sun,
  into the night.

Frank Miller calls the surfer:

... mother's fumbling
  curly-haired
  tubey-laired
  son.

"Ooh, offshores—," writes Reno Abbellira, "where wind and wave most often form that terminal rendezvous of love—when the wave can reveal her deepest longings, her crest caressed, cannily covered to form those peeling concavities we know, perhaps a bit irreverently, as tubes. Here we strive to spend every second—enclosed, encased, sometimes fatefully entombed, and hopefully, gleefully, ejected—Whoosh!"

"An iridescent ride through the entrails of God," says Gary L. Crandall.

I am relieved that the surfers keep asking one another for descriptions. I also find some comfort in the stream of commuter traffic, cars filled with men over twenty, passing Sandy Beach on their way to work.

HAWAI'I AT THE EDGE

JOHN L. CULLINEY

ISLANDS are clothed by the sea. Around the Hawaiian archipelago, in sunny, trade-wind weather, they flaunt their finery. Blue gowns flecked with white billow to the horizon and at a distance merge with one another in epipelagic swirls. Hidden below is a seductive world where scientists, explorers, and island lovers are enticed by mystery and beauty. Here, too, we find evidence of origins—of earth, of life, of our vertebrate selves. Sometimes, if we dare, we sense human proportion and planetary perspective and, swimming deep in earth's ancient biospheric womb, confront our own infancy as a species.

Roam where you will on the edges of the islands, the wonderful variations in coastal topography—dramatic cliffs and canyons, long sloping ridge lines, wide beaches of powdery sand, and ramparts of boulders—are extended in underwater landscapes. To be sure, much of the scene below the shoreline is softened; starkness and contrast are muted in the filtered light; steep and jagged landforms assume rounder contours as they accumulate falling sediment. One's perception of scale also changes. Oddly enough, on land an explorer looms large over the path being followed, feels large amid the immediate surroundings. For me, this is the case even with a one-hundred-mile view across mountains, above timberline. In the sea, however, it can be just the opposite despite a miniscule panorama. Off the Kona coast, I feel small indeed as I hover in what seems vast blue space above a slope that plunges down into darkening obscurity, where I can see perhaps two hundred feet. Touching the bottom or standing on it doesn't change this perception—the compression of human stature seems inherent in descending to the floor of the sea—but this solid ground does provide a connection to the island that extends up through the ocean's surface to well-known, long-charted realms, and also down to indistinct and uncertain boundaries where Hawaiianness merges imperceptibly with the deep world ocean. The nature of these waters and dusky lands on the hidden flanks of the islands is of special interest to a naturalist because this is the last of primeval Hawai'i. Above the sea, Hawaiian endemic nature has been long despoiled, even eradicated in many areas. Only beyond and below the shore are there still habitats and wildlife virtually the same as they were before the arrival of the first Polynesians.

Traveling the islands with mask and snorkel (scuba is a luxury), I look for some cove or rocky headland I have not yet visited, and for a short time I leave behind the hard perimeter of the land and the harsh light of the shore for a quiet and languid tour. This immersion plays in dreams, and perhaps for a lifetime it will continue to replay. Slow-motion flight over a dappled landscape is a constant feature of this dream, but I seem to replay specific scenes as well: a swarm of black triggerfish far out on the shallow eastern reef fringe of Lāna'i; a huge green sea turtle grazing algal turf in a coral grotto off Olowalu, Maui; a chaotic mix of colorful tangs, wrasses, and butterfly fishes over black shelving lava off Captain Cook's monument at Kealakekua Bay. In such places, the wildlife is rich and endemic, the setting pristine and atavistic. These are scenes the first Hawaiians saw, then and now a world apart from the land, just a plunge from island shorelines where life is overwhelmingly composed of alien species now, plant and animal weeds of the world's lowland tropics.

I often wish I could take others—those unfamiliar with undersea life—on a tour of this side of Hawai'i, where there is a compelling wildness. Such a tour could only be an orientation, an introduction. Many years, even decades of close study are needed to begin to comprehend even a small part of the complexity of undersea life. Hawai'i, however, is an ideal place for such a study to begin. Because of the proximity of the shallows to the deep sea, in some places an energetic half-hour swim out from shore can take you into waters where the bottom lies more than a mile below. The tour would start close in, just below the edge of the sea, in the region I will call the undershore. From here it would pursue the increasingly deeper realms of this side of Hawaiian nature, its structure, its riches, its boundaries, and increasingly its vulnerability to human disturbance.

The first stop of the tour would be the coral reef, arguably the lushest and liveliest terrain of the Hawaiian undershore. Precipitated from clear, warm seawater, the reef houses tremendously complex ecosystems with many hundreds of different life-forms contributing to a welter of geobiological processes. But the permanence and preeminence of coral reefs are not due to the coral alone, but to the combined life forces of those simple animals and the primitive plants called algae.

The coral itself is a thin, living tissue in two layers stretched over stony skeleton, like bed sheets stretched over a mattress. The soft tissue layers are contiguous with tiny, hollow, flower-like pouches called polyps—up to thousands of them distributed more or less evenly on the surface of a mature coral. The polyps are fringed with stinging tentacles that serve to capture and consume food in the form of minute planktonic organisms. Reef corals commonly feed at night. During the day, polyps are usually retracted and tightly puckered so that they are virtually unrecognizable. Each puckers down into a calyx—a star-shaped opening in the skeleton—whose form varies among coral species. Calices are shaped by their polyps and cover the skeletal surface of a large coral like a well-ordered galaxy.

Modern research has confirmed that the algae are at least as important in reef formation and maintenance as the corals. Two categories of algae are involved. The first are the symbiotic zooxanthellae, single-celled forms that live within the tissue-thin flesh of corals. Covered by translucent membranes at the very surface of the coral, these algae bask in a protective living greenhouse. Zooxanthellae typically give corals a brown or yellow hue and, more importantly, they absorb coral waste products permitting rapid, robust growth of the coral's skeleton, the limestone framework of the reef. Many coral species lack zooxanthellae and remain puny beside the reef builders. The reef framework—rough pavements and walls of living boulders, irregular stony plates, and antler-like growths—is mainly the result of the coral-algal partnership, which has evolved to the point where neither organism can survive naturally without the other. Biologists have begun to argue that the partnership is so tightly integrated that it represents not merely the symbiotic sum of animal and plant, but an emergent new kind of hybrid organism.

Comprising the other category of algae vital to reef formation is a collection of independent plants described as seaweeds—although many of them are passing strange for the genre. Swimming over the reef, a diver sees them as brittle stony balls and pompons, sprigs of tiny green plates articulated like cactus pads, and—least plantlike of all—brittle coatings on rock that look like painted surfaces and dribbles of putty in pink and purple hues. The common contribution of these cryptic water plants to reef building is their precipitation of limestone at a rate far faster than any coral. However, as fast as these brittle organisms grow and proliferate in the intense sunlight on the reef's surface, they die and fragment into fine sediment, unlike the framework corals, which largely remain a stony mosaic matrix in the reef. These so-called calcareous algae are the greatest sediment producers on most coral reefs, and this sediment—which also comes from a great variety of other shelled creatures, animals that swim, glide, hop, and crawl about the living rockery—often contributes more than half the bulk mass of the reef. It is filler, the sweepings and midden debris of the ecosystem, that settles into the irregular voids and cracks and crannies among the framework growths of the corals. Eventually, well below its living surface, the reef's internal mass—bouldery framework and in-filled sediment alike—cements itself into a hard limestone conglomerate.

In the presence of a great reef, one recognizes the nearest shape in which any life-form comes to immortality. Evolution seems to favor simple life-forms with tenure on our planet, but few proclaim their dominance with megalithic constructions like these. In leaving such earth-shaping works to ecological posterity, reef-building corals rank high indeed among the ruling organisms of our natural world. And unlike the statue of Ozymandias, the reef in its element confronts a traveler with a monument always bright and articulated. Self-renewing and adapting, it may persist for tens of millions of years in tropical sunlight and clear, warm environs beneath lone and level seas. Even in an afterlife of fossilization, and tectonic resurrection from the sea into continental limestone mountains, an ancient coral reef often displays, albeit with microscopic humility, the signatures of its tiny polypoid builders.

Of course, no reef in the main islands of the Hawaiian chain can claim great antiquity. You have to go far to the northwest, down the chain of former high islands now mostly submerged and shrouded with reefs, to find the truly old structures. At the end of the line are the Midway Islands and Kure Atoll, whose main reefs have been growing—with time off during occasional episodes of slowly falling sea levels, when the corals retreated to a narrow outer rim—for nearly 30 million years.

While we naturally take a monolithic perspective in considering the building of reefs and their persistence in geological time, ecotourists, hovering over a flourishing reef, would discover that the reef has two living layers. One is rugose, gritty, comprising the solid reeftop itself, virtually a still-life arrangement on the floor of the sea; the other is fluid, evanescent of shape and color as its living components twist and turn in the clear water.

The second layer belongs to the reef no less than the landscape of framework corals, algae, and sedentary animals that are fixed to the sea floor. It is a satellite layer dominated by fishes. Some remain close, seeking the bottom for food and protection, while others orbit far out into the blue abyss and return in cycles that range in duration from hours to months. The wanderers no less than the other fish may benefit the reef. For example, species that daily forage away from the reef and then return import vital nutrients. Marine biologists have shown they provide additional elements for the fertilization of algae. And those prodigals that return after spending longer periods away from their reef and growing significantly in remote oceanic provinces bring back wholesale quantities of new flesh to the food economy of the reef. This process, which coincides with the production of each new generation of a wide variety of reef fishes, has presented marine biologists with a deep mystery.

Most of the small, often colorful species known as reef fishes appear tethered by invisible bonds to the shallow sunlit landscape of the undershore. In this behavior, they resemble the birds that inhabit upper-elevation forest on a high mountain rising out of a desert. Such creatures—bird or fish—seem content with their isolation and are rarely seen crossing the great hostile distances to reach the blue-green heights of another mountain. However, many of the fishes that a snorkeler sees everywhere in coastal bays and over the reefs have led an errant childhood, roaming widely in the open sea. At birth, they are launched from the reefs by the billions in microscopic life-supporting capsules that vanish from the shallows without a trace. The embryos grow and hatch into planktonic larvae, diminutive inner-space drifters, the spawn of wrasses, parrotfishes, goatfishes, butterfly fishes, tangs, filefishes, and others. The larvae spend the early part of their lives suspended over ultimate deeps many miles from the islands. They consume an oceanic gruel and grow as they travel on unknown looping journeys before they at last return to the reefs.

Initially, at the point these fishes migrate offshore, marine biologists find it impossible to identify them in their element. Starting on their uncertain trajectory into the blue void, they appear as drifting motes—eggs and larvae, some no larger than the letters on this page—before the diver's mask. Even back in the laboratory, after fishing them out of the sea with a fine-mesh plankton net, I often have trouble telling one species of big-eyed, translucent hatchling from another. Under the microscope they resemble figurines wrought in milky glass; each species is different, but none even remotely resembles its adult form.

Weeks to months later, the next generation of these fishes appears near the surface as young-of-the-year juveniles. Many of the reef fish babies, now an inch or two long, are still hard to classify in their species. As they begin to make their way back to island shoal waters from somewhere offshore, they resemble miniature finned gargoyles and are categorized as nekton, or active swimmers, rather than passively drifting plankton. Growing as they migrate back toward the islands, many become important prey for offshore denizens, including tunas, barracudas, jacks, and a variety of Hawaiian seabirds (among them terns, noddies, boobies, and petrels). But *en masse* the small migrants are survivors. Some, such as goatfishes and filefishes, are highly conspicuous as they appear along the reefs during the summer months.

Once they arrive at the reef, however, a reckoning is at hand. Baby goatfishes called 'oama, several inches long, are avidly sought by Hawaiian fishermen and other predators on the reef itself. Though this rapidly reduces the goatfish populations, enough survive to sustain the species on the reef. Filefishes, however, sometimes suffer a fate that is less satisfying by conventional (or at least popular) ecological aesthetics. Millions of the little orange-tailed juveniles apparently overgraze their food supply (various algae on the reef), then starve and wash in to die on island beaches. The ocean proposes and the reef disposes mainly to the benefit of shoreside bacteria, the ultimate scavengers. Nature guarantees nothing, even to creatures that defy all odds to reach a world of seeming security, and nature in this case delivers everything to those that dumbly wait under the sandy shore.

Biological oceanographers are unsure how the reef fish babies manage to return at all. A wide, steady current moves past and threads among the Hawaiian Islands, flowing from east to west into the empty central Pacific. Large eddies that form near the islands—both horizontal and vertical looping currents—have been invoked to explain the return of each new generation of Hawaiian reef fishes weeks to months after the larvae disappear from the shallow undershore spawning grounds. By whatever means they use to reach the offshore pelagic realm, they must be shuffled considerably among the islands before returning to grow into adulthood on the reefs. The exact mechanism that conserves them around the archipelago at large remains a mystery, but it seems likely to represent a fine example of ecological circuitry, composed of linkages that couple the fates of reef dwellers with those of fishes and birds of the blue epipelagic, out to where a high island is only an uncertain smudge on the horizon.

Our acquaintance with the sea is so limited by vast opacity that modern exploration of the earth may soon lag behind what we accomplish on other planets such as Mars. Even in such accessible habitats as the coral reef we are often limited in our observations and understanding of the ecosystem. For example, because our images of the reef and our explorations of its intricacies are primarily influenced by daylight vision, we miss a great deal of the life and dynamism of the underwater community. Equipped with underwater lights, we should visit a reef at night and gain a first impression of its strange ambience.

I once dove with scuba off the southeastern coast of Oʻahu to observe the crepuscular transition. This is the marine ecologist's phrase to denote the shift between night and day (or vice versa). The water was shallow, no more than twenty-five feet deep, so that my partner and I were able to stay below for nearly an hour and a half.

We began just before dawn with bright stars but no moon. The darkness within the sea was as I had seen it on previous night dives. My existence and progress were focused within the narrow yellow beam from my underwater light. We swam over a ledge and down a gently sloping bottom of smooth limestone swept bare by the surge from occasional large surface waves. Stopping on a smooth sandy plain, we momentarily switched off our lights. In the dark water in front of my mask, tiny flashes and trails of light appeared and multiplied by tens to hundreds at a wave of a hand. Disturbed by the clumsy play of giants, bioluminescent plankton, elementary particles of life, were streaking and spiraling through turbulence in the dark watery cosmos. Do these tiny fireworks signify irritation? Alarm? Exhilaration? And to what end? Looking up, with our eyes beginning to adapt to the darkness, we could see, very faintly, a darkly textured ceiling scattered with scintillations in patterns wider than those produced by the plankton—refractions of starlight from the clear Hawaiian night above.

Trapped in narrow laws of physics, the real starbursts seemed less intriguing than those that came from living cells.

Swimming toward a coral-covered platform, we now perceived a huge difference between night and day on the reef. The living layers of the reef had undergone a dramatic shift. The fishy layer, extremely active and diverse by day, had all but disappeared, while the solid, gritty surface had come to life. Coral is especially transformed at night, when its animal nature asserts itself. Tentacles extend radially from every polyp and converge to form a stinging geodesic—a deceptively lacy trap for tiny prey—that virtually covers the coral surface.

The business of our dive was to observe and collect cones, predatory snails that are primarily active at night, and we succeeded in finding several live specimens, primarily the large fish-eating species, *Conus striatus*. At night, it sniffs out its quarry—a small fish resting on the bottom—with its periscope-like siphon that rises into the clear water. It then harpoons its victim with specialized, venom-containing darts that have evolved from small scraping teeth common to many kinds of snail. Because of its large size and predatory focus on a fellow vertebrate, the striated cone, among a few others, has a sting that can be dangerous to humans. Although cones are slow to react, we watched our fingers as we handled them; they were very shy and retreated inside their shells. The powerful effects of cones' venom on cells and tissues of vertebrate animals has attracted the interest of the pharmaceutical industry, which refines and tests such natural materials for potential use in treating neurological and cardiac disorders.

Both of us were alert to other denizens of the night reef rarely exposed by day. A motionless five-foot moray eel faced us down in a narrow alley; its aggressively toothy breathing motions suggested, "Do not even think of trying to swim past here!" A large octopus flowed over a coral-studded pavement, centered in my strong beam like an entertainer illuminated by a spotlight on a darkened stage. Cowries, hidden in crevices and caves during the day, were out in numbers, grazing on algal turf. In a nearby sand channel, hugging the edge of the rocks, a pair of huge-eyed squirrelfish swam slowly, apparently mesmerized in the bright light of my beam.

Some animals don't seem to care whether it is light or dark. I discovered a crimson-and-cream, six-inch-long Spanish dancer, a large nudibranch, completing the final whorl of a spiraling pink deposit containing thousands of its tiny eggs. This creation resembled a fancy chiffon dessert, but edible it apparently is not. The dancer and its eggs remain exposed both day and night, yet never seem to be threatened by predators. Bright colors and bold patterns of many such animals seem to warn of distastefulness and/or toxicity. This kind of animal with chemical defenses is another creature of potential use in the search for medicinal drugs from the sea.

Overall, there were far fewer animals out in the open than I remembered from dives during the daytime in this area. I began to find some of the missing daytime species deep in recesses and caves. In one cramped crevice, a school of large blue-tailed tangs swam nervously in tight circles, obviously disturbed by the bright light of my lamp and the pressure waves from my clumsy, sweeping, stabilizing movements in the surge.

These fish and hundreds of others, nearby but unseen, were waiting for the dawn, which was not long in coming. I recall looking upward to the surface little more than twenty feet above and seeing the first light of day as a swash of textured pewter, faint and absorbing its own reflection. As yet no illumination reached me and my surroundings. Night lingered even at my shallow depth. But now I swam with anticipation and looked intently on all sides for day to come to the reef. It was a slow and subtle dawn; the light sifted and washed feebly into the undershore as if impeded by the density of the medium. My first views, unaided by the

diving light, were reminiscent of a strange cityscape on an over-
cast and snowy morning, where edges of streets and buildings are
soft and indistinct, without color. The sand channels, projecting
rock shelves, pinnacles, and rugged pavements of the reefscape all
possessed an alien, dreamlike lack of geological definition. Even
solid bottom seemed fluid in those few minutes.

Color came as blue or, more precisely, *blueness*, slowly
emerging from all around, out of the erstwhile gray hues of water
and rock, and was absorbed more and more until the water almost
glowed with blueness. And then, in minutes, came the daytime
fishes. From the refuges of the night, the caves, and the sand itself
(where some species of wrasses and others hide) fishes seemed to
materialize in the water. Their colors and those of the corals and
algae—reds, oranges, yellows, greens, and many blends—quickly
emerged as the water continued to emit the ethereal blue of the
watery dawn. It is a color that does not last, as I have often veri-
fied. Now, my partner and I, godlike in this realm for the previous ninety minutes, found our powers ebbing. The air almost
exhausted in our tanks, we rose above the bustling city in the sea,
with its sandy thoroughfares and alleys, grottos, and rough
pavements, filled with active life, browsing, migrating, schooling
on a new and timeless day.

As colorful and diverse as the coral regions are, the environs
where coral reefs have not become established are equally
dramatic. Although wide and extensive reefs occur along some
coasts of all the main islands of Hawai'i, they are interrupted wherever rocky points and ridges thrust into the sea. In fact, the control of reef formation by island topography is striking. If they are
present at all, reefs are barely developed off coastlines that rise
steeply from the sea. Thus, for example, Maui's reefs are notably
limited, and the youngest island, Hawai'i itself, is largely bereft of
coral reefs, except off the gently sloping North Kona coast.

Steep and rainy shores, for example, present a combination

of factors that prevent corals from establishing a contiguous framework. In such places as along the Hāmākua coast, north of Hilo
on the Big Island, muddy torrents frequently pour into the sea.
There, as in other places, both fresh water and smothering silt kill
developing coral. In other locations, fresh water is carried under
pressure in subterranean aquifers, and these may open on the sea
floor, even off normally dry coasts. Near Diamond Head on O'ahu,
at forty feet I once swam through a large volume of fresh water
seeping out of the rocky bottom. The seep filled an irregular, room-
sized space with a cold transparency. Inside were only gray rocks
devoid of obvious life; along blurry borders formed by the
mixing of fresh water with salt, fish played skittishly. In some
locations, springs opening under the sea are large enough to create
surface boils of fresh water. Early Western explorers reported that
Hawaiians traveling waterless coasts dove to these sources to
obtain drinking water. They wrestled an empty calabash below
the surface, keeping a thumb over the opening until they reached
the freshwater plume.

Where steep terrain prevails along the coast, rock debris
accumulates in the undershore, and storm waves create a chaotic,
bowling-alley milieu on the bottom—an impossible environment
for reef development. In zones of active vertical faulting, especially prevalent on the Big Island, coral reefs may be carried by
seismic quakes down to killing depths (zooxanthellae are rapidly
enfeebled by fading sunlight only a few dozen yards down). This
may be what happened to extensive coral reefs that grew perhaps
10,000 years ago along the Big Island's northeast coast. There,
dead reefs, their surface-loving species of corals turned to bleached
headstones in a natural graveyard, now lie roughly 3,000 to 5,000
feet deep on the Kohala Submarine Terrace.

There are places along the coasts of Hawai'i beyond the
undershore where scuba-equipped explorers can briefly glimpse
regions of great depth, the twilight Hawaiian deeps. One such

vantage is off the South Kona coast of the Big Island. There are plenty of scattered coral colonies, or heads, growing on bare lava here, but there is no reef. Right from shore, you descend along the island slope itself. Over a bottom of shelving lava and sand rivers, fishes of every color crowd water that seems clear as air. Most of the obvious life is concentrated in a layer about seventy-five feet deep. At 110 feet, a fantastic school of red-orange 'ū'ū, a species of squirrelfish, mills chaotically beneath a rock shelf. Their vivid color exists only in the beam of a diving light (it also emerges if these fish are brought to the surface). Seen naturally, everything on the bottom here looks bluish gray, owing to absorption by water of all the more colorful wavelengths of the spectrum. Passing 160 feet, there are a few smallish snappers in the middle distance; a species of whip coral resembling five-foot lengths of haphazardly bent wire sprouts from the rocky ground. At 200 feet, even with your companions you feel alone in an empty wilderness, like climbers above timberline, and you have two minutes before you must ascend to avoid running low on air and risking the bends. Here, the water seems to press heavily, yet is so clear that your boat is visible, remote and toylike at the surface near a large circular patch of light from the noonday sun. This light breaks and melds constantly, its fierce tropical energy teased apart and diffused in the sea.

Two hundred feet below the Kona shore, you feel as if you are approaching the edge of creation. In the cool gelid hydrosphere, nothing seems to move; bare rock and barren rubble are evident all around; life has become, if not scarce, far less conspicuous than in the teeming shallows. Indeed, this last diver's outpost overlooks the boundary of the Hawaiian submarine world. The terrain drops away into the thickening twilight, followed by the cold, heavy night of a generic Pacific that one imagines reaching to the antipodes. Yet, nearby, a uniquely Hawaiian creation continues—the old gods of the islands are still active. To the south and east, over the submerged shoulder of the Big Island, some thirty miles offshore, down in the cold and the dark, the Hawaiian gods are rapidly raising a new island.

This is the work of primary gods, unknown even to Polynesians. For eons, in silence, they have raised islands-to-be from the deep sea floor hereabouts—upward toward the boisterous demigod Maui with his mighty hook and the flamboyant goddess Pele with her hot coloring. In our time, the silent gods have raised the seamount called Lōʻihi within three thousand feet of the surface. Maui will set his hook when the seamount grows to just a few hundred feet below the surface. There, the diminishing water pressure begins to permit superheated water to flash into steam, and with each eruption the young volcano will approach the surface more and more explosively. Always intolerant of the sea, Pele will finally dominate, when an island breaks above the surface. Geologists estimate that she may begin to rule Lōʻihi in as little as twenty thousand years.

Eventually, even Pele's powers ebb. Over time, Lōʻihi's quenched lava will develop virgin reefs and teeming undershore communities. The gods have a long view of time and of the effort they lavish on the shaping of Hawaiian ecology. It is therefore startling to reflect how, in a tiny fraction of the time it takes these gods to raise a new island—let alone in the time it takes for a coral reef to grow on its flanks—all the gentler places of an island may fall under human domination; and when this occurs, destruction vastly outpaces creation.

In the shallow undershore of Hawaiʻi, marine resources have been exploited for centuries. Polynesian colonists from the South Pacific, the original Hawaiians, arrived in the islands sometime between 200 and 500 A.D. Archaeological evidence indicates they fished and gleaned much of their dietary protein from the reefs and coastal waters. They also seem to have deforested steep hillsides along the coast, triggering massive erosion that filled shallow marine bays and may have smothered some reefs under a blanket of silt.

Indirect evidence leads to the suspicion that some species may have become scarce during the aboriginal Hawaiian period before the arrival of Captain Cook. Such evidence includes a system of traditional Hawaiian fish and game laws that came under the general heading of chiefly or royal kapu (or *taboo* in the vernacular of early Pacific seafarers). The term meant "forbidden" and could be used to reserve anything a chief wanted for himself. This was probably the case for the kapu placed on sea turtles and certain other delicacies; but the kapu system may also have been applied in cases involving the perceived good of society. In this context, a kapu that was widespread and that regulated fishing for certain species in their breeding seasons could have functioned as a conservation law.

The kapu system in part suggests that the Hawaiians were responding to the threat of depletion. By the time of Western contact with Hawai'i, very large population centers had formed, and overfishing in regions such as Honolulu, Lahaina, and Kailua-Kona could have been severe.

Overfishing on the reefs, together with siltation and pollution from domestic and agricultural wastes, have all greatly accelerated, and are now immensely greater than any such effects engendered by the organic subsistence culture of the old Hawaiians. Still, for all the decades of destruction, the environmental history of Hawaii's undershore is as yet in a formative period. So far, few if any marine species have become extinct in the time that humans have inhabited the islands. But some, such as the monk seal, are endangered and others are close to that status. In terms of environmental degradation, the reefs are perhaps a century behind the Hawaiian mountain forests and several centuries behind the old coastal forests.

At present, distressing trends are increasingly affecting the

Hawaiian undershore, especially around Oʻahu, where the reefs have suffered major damage. Owing to the intensity of modern environmental disturbance, the reefs may finally be destroyed at a much faster rate than the native Hawaiian forests.

At the end of our imaginary tour, back in the coastal shallows, our senses might well be sharpened enough by our passage in the pure sea below the Kona undershore to begin to recognize the onset of this despoliation. Most underwater environmental changes are undramatic. Roaring fires do not consume ecosystems here; grinding bulldozers and shrieking chainsaws never threaten the coral reefs directly. But the reefs begin to die nonetheless after those machines and others have created massive changes on nearby coastlines.

Uncontrolled siltation of coastal waters, runoff of toxic chemicals from parking lots and golf courses, and even the increased presence of divers—all now threaten Hawaiian reefs and undershore environments in formerly remote and pristine places. The 1980s and 1990s have witnessed an unprecedented growth of new coastal resort construction, most of it on the dry leeward shores of the islands, which in turn creates ease of access to these environments. Reefs that were once largely inaccessible are now being mobbed by snorkelers, spearfishers, and shell collectors. Except for a handful of little-enforced laws on sport fishing, the undershore ecosystem is unprotected, and becomes a new kind of tragic commons. Imagine for a moment a city park with attractive flower beds in which large numbers of visitors not only pick all the flowers they like, but remove whole plants and rocks, cut down trees and shrubs, and shoot the birds and squirrels.

The most destructive kind of fishing in Hawaiʻi is done with monofilament gill nets. Once employed by relatively few commercial fishermen, these "walls of death" have proliferated tremendously with little regulation. They are often linked end-to-end to reach a mile or more, becoming deadly fences that kill fishes indiscriminately all across a reef or coastal bay. Sometimes, as in the case of deep-ocean fisheries, they are lost, and the subsequent, wholly wasteful "ghost fishing" continues indefinitely, for the synthetic meshes do not decompose. Many fishery conservationists now blame the use of these nets for much of the demonstrable decline in Hawaiian reef fishes, especially on O'ahu.

Despite signs of decline in fish populations and whiffs of biocides and petroleum products as we come ashore after our lengthy sea trek through Hawaii's hidden wilds, there is the realization that we have visited one of the few remaining regions of the islands that can remain in a largely unspoiled state of nature. Here, we still do have the chance to coexist successfully with part of our native planet. It is not yet too late. We can control overfishing; we can minimize the impact of coastal development. Much of the rest of Hawaiian nature has been destroyed or is badly degraded. Here, among the lovely reeflands, the blue vistas, and the deep twilight slopes, our last chance may exist to save a large part of Hawaii's natural heritage for future generations. The true Hawaiian places and things that still remain are, sadly, mere vestiges, while artificial amusements and plastic satisfactions abound. Consequently, the native places, on land as well as in the sea, appreciate in value just by remaining the way they are. These islands, which display so much of our planet's dynamism and hospitality to life, have come to represent common ground and environmental hope worldwide. How well we protect the remaining natural essences of Hawai'i, and learn to live here within our ecological means, will foreshadow our success in preserving the vital systems of our ultimate island, the Earth.

CAPTAIN COOK'S PORPOISES

KENNETH S. NORRIS

"SPIN, spin, spin, head over tail, nose out, spin," Tom chanted faster than I could write. To take notes, I made up a kind of instant shorthand on the spot. Tom Dohl, my colleague on this project, was watching a school of Hawaiian spinner porpoises that played forty yards off the bow of the SSSM [a small, mobile observation chamber, nicknamed the "Semisubmersible Seasick Machine"], close to the cliffs of Kealakekua Bay, Hawai'i. His ever-present pipe in hand and his angular body folded up on the little seat over the conning tower, Tom called out the different kinds of aerial behavior to me below deck, where I sat taking notes and watching them below water.

The porpoises, all thirty of them, had just shaken off a sort of midday doldrums. Minutes before they had been spending nearly all of their time under water, surfacing quietly for three or four quick breaths before diving for up to four minutes. Their school had been a tightly packed mobile amoeba of porpoises, with some animals so close they seemed actually to be touching. They had been in this formation for four hours and not a porpoise had jumped. Now, suddenly, they rocketed out of the calm sea in their peculiar spins, one after another. Often two or three were in the air at once.

"Sleeping time is all over, Tom," I said. During weeks of watching we had begun to feel that this midday quiescence was what passed for sleep. After that rest period came what we called "zigzag swimming." Once the porpoises began to leap, the entire school raced back and forth, sometimes in and out from the cliff, and sometimes taking long traverses back and forth parallel to the coast. Always it was a strenuous affair with much leaping and usually any time one looked, one or two animals were slapping the water with repeated blows of their flukes—"tail slapping," we called it.

Sometimes the whole school seemed to decide upon a course and moved rapidly from the bay and out to sea. I once watched such a movement from our cliff-top camp. There, at the brink of the five-hundred-foot lava escarpment overlooking the mile-wide, almost semicircular bay, I watched the school leave, passing the little fishing villages of Nāpoʻopoʻo and Keʻei, past Palemanō Point at the southern tip of the bay, and swimming straight out to sea. The day was calm, as it usually is on the Kona coast of Hawaiʻi. As far as we could see them with binoculars, the school plunged along. Animals out on the flanks spun and fell back amid spreading masses of foam that marked their path with white splotches on the flat sea. At last sighting they were about two miles beyond Palemanō, or four miles from our perch, leaving tiny blips of white against the steel-gray water. Then they were lost amid the wandering breeze trails and slicks.

More often the porpoise school turned south around Palemanō Point, hugging the rugged lava-bluff coast. The school then moved in procession, many animals so close to the bluffs that the rising swell lifted them high as the water surged up against the jagged black rocks. Somewhere near the fabled ancient Hawaiian

City of Refuge the porpoises turned and retraced their path, only this time crossing Kealakekua Bay at its mouth and going north-ward. We came to believe this maneuver allowed the school to gather in little subschools that had been resting at various points along the coast, for the school obviously grew in numbers until, at dusk, it numbered about a hundred animals and spread over half a mile of water.

These Kealakekua porpoises represented one of those rare opportunities a naturalist occasionally encounters. Sometimes a rare or difficult-to-observe species presents, at some special place or time, an unparalleled chance to look into its life patterns. The trouble with watching porpoises is that they are shy and fast-mov-ing. One may spend the greater part of his time simply trying to find his animals, as we had done off O'ahu. These Kealakekua Bay porpoises came in virtually every day to rest, and equally im-portant, they did so in a limpid bay that is usually flat calm. We could watch to our heart's content without getting seasick.

The local fishermen knew about the porpoises, but they didn't harass them, so the animals were not frightened of people or boats. Here, it seemed, was a chance to look at the ways of life into which the mysterious intelligence of the porpoise presumably fits. Here, if we looked hard enough, lay the uses of the remarkable sound systems of Kathy or Alice or the learning capability of Pono or Keiki. Here the affection and trust of Pono had its place. A school like this *was* the world of a porpoise, if we could only have the wit to understand it.

My frustrations with the O'ahu school made me decide to check on repeated stories about the porpoises of Kealakekua Bay, which were said to be tame and to live all year in the bay. One young man even told me he had fed these porpoises by hand while swimming in the water with them. Another told of the porpoises lining up around him as he treaded water, so close he could touch them. Later I came to doubt these stories, but at the time they were intriguing.

So Tom packed the SSSM aboard an interisland barge, while I scheduled the *Westward,* the Oceanic Institute's ninety-foot brigantine. At the little port of Kawaihae the SSSM was reassembled and slipped into the water. The *Westward* took her in tow for Kealakekua, sixty miles distant.

At first it was choppy and progress was slow. Once we had passed the great, spreading lava fan of Keāhole Point, the water turned calm and the great volcanoes of Hawai'i rose along the shore. A few miles farther, where the vast, coalescing lava slopes of Mauna Loa and Hualālai volcanoes had long ago flowed together, was the mile-wide indentation of Kealakekua Bay. It is a snug, crescent-shaped jewel of sparkling blue water, of bright reef fish, and of history. For centuries a procession of thousands of lava flows had poured down the slopes of the two great mountains. Their crests were now, as almost always, shrouded in clouds. The flows met at this point to form a precipitous five-hundred-foot, layered black cliff that drops abruptly into the sea at the back of the bay. Two smaller flows, just above sea level, spread out from either end of the cliff to define the cusps of the cove.

The dark cliff is pierced by dozens of lava tubes, each of which once sluiced lava into the sea in a fury of steam, smoke, and light. They have long been cool. Aboriginal Hawaiians used their cool interiors to bury their dead. Even today, we are told, some Hawaiians scale this cliff at night and go through the old ceremony of reburial of the carefully cleaned bones. At any rate, deep in the dusty cave recesses, sometimes hundreds of feet above the water, the sacred bones of the dead still lie wrapped in ancient tapa, the pounded bark of the paper mulberry tree, bound in palm fiber or sennit. Mummies of babies, we are told, are held in tiny wooden cradles whose pieces are also lashed together with sennit. The modern Hawaiians are quick to tell you of the spirits that abound in the place, guarding the bones of the ancients. Disturbance of the bones, they say, means the marching of the dead. Legions of giant Hawaiian ghosts will then be heard in the night, pounding their drums. Especially sacred are the bones of Kamehameha I, the first conqueror of the Hawaiian Islands, which are said to lie buried somewhere near here in a cave whose entrance was once marked by a single sandalwocd tree.

A temple to Lono—a heiau, or stone platform, built by hand of large lava blocks with almost unbelievable expenditures of energy—rises above the beach next to Nāpōʻopoʻo. Its priests were repositories of the secrets of the god Lono. They said Lono would one day return to the Islands borne on white wings. In 1787 Captain James Cook came here and, because of the white sails of his ship *Resolution*, he was understandably thought to be Lono. When a Hawaiian was killed by others in the Cook party, they turned on the Captain, spearing him and dashing his brains out in the shallows of Kaʻawaloa, the village that once occupied the north limb of the bay.

From the deck of the *Westward* we could look up the hill above our anchorage and see the small stone temple where Cook was ritually dismembered, cooked, and, in part, eaten. With Cook were two other famous figures in Pacific exploration: William Bligh, whose exploits would lead to mutiny on his ship, *Bounty*, and the incredible saga of his seamanship in successfully crossing half the Pacific in a longboat; and George Vancouver, who would later explore much of the Pacific coast of North America. All these events, these historical figures, and the natural beauty and calm combine to make a visit to the bay a powerful experience for most people. I felt its aura each time we dropped anchor off the beach of Kaʻawaloa.

Our first porpoises were gamboling along the shore about two miles north of the bay. They flirted briefly with our bow and left us. So we continued into the deep arc of Kealakekua, dropped anchor, and began to ready the SSSM. As Tom and I watched from her meager deck, the porpoises rounded Cook Point and came toward us. They began the patterns we would only begin to understand months later.

These patterns and the Kona porpoise schools are probably historically very old, certainly antedating the advent of white men. The burials, the coming of Cook, and perhaps even the fiery formation of the bay itself must have occurred with a complement of porpoises in attendance. Some hint of this antiquity can be gained back down the coast, near Keāhole Point, where there lives another spinner school. The ancient Hawaiian name for the ground to which they come to sleep is nai'a ke'e, or "the place [nook] to which porpoises are drawn." The nai'a ke'e is formed in old lavas that flowed into place several hundred years ago, but I suspect the porpoises come not because it is old but because, as we shall see, its coves have the proper shape. Mark Twain, when he passed through Hawai'i a little more than a hundred years ago, noted of our Kealakekua school:

> We dashed boldly into the midst of a school of huge, beastly porpoises engaged at their eternal game of arching over a wave and disappearing, and then doing it over again and keeping it up—always circling over, in that way, like so many well-submerged wheels.

Every fisherman now living on the coast has seen them as long as he can remember.

Tom and I, not thinking about history, were merely elated to find porpoises so easily. We watched quietly as the porpoises swam into the shadow of the cliff, a dozen yards from its base. A fortuitous gift, for one day we would look down at the porpoises from a vantage point five hundred feet above, on the cliff rim.

Even though our attention was riveted on the porpoises, I had time to muse with pleasure about the calm ride I was getting in the SSSM. The ungainly craft slipped through the still cove with scarcely any of its usual movement. This is more like it, I thought. I knew I could watch for hours in this place with no discomfort.

The triangular fins of the school lazily cut the water close under the cliff, less than two hundred yards away. The animals came willingly to our bow and cut back and forth ahead of us, showing no signs of the skittishness that had become the hallmark of the Oʻahu animals. From my seat in the observation chamber I looked out on a mother and baby. The three-and-a-half-foot-long young had a broken upper beak, bent to the side three or four inches back from the tip. We named him Little Cross Beak and were later to see him many times ahead of the SSSM windows, always swimming close to the flanks of a big female, who was probably his mother.

Little Cross Beak became a personality to us, showing us some of the subtle details of life between mother and child in the porpoise world. We saw her discipline him with a petulant slap of her flukes, and we saw him slip back along her side, his little flipper touching her undulating tail stock, and come to rest with his tiny flukes on top of hers, passively following the beat as she propelled them both along. In spite of his grievous injury, he was sleek and full-bodied. We wondered how he managed to nurse, but never saw him try. And we wondered what would happen to him when the time came to be weaned. By that time, a month or more away, he might have learned to catch fish and squid with his partial beak and thus to make his way.

The outcome, however, is clouded. Three months after we first sighted him, Little Cross Beak disappeared, and we never saw him again. He could have perished, as we might expect him to, considering his injury. But he may simply have joined one of the juvenile groups we could recognize from the surface. Their little rounded fins revealed their age and we saw them often. But always they were shy and refused to come in to play at the SSSM. So there remains the hope that we may see him again when he emerges into adulthood.

Little Cross Beak was not the only injured animal in the school. In fact, so many animals bore the scars of past injury that Tom and I were able to compile a dictionary of scars and marks that came to include more than fifty animals. Many bore distinctive circular scars, like those that caused us to call *Steno* [*Stenella longirostris*, Hawaiian spinner dolphins] the "polka-dot porpoise" and that are now suspected to be the work of an insidious little fish we have called the "cookie-cutter shark" (*Isistius brasiliensis*). Everet C. Jones of the National Marine Fisheries Service discovered that this strange eighteen-inch shark is remarkably adapted to bite into the bodies of fish and porpoises, having a symmetrical circular row of sawlike teeth on its lower jaw. Then, using suction, it literally forces these teeth into its prey, scooping out a one- to two-inch disk of flesh or blubber before it can be shaken off. Most Hawaiian porpoises and whales are dotted with scars from this source, especially those that live far offshore and those that feed deep below the surface. Jones feels that it may mimic squid, allowing it to get close enough for a dash to the unwary animal's side, a quick attachment, and then flight with its disk of flesh.

Other sharks, larger and more dangerous, obviously take their toll of porpoises in Hawaiian waters. Some recorded scars are ugly lunate rows of tooth marks, so broad the porpoise's whole tail must have been grasped by a giant shark before it somehow shook loose. Fins and flukes, too, are rather often tattered in ways that suggest shark attack. The communal alertness of the porpoise school, we realized, is an essential component of survival in these shark-filled waters, and even that sometimes is not enough.

After seeing the porpoises swim so close to the cliff base, we knew we needed a cliff-top camp. Somewhere along the imposing rim there should be a vantage point where one could observe and photograph, wholly without disturbing the porpoises. So one sunny morning Dave Bryant, Tom's quiet young assistant, and I started up the back slope of the cliff. It proved a long, hot climb through shoulder-high tussock grass growing from a hidden mass of jumbled boulders. The pitch increased until Dave and I were on hands and knees swinging from clump to clump. Then, finally, we reached the crest, and a lovely, savanna-like parkland opened before us. Undulating grassy slopes studded with spreading monkeypod and 'inia trees provided cool shade for sleepy cattle. Our passage jarred their slumbers, but soon we left them and plunged into a dense koa haole thicket that skirts the cliff edge, making our way by parting the bushes at each step. Finally, the brush thinned at a little promontory on the cliff edge.

A ledge of huge lava blocks hung over the sheer drop. Dave scaled a stone out arcing into the air, and we listened until it whumped into the water below. The whole character of the bay was different when one looked down upon it, rather than across its surface. Close against the cliff shore castellated domes of submerged coral showed clearly, flickering beneath the water: green, yellow, and white, each with its halo of fishes. Dozens of black triggerfish that the Hawaiians call humuhumu 'ele'ele cruised just beneath the surface, while deeper yellow flashes came from butterfly fishes and tangs. Beyond the shallows the coral became a tracery between the light blue of coral-sand "meadows," and then beyond all deepened to indigo where deep water lay.

Later, with the gracious help of the local ranger, Sherwood Greenwell, camp was made nearby. We pitched a tent, suspended shade awnings, built ourselves a big stone fireplace for an evening campfire, and began regular observations. With this work and the SSSM observations we could piece together a daily routine for the porpoises. We knew now that they enter certain bays around all of the Hawaiian Islands in the morning. They come in from the sea in a broad rank, many leaping and spinning. At this time they are sociable and, in fact, are usually divided into small social groups that will ride the bow of the SSSM and will sometimes peer in through the capsule windows to make their own observations of the strange air-encased creature inside. Their stomachs are full, and soon the water is filled with contrails of fecal material as the night's catch of lantern fishes, squids, and shrimps is metered through the digestive tract from storage stomachs, where it had been packed during the night. Gradually the school slows and the spins become less ebullient. In an hour or so no leaping animal can be seen. A desultory slap of the tail or the head is all we see. Then that too is gone. The porpoises quietly rise to the surface and dive as one. They begin to surface and for so brief a time that it is easy to miss them, even though they swim in calm water directly below us.

A curious thing happened during this subsidence into porpoise rest, or "sleep." They ceased to act like porpoises and began to act like herrings. When the animals entered the bay, they swam in little subgroups, roughly abreast of one another. Each of these subschools dove and swam as if partly independent of the school as a whole. One subgroup or another was usually at the surface. This is what the observer normally expects to see in porpoise schools. But by the time the porpoises slowed into the resting pattern, they came to dive in unison, and subgroups were no longer evident. The school became a tight disk of animals, quite as structureless as a herring school and without any apparent leaders.

This became obvious when Tom brought the SSSM near one such school as it swam quietly close to the cliff base. Even though we bobbed silently in the water with our engine shut down, the porpoises were fully aware of our presence. They always are, by the way, no matter how stealthy one tries to be, even from hundreds of yards away. The school surfaced, and we could see that the disk of animals was dented inward on the side nearest us, as if our presence had forced animals away from us from a distance of thirty yards. The school moved down the sixty-yard corridor between our vessel and the cliff. It stretched out into a dumbbell shape, bulging out on either side of us, as if the cliff and our little craft had combined to squeeze the school almost to the breaking point.

Beyond us a passing motorboat caused the school to reverse its direction abruptly, so that followers instantly became leaders. I feel that this kind of behavior represents what I call "sensory integration"—that is, in the absence of a leader, each school member receives sensory information about the surrounding world and reacts to a greater or lesser degree depending upon how close he is to the source of disturbance. Then, because schoolmates also react to each other, the school as a whole moves in a useful way. Probably such an arrangement requires less individual alertness than for a single porpoise to make decisions independent of the whole school. Thus, I suspect that when the porpoise school subsides into rest, a measure of relief comes to each animal—they needn't be alert in the same way as in a socially structured school. It's not your sleep pattern, or mine, but perhaps it's the best a porpoise can afford in the hostile world of the sea. It's probably why they enter calm coves, such as Kealakekua Bay, where some of the awesome predators of the deep sea are absent, or at least scarce, and where the protective sea bottom is close at hand.

Then, as I described earlier, after three to five hours of rest all the porpoises abruptly become alert again, begin aerial behavior, resume their socially structured school, and begin zigzag swimming. Toward dusk the porpoises begin to edge out to sea, sometimes directly, and sometimes angling slowly away from the coast. As they do so, their school spreads and a new diversity of social activity begins to appear.

At twilight from the bow of a ship traveling with such a school, it is possible to see all kinds of social encounters, whose meanings are mostly hidden from us. Porpoises swim upside down, slapping their flukes on the water surface while emitting streams of sound so loud an observer above water can hear them as high-pitched air-borne squeaks. One baby seems to be practicing his spinning technique as he vaults from the water repeatedly, com- ing closer to the ship with each leap. Finally, when he is all but in the bow wave, he "looks up" to find the boat bearing down on him and quickly veers off. Chases and matings are common.

As night comes, the school has spread across a great swath of sea. Its parts can be located only when animals leap or when a few black fins can be seen out on the graying sea. Even though the animals are spread over a mile or more, all know precisely the position of all parts of their school, for often the school chang- es direction, and the new course will be quickly taken by all the far-flung groups of porpoises. Our ship turns belatedly, like a member of a platoon who didn't hear the command "To the rear, march!" Soon, as darkness closes over us, the only hint of the school comes when a few animals race into the ship's bow for a brief ride.

By this time the ship is usually two to four miles at sea, over water varying from a hundred to a thousand fathoms or more in depth. A look at the chart will show that whatever the depth, the animals have taken up station over an underwater cliff or slope; a vast dropoff in which the submerged base of the island descends into the true abyss. It is here, we and other cetologists such as Bill Evans think, that deep-sea fishes, shrimps, and squids which form the porpoises' diet rise in greatest abundance toward the surface. Together these deep-sea creatures form what is called the "deep scattering layer," so called because in certain parts of the world the sheer mass of this rising cloud of animals is so dense that fathometer sounds beamed downward against them return echoes that have led mariners to talk of a "false bottom." Each night this deep scattering layer (or DSL) rises from dark waters over most of the oceanic world away from the poles. Its organisms feed on the abundant planktonic food of the surface at night and descend again before daybreak.

By the time darkness comes, our porpoises are swimming

over this layer with their food rising toward them. They don't wait, though, but begin to dive far down to meet it. Other scientists have made echo traces that show porpoises descending to such a DSL, and one can clearly see the animals on these records in the midst of the rising mass of scattering layer organisms, as deep as seven hundred feet below the surface.

Subtropical waters such as those of Hawai'i are not noted for having dense scattering layers, so we decided to see for ourselves how difficult it would be for a porpoise to find enough food. At dusk the *Westward*'s lines were cast loose and she took us a few miles offshore. A big light and reflector were rigged over the water from a spar. Soon fish began to dart in and out of the halo of light. At first surface creatures like flying fish came in, their long wings folded against their sides for speed; small barracudas and needlefish skittered in tight against the surface. Later came the first lantern fish from the depths. These strange light-bearing creatures darted in rapid, erratic paths beneath the light. A swift swoop of a dip net and the three-inch fish lay flopping in the meshes. In the dark, away from the boom light, one could see rows of gleaming bright-blue jeweled buttons running down its belly and scattered over its head. Each tiny light was directed downward as if to signal those beneath. It seemed able to turn the light on and off at will—cold, strange, beautiful light from another world, and a sight to stir the wonder of the naturalist.

We know that squids formed an important part of the diet of our porpoises, yet at first we saw none under the light. Then we noticed, out at the light perimeter where the disk of light faded into darkness, forty shining amber eyes staring at us—squids at the ocean surface and too timid to enter that glaring disk. Later some came in—darting, milky arrows. A few were caught in spite of their speed, perhaps because the light blinded them to the danger from above. Some of these creatures, too, had bioluminescent lights. As they lay before us with pulsing mantles, spots of light glowed, showing that they too were dwellers of the depths and not surface squid. Some scientists have even dipped up the cookie-cutter shark in these same waters.

At any rate, even though the DSL is a faint trace or none at all on fathometers in Hawaiian waters, we knew it was there, part of the vast worldwide movement taking place every evening and morning around the globe. And from the variety and numbers of organisms we have been able to catch, we surmised that a much more adept porpoise would have little trouble making a living.

Perhaps the most perplexing feature of our porpoise school is its habit of spinning. No one really understands its meaning. Porpoises of the group to which ours belong occur around the world in tropical and subtropical seas, and wherever they occur, they seem to spin like dervishes. So there is almost certainly a genetic aspect to the behavior, a racial memory of the patterns involved.

Actually the Hawaiian porpoises do much more than spin. Tom and I have catalogued eight different kinds of aerial behavior. The simplest is the desultory tail slap, in which an animal lifts its flukes free of the water and smacks them down again, sometimes with a resounding slap that can be heard for dozens of yards. Another common behavior, a bit more energetic, is the head or back slap, in which the animal lunges from the water for three-quarters of its length and then slaps its body back against the water, producing a cascade of spray and a sharp, slapping sound. But these minor displays are not even worth watching when a school member begins to spin. To perform a true competition-grade spin, the porpoise swoops down deep beneath the surface and comes up in a swift arc. At the very last instant, as its body darts free of the water, it tilts its flukes, catching the water and sending its body into a dizzying spin that may cause it to revolve four or five times around the long axis of its body before it crashes back into the sea. Usually, as it lands, its rotating body scoops out a hollow of water which claps together over it as it sinks, jetting a column of white water upward from its entry point like a boy doing a cannonball dive.

But for sheer grace and athletic prowess I prefer the head-over-tail leap. This magnificent leap can often be seen when a school is in the height of excitement. The animal leaps free of the water in a graceful arc, and when seven or eight feet above the water whips its tail over its head, slinging trailing spray for many yards into the air like the sparks from a pinwheel, and enters the water tail first. Exhibitionist porpoises sometimes combine the spin and the head-over-tail leap. This is too complicated to be beautiful, but I suppose it must represent a joyful degree of bodily control for an animal.

To suggest, as some of my friends insist, that pure joy motivates the leaps is, I think, begging the question. Even so, the best I can conjure up as half-hearted explanation is that the intensity of leaping indicates rather precisely a level of "school excitement" or alertness. A resting school leaps not at all. A fast-moving school in deep water will usually leap more than one swimming more slowly in shallow water. The leaps are most common when the schools are spread far across the sea. Their slapping return to the sea may produce underwater sounds that let schoolmates know where others are. They may serve to shake off parasitic fish like remoras and maybe even the cookie-cutter shark. I don't know. All I know is that so far I'm unsatisfied that I understand them. But seen in evolutionary perspective, it seems clearly a pattern that has evolved through time. And such things do not happen just for the joy of it.

From my studies with Alice and Kathy I knew that sounds probably controlled much school behavior. So we rigged hydrophones, tape recorders, amplifiers, and the like and began to listen to what the porpoises in our school had to say.

As an aside, before telling what we heard, I want to explain that in all my work with porpoises I have never seen any evidence that suggests to me that they have a language like ours. I'm not surprised about this, either, since our strange method of acoustic communication is almost grotesquely clumsy and difficult. What other creature, for example, would want to wait around for the message involved in a long sentence; to wait until all the little abstract symbols like prepositions and adverbs and participles were arranged according to an arcane plan before meaning could be extracted? Only, I suggest, an animal deeply involved in cause-and-effect sequences, like those that result from and allow the use of tools. Each time we use a tool, we make a set of predictions to ourselves: "If I turn this screwdriver so far, it will release the window screen, and if I don't step aside now, it will hit me on the head." We are predictive animals par excellence, and nearly everything we do, from our technology to our language, involves looking at time spans longer than the moment just before us.

Porpoises are almost wholly nonmanipulative, as one would expect from an animal whose fingers are encased in a smooth glove that makes their hands into diving planes. Probably, like most other animals, it is likely that most of what they think, do, and say is related to relationships and emotions and not to complicated abstractions. Certainly I have seen no evidence to the contrary.

Purely as a prediction, I suggest that when we truly understand the sounds of porpoises and their meanings, we will have found that they have incredibly refined capability at "seeing with sound," to the point that they form sonic images of their environment. Further, it is already clear that they can hear the composition and texture of objects around them. I suspect they look into each other in eerie ways, inspecting the contours of internal air spaces like lungs and upper respiratory tract spaces, and that information about emotional states is to be gathered this way, even though the external surface of the animal is smooth and expression-free, having been dictated largely by the demands of hydrodynamics.

Then, I suspect that their whistle signals will be found to carry a variety of meanings, like the cries of wolves which carry information about the state of the chase—"I'm closing in now"; "The prey is a long way ahead"; and so on.

So it was with these personal prejudices (in my case at least) that we began to listen to the Kealakekua Bay school. One of our hydrophones was affixed to the hull of the SSSM, just in front of the viewing windows. Its cable ran through a stuffing gland in the hull to the tape recorder lying on the little shelf in front of the observer. With Tom topside steering us toward the porpoise school, I spoke into the microphone to identify the sequence for the later time when we would analyze it in the laboratory.

> May 2, 1970. Observers are Tom Dohl, Larry Hobbs, and Ken Norris. We are approaching a school of approximately 30 *Stenella longirostris* that entered Kealakekua Bay, Hawaii, at 8:15 A.M. It is now 8:35 A.M. and the animals are still in rank formation headed for Observation Post No. 1, 1500 yards offshore. Occasional spins and head slaps can be seen. The weather is clear, sunny, and calm. Recordings are being made with an LC32 hydrophone, a 466A Hewlett-Packard Amplifier set at 7-1/2 inches per second. The animals have just come in sight of my capsule at 11 o'clock. They are swimming toward the bow of the SSSM. Recording starts.

One five-porpoise subgroup of the school cut toward us, swinging around a few feet from the windows and taking up station directly ahead of our bow. Their tails beat up and down a foot or so in front of the Plexiglas windows. The sleek porpoises jockeyed for position, poking each other with the tips of their pectoral flippers, or occasionally nudging one another body to body. A stream of bubbles issued from the blowhole of one and trailed back past my capsule. At the same instant a chirping whistle, so high I could scarcely hear it, issued from the tape recorder speaker. I heard no clicking sounds until another group joined the first, and when they came in, heading directly toward the capsule, a barrage of clicks, like rain on a tin roof, hit my capsule. As the animals turned their tails toward me to take up station, the sounds ceased. Their directional beams now shot forward into the water ahead, out of my hearing.

Hours of listening to a resting school revealed no sounds other than desultory clicks when a school headed toward us. But after they aroused themselves, whistles became prominent. Once, when a newly aroused school had begun zigzag swimming out into Kealakekua Bay, we still heard nothing but clicks until another school, alert and leaping, approached them from across the bay. This record is then dotted with a peculiar double-parted whistle that we have yet to hear again. The two groups joined and left the bay, heading for Keawekāheka Point to the north.

Fully alert traveling schools are sometimes very noisy indeed. We encountered such a school several miles south of Kealakekua Bay, in the deep-water cove called Ho'okena. We swung the skiff just ahead of the leaping, spinning animals and dropped our portable hydrophone in the water. Moments later we had drifted to a stop, and as the hydrophone hung quietly a few feet below us, cascades of clicks could be heard. Clearly by now the porpoises knew all about us. Still, they came toward us. Some were within a few yards when the clicks subsided and a weird chorus began. Bleating and quacking sounds issued from animals up and down the passing rank, and an undulating chorus of very high-pitched whistles arose, rising and falling in volume as animals closer and farther away spoke their piece. Presumably they were reacting to us, since once they passed abeam the sounds ceased.

Later, by slowing the tape recorder, these sounds could be brought down to levels where humans could hear them easily. The bleats became moos that sounded for all the world like those of a barnyard. The high, squeaky whistles resolved into long, rising, pure-tone whistles coming in sequential chorus. The whistle of one animal seemed to evoke that of a nearby animal, and so on down the rank and back again.

What do the sounds mean? That very difficult question is a long way from solution in our work, or, for that matter, in the work of all others who study porpoises. At last we can begin to relate certain kinds of sounds to certain parts of the daily activity cycle. But I suspect it will be a long time before we can truly unravel the intricacies of porpoise sound communication.

Many other questions remain. We know that in late summer and fall all the porpoises from the lee side of Hawai'i seem to gather in a sort of "Porpoise National Convention," usually off Keāhole Point. Many young appear about that time, but birth seems clearly not restricted to such a short time but is instead spread over most or all of the year.

Even with the SSSM and our cliff-top observation post, most porpoise social behavior remains a mystery to us. For instance, most of the subgroups we see in active schools have no clear function. Are they family groups, play groups, are they divided by sex or age? As yet we have few answers to these questions, but we must continue to learn, in order to understand wild porpoise life.

What is it that regulates porpoise school numbers? Why don't their schools grow and grow until every scrap of natural resource is used, as humans are busy doing? What racial wisdom, somehow lost by humans as they adopted civilization, keeps them in balance? If we can answer that by watching the Kealakekua porpoises, they will have told us a great deal.

THE MOON
BY WHALE LIGHT

DIANE ACKERMAN

R OGER PAYNE was not hard to spot at the airport on Maui
that February day in 1990. He was the only person who looked
as if he had just flown out of a war zone. His left eye bore a
half-moon bruise below it, a small piece of gouged forehead had
been pushed back together, and an angry cut was just starting to
heal above his mouth. One evening earlier in the week, he had
strolled across the lawn, hands tucked in his pockets, regarding
the beauty of the Hawaiian night sky, forgotten about a low rock
fence, and tripped squarely onto his face before he could pull his
hands out to break the fall. His glasses fell, too, and cracked at the
nose bridge. Repaired repeatedly with Krazy Glue, they now sat
at several angles on his face, one lens tilted forward, the frame
slightly askew. So it was an unlikely apparition holding a red-and-
yellow lei of plumeria blossoms that greeted me in the poly-
glot hubbub of the airport. But it was also someone I had waited
a dozen years to meet, ever since the night in the mid-seventies, at
Cornell University's Bailey Hall, when I attended his lecture on
the songs of humpback whales, which he concluded with a duet

for cello and whale song. He was clearly an expert and talented cellist, but it was the whale songs themselves—great booming ragas of creaking and moaning and seat-shaking bass—that captivated everyone with their beauty and mystery.

Leaving the overhanging shadows of the terminal, we strolled out into the sunlight and drove to the town of Kihei and an oceanside house owned by Ani and Jerry Moss, two whale enthusiasts. Over the years, Roger had traveled the world, recording and analyzing the songs of humpback whales and studying the habits of other whales. By his definition (derived from Melville), a whale is "a mammal in the sea that has a horizontal tail and spouts," so it includes both the large animals we usually think of as whales and also the small whales we describe as dolphins or porpoises. Whales have the largest brains on earth, brains every bit as complex as our own. They have culture, and they have language. They sing songs that obey the kinds of rules one finds in classical music. What does a creature with the largest brain on earth use it for? Why does it sing? What do the songs mean? Almost everything about whales is a tantalizing mystery. We ache to know about other forms of equally intelligent life in the universe, and yet here are creatures as unknown as extraterrestrials right among us, moving in a slow-motion ballet under the oceans, hidden from our view. Questions about mind and music had been plaguing me for some time, so although I had never met Roger Payne before, I had met some of his fascinations and questions and considered them old friends.

Turning onto a shore road, we found the Mosses' home, set among trumpet flowers and bougainvillea, sprawling on a promontory above the sea, with its own small sandy beach and ragged shoreline. Jerry, one of the founders of A & M Records, had just left for Los Angeles, but Ani was still there, along with her sister, Katy. Ani was a tall, thin, beautiful, fey, fawnlike woman of unidentifiable age who had once been a *Vogue* model (and still looked the part). Her sister, also thin, pretty blonde, was an accountant from Salt Lake City, who could, as it turned out, tell off-color, working-class jokes with such wide-eyed innocence that they packed a double whammy. The plan was for Roger and me to rent a Zodiac and go out to find some of the singers. Each day, we would rise at 5:00 A.M., phone the National Weather Service's general- and marine-forecast recordings, and even the pilots' Flight Service Station, then scan the ocean through binoculars, and see whitecaps too treacherous to risk. A trough had settled over the islands, bringing steady rain and high winds; the seas were eighteen feet, and the storm system was unyielding. So, since we were housebound, Roger worked in the water, installing an offshore buoy to which he had attached a hydrophone; an antenna hitched outside the Mosses' house led to a receiver in their living room, and this would allow them to record whale songs for him continuously in season or tune in whenever they were just in the mood for a concert.

Roger was a tall, slender man with sturdy shoulders, enormous hands on which the nails were neat and trimmed, a long stride, and a slightly rocking gait, probably the result of a knee operation he had had the previous year. When he walked fast, his hips sometimes seemed to be balancing along a spirit level. Parted on the left, thinning a little on top, his slate-gray hair looked slightly windblown even when freshly combed. He had a large forehead on which four evenly spaced lines formed when he was concentrating, hazel eyes that more often looked brown than green, and a small, neat nose. Sometimes, in repose, his face was undisturbable and fifty-something, but when animated it often became that of a rompy, mischievous twenty-year-old. Although he spent many months out of doors, he had the kind of front-only tan that one acquires accidentally. His clothes were freshly laundered and ironed, his gray-green pants had a small constellation of holes on one leg, and both pockets on his blue shirt were frayed.

He slipped into a Brooklyn accent from time to time in conversation, just to emphasize the silliness of something or other, but his normal speaking voice was unusually resonant and poised like a singer's, and indeed he was a madrigal singer. What dialect he spoke would be hard to pin down. In a cosmopolitan vernacular that shifted easily among classes and cultures, his vocabulary was peppered with scientific jargon, sixties lingo, literary allusions, musical terms, poetic images, casual down-and-dirty cursing, plus the verbal dressage needed for courtesy or protocol. A word like *groovy* or *bozo* mixed naturally with the down-home expression "right quick," such British TV sitcom exclamations as "Lord love a duck!"; a heartfelt "Bless you" by way of thanks; or an unexpected leave-taking like "Let's blow this Popsicle stand." "Well, that sucks the big one," he could say unselfconsciously, and the next instant utter a string of well-groomed clichés. In situations that required the delicate handling of people, he glided into a tone of casual high regard that was intense, warm, and smooth as flowing lava. His father, an electrical engineer at Bell Labs in New York City, had been every bit as absentminded as Roger freely confessed to being. His grandfather had been a logger, his mother a violinist and violist, beside whom he often sat when they played string quartets with friends. Before she married, she had taught music at the Mannes Music School in New York.

For days, telephone calls had been crackling back and forth between the house and a ship at sea. Roger, who was director of the Long-Term Research Institute, in Lincoln, Massachusetts (an affiliate of the World Wildlife Fund), had been trying to acquire a boat equipped with directional sonar. But the boat needed expensive and unexpected repairs. Now it seemed a smaller but more workable boat might soon become available. This new forty-six footer was built in Sri Lanka, had directional sonar, a directional hydrophone, ten halogen lamps built into the hull to illuminate the ocean, and other desirable fittings. Roger was also trying to coordinate trips to Japan, the Galápagos, Alaska, and Hawai'i, and to review whale research from all over the world. The International Whaling Commission declared a moratorium on commercial whaling in 1982, ten years after the United Nations Conference on the Human Environment called for one. But the IWC moratorium didn't take effect until 1986, and it left a loophole: Countries could "kill, take and treat whales for purposes of scientific research." Japan had been especially unscrupulous about taking advantage of the loophole, and Norway was another offender. So much of Roger's time was also spent trying to save endangered whales. His days brimmed with commotion and he must have felt like he was living in the middle of a Charles Ives symphony. Most of his recent research efforts had focused on the humpback whale's songs and the family life of the "right whale," but all whales intrigued him, since scientists still knew so little about them, and nonscientists even less.

If you ask someone to draw a whale, she will probably draw a sperm whale, the bulbous-headed whale made famous in Melville's *Moby Dick*, a book that is as much a treatise on whales as it is a piece of fiction. But whales come in many shapes, sizes, and colors. There are two basic groups: the toothed whales (Odontoceti, from the Latin for "tooth" and "whale") and the baleen whales, (Mysticeti, from the Latinized Greek work for "whale"). Toothed whales include the sperm whale, the dolphin, and the orca, or killer whale, and they have a single external blowhole, which in the course of evolution has migrated to the top of the head. They echolocate just as bats do, using sonar to scan their world, find their prey, and map their underwater landscape. And they have teeth, which they use to hold on to such prey as fish, squid, and shrimp. Whales swallow their prey whole, so the teeth are for grasping rather than for chewing.

In contrast, baleen whales don't have teeth but hundreds of tightly packed, springy baleen plates (made of keratin, the same

substance as human fingernails), which grow down from the upper gums. Baleen whales have paired blowholes—nostrils, in fact—
which are on the top of the head. Some baleen species graze
peacefully as they move through the water, rolling slowly through
the surface with their mouths yawning open. Because the baleen
has a smooth outside edge and a bristly inside edge, water can
flow freely through the whale's mouth, but krill, plankton, and
small schooling fish get caged inside. Other species have pleats on
the throat, so that they can stretch their mouths open even wider,
like valises, and when they're feeding they roll on one side, take
in a huge amount of water, expand the pleated throat, force water
against the roof of the mouth, and press the water out, leaving
the meal behind.

Those two large groups, Odontoceti and Mysticeti, include
seventy-seven species of whales and dolphins—all that inhabit
the earth. In a rather ghoulish twist, one of those species, the right
whale, Mysticete, gets its name because it was "the right whale
to kill." Ignorant about whale species, new whalers would look
out, see a whale, and ask if that was the right whale or not; in
time, the name stuck. When right whales were killed, instead of
sinking as most dead whales do, they float; they don't struggle
much in battle, either, and their baleen was extremely valuable.
Now the right whale is one of the rarest whale species, and it has a
special distinction in the history of human affairs. Every species of
animal that we have brought to extinction has occupied a limited
area—an island, an archipelago, a continent. We have never in
our tenure on earth brought to extinction a truly cosmopolitan
species, one with a worldwide distribution. "The closest we've
ever come is with the right whale," Roger explained over dinner,
"and we came so vanishingly close. It would have represented a
new benchmark, a new low, the lowest, the most careless, the
most outrageous thing that humanity had yet done to the planet.
The fact that our generation is now making the effort to prevent

that extinction is evidence that we're waking up at last. In that sense, the right whale is an important bellwether of the human condition."

Another species of Mysticeti, the gray whale, became extinct in the North Atlantic by the end of the seventeen hundreds, at the hands of Basque whalers, the founders of seagoing whaling in the West. It was almost certainly those whalers, and the Vikings, who first discovered America, not Columbus. Roger quipped that what Columbus really discovered was "public relations." When the gray whale was formally "discovered" in the nineteenth century in the North Pacific, it was called the devilfish. Captain Charles Scammon, a naturalist, found its major breeding areas in the lagoons of Baja California, and furiously hunted it; the grays killed several men and smashed all his boats in very short order. This same species is now noted for what's called "the friendly-whale phenomenon." In 1977, a single gray whale in San Ignacio Lagoon, near Scammon's Lagoon, off Baja California, became "chronically friendly," as Roger put it, and allowed itself to be patted by passengers of all the whale-watching boats that could find it. During the next several seasons, the number of friendly whales soared, until anyone who wanted to pet a whale could do so. Though no one was keeping count, in the previous winter there had been hundreds of gray whales approaching boats for cosseting and stroking. Now it seems to have become part of their whale culture, something they've learned from each other. In the lagoons, where gray whales gather in high numbers in the wintertime, it can grow terribly windy. Tourists in a whale-watching boat near a gray whale may find the wind blowing them along the surface. The whale isn't borne along by the wind, and it will go through contortions to stay with the boat, presenting its belly to be scratched and rubbed. Many times a day, this will happen, with boatloads of people leaning out to touch a whale. Originally, the friendly gray whales drew tourists, but it soon was the other way around—the presence of the tourists drawing the whales, who actively searched for boats. The whales rush out and will even ram into a boat and then quickly roll over like puppies, belly-up, because they love to be patted and rubbed and scratched. To Roger, they were the classic example of how wrong our conceptions about whales had been: "Imagine, it was the devilfish, the malicious animal that had the gall to kill people who were attempting at that very moment to reach its heart or lungs with a spear so that it would bleed to death internally. Not a very strong sign of aggression, I should say. How could we have been so wrong to name this animal the devilfish when it turns out to be so friendly?"

One genus of whales, *Balaenoptera*, includes five closely related species—sei, brydes, minke, blue, pygmy right—which are essentially small, medium, and large versions of the same body plan. The minke whale is the smallest baleen whale. The pygmy right whale, a rare creature about which little is known, is so similar to minke whales that it's hard for scientists to identify in the wild. But the blue whale is easier. It is the largest animal ever to exist on earth. It can grow to as much as a hundred feet long. Its tongue weighs as much as an elephant. To execute the simple maneuver of putting its head down—that is, going from horizontal to vertical in the water—it first has to be in a hundred feet of water. When it does that or stands up on its tail, it experiences a difference in pressure from the tip of its nose to the tip of its tail of three atmospheres. The heart of the blue whale weighs several tons, and on a factory ship it often took six brawny men to drag the heart out with flensing hooks. The aorta leading from its heart is large enough for a child to crawl through, and the major blood vessels appear to be about the size of a sewer pipe. A salmon could comfortably swim down them.

The blue whale makes loud, low-frequency sounds that can travel enormous distances. The ocean transmits sound in strange and unlikely ways. There is a layer of water, known as the deep sound channel, in which sound waves can be trapped and spread great distances because they bend back into the channel over and over, without losing much energy. Under those circumstances, whale sound can travel as much as five hundred miles before blending into background noise. These days, the oceans are polluted by human sounds. But in the tens of millions of years before the advent of ships (during which about 99.9 percent of the evolution of blue whales took place), whale sounds might have traveled out to distances of several thousand miles, so that two whales could have sat on opposite sides of the same ocean and been in contact with each other. Those wouldn't have needed to be complex conversations. They would not have been chitchat, either, but simple exchanges of information about where food could be found. If a whale had been hungry, it might have remained quiet; if it had been well fed, it might have spoken. Then, all a hungry whale would have needed to do was swim in the direction of the loudest sound. If a whale had had too much to eat, it would have been to its advantage to share excess food with its kin; next year, its kin might have returned the favor.

Finally, there is the humpback. Although it has long, paddlelike white flippers and a huge tail with markings unique as fingerprints, its most arresting feature is that it sings—sings complicated, beautiful songs. A bird will sing a song, grow quiet, and then perhaps sing its song again; but a humpback will sing a long, complex, sustained song and then go back and start again without any break, singing continuously. When it dives, it flexes its back sharply and appears to have a hump on its back, hence the name. It is acrobatic when it breaches. Sometimes, it will roll onto one side and wave a long flipper out of the water. At others, it will stick its head out of the water in a "spy hop," to look around. When a humpback feeds, it swims in a tight circle, spinning a net of bubbles around a school of krill or fish, which become alarmed by the bubbles and clump together, whereupon the humpback swings toward the center, mouth open, and gobbles them up.

Whales are mammals: They breathe air, bear live young, nurse them with milk, and have hair. People don't think of whales as hairy, but they do have a few whiskers. And though we picture whales wobbling with blubber to keep warm, a whale's real problem is staying cool. A whale is like a house with a too-large furnace and too few radiators. When a whale exercises in warm equatorial waters, it can die of overheating. If it races hell-for-leather in pursuit of prey, it can become so hot it virtually blows up. After a whale is killed in the Antarctic, it is eviscerated with a long, sharp flensing knife. The entire length of the whale's body cavity is opened up so that the icy water can wash it thoroughly. Then it's tied tail first to the bow of the catcher boat and dragged back to the factory ship, where it will be hauled aboard and cut up. If the trip back to the factory ship takes too long or if the whale is left in the water for too long, even though it is lying in icy water, its bones will be charred by the heat of its internal decay. When that happens, it's referred to as a burnt whale. Imagine an animal generating so much heat that even though lying under icy water with its belly cut wide open, *its bones cook.*

Sperm whales, most of which live close to the equator, cool off by diving to unimaginable depths. Plunging down to where the water temperature is close to freezing, sperm whales feed on squid or large fish, sometimes swallowing sharks whole. In the strange realm of pressure and near blackness, a sperm whale swims like a spaceship through slowly moving galaxies of luminescent fish—a world difficult for us to imagine. Small wonder that whales seem magical.

As Roger sprawled on the rug, adjusting the receiver, whale songs filled the house with otherworldly music, produced by singers who had been his often invisible companions for nearly thirty years. Although he had a photographic "fluke record" of many humpback whales, and could also identify some singers by their phrasing of the songs, he had most often heard the songs without being able to see the singer or guess who it might be. In that sense, the songs were like those of the troubadours, who wandered through the Middle Ages regaling people with songs anonymous but unforgettable.

Why do whales sing? One theory argues that humpback whales use their songs as other animals use their horns. The whale with the longest and most ingenious songs wards off competing males. Another theory has it that the songs are more like peacocks' tails—the whale with the best song is the one most attractive to females. But that doesn't explain why whales revise their songs. I wondered if whales changed their songs for the reasons humans do—for sheer variety, or to include new myths or folk wisdom, or out of a kind of mental fidgeting, or as a way to give the group a stronger sense of community, or simply as a form of play, or as a method for generations to set themselves apart, or to pass along new information about their changing environment, or for reasons as whimsical as fashion. They live at such great distances from one another. Maybe singing is their equivalent of shepherds' whistling or yodeling across valleys with news—or just so they don't feel quite so alone.

"Could they be changing their songs for the same reasons human beings do, in an intelligent way?" I asked Roger.

He glanced at me over the top of his glasses, then returned to a delicate soldering job and said, "Maurice Ewing, who was head of the Lamont-Doherty Geological Observatory, in Palisades, New York, and is one of those who really synthesized the details and facts that led to plate tectonics, spoke of what he called 'brutal facts.' A brutal fact is one that goes against your natural inclinations and beliefs, yet you're forced to pay attention to it and recognize that it's telling you something wholly unexpected and very powerful. Well, some brutal facts associated with whales make it very difficult to figure out what the songs are all about. Let me give you a few examples. The songs are incredibly complex. They change every year, and they're very beautiful. For us, they trigger many ideas and emotions—some people respond to whale songs by weeping. But another brutal fact is that they're monotonous. They repeat endlessly. It doesn't sound that way to a casual listener, but if you sit for an entire season listening to whale songs, you can get roundly sick of some of the variations you're hearing. A song won't be completely different for several years, so you must keep in mind that whatever it means, its message is bound to be very monotonous."

"Do you think their monotony makes them less aesthetically pleasing to the whales?"

"Oh no. Not at all. What could be more monotonous than a teenager's playing the latest heavy-metal tape three hundred times in a row, until it's worn out or demagnetized? No, if you tune in and are a regular listener to pop music, you'll hear the Top Ten songs played most of the day on many stations. That doesn't affect aesthetics. What I'd like to know is: What's the evolutionary advantage of this monotony? Of course, it's just as hard to say why people sing. In the case of rock musicians, you can see that it greatly improves their reproductive fitness," he said, laughing, "but not all of us are rock musicians." Roger unfolded his long legs slowly, one at a time, with the care of an afghan hound standing up, and ambled over to the electrical closet to test another receiver. There, among fuses, wires, and electronics, sat stacks of New Age music, all published by A & M records. With one hand he twiddled a knob on a control panel, cocked an ear, listened intently, then returned to the spill of wires, boxes, and screws on the rug.

"Suppose human beings evolved two forms of communication," I said, "one that is direct emotional communication—music—and one that's analytical and verbal, which we call languages."

"Now you're exactly on to what I'm suggesting. I like that

idea. It would be wonderful to be able to look at someone and make those noises that are deeply evocative of a particular kind of emotion and thus lock the other person to the emotion you're feeling. And we *do* do that to some extent. If we see someone weeping, our urge is to weep with him. Or if we see someone yawning, we may yawn as well. Such things help to synchronize the behavior of the group. I've done a lot of madrigal singing, and in some of my favorite songs you're saying fa-la-la-la-la a lot of the time. Tiddly-pum, tiddly-pum. It doesn't *mean* anything. But it's just right. It has tremendous artistic importance and meaning, which people memorize and love. There don't have to be words in these songs, or any direct meaning, for the songs to be meaningful and selected by evolution. But then there's that monotony. It would be almost as if you sat each day and told the story of some terrible trauma—or wonderful love or deep disgrace—over and over again, while everyone around you was telling the same story."

"Birds and other mammals get along perfectly well with songs that don't change all the time," I said. "Why is it so important to whales to change their songs?"

"I could make up a sort of half-baked answer. I could say, for instance, that if one male comes up with a song that's attractive to more females, the other males in the area will soon recognize that Joe is doing a lot better than they are and change their tune to copy Joe, so then Joe loses his advantage. And the others, or Joe, would then try different versions that might give them an advantage over the competition, even if it's just a momentary one."

"So we don't know why they sing. But it's only the males that sing, right?" I pictured an oceanful of cetacean Pavarottis.

Roger smiled. "There's some confusion over that. We have thirty-five singers of known sex and they are all males, except one. An adult and a calf were seen by a highly reliable observer, Graeme Ellis. Singing was coming from the adult. Graeme dived to observe them, and as he watched, the calf went down and appeared to nurse, and the adult released what seemed to be milk into the water. A puff of milk should be a pretty good indicator of sex. But the trouble is that even though Graeme is a totally experienced observer—and I completely accept his interpretation of what he saw at face value—I am an experienced observer, too, and I've been so badly fooled so many times by what whales were doing around me that I know how badly anyone can be fooled. For example, in Argentina, where you can sit on cliffs and look directly down through the water, I saw a female and a calf underwater with no other whale around for as far as I could see, and suddenly a male was there, underwater, right next to them. He messed around with them for five or ten minutes and then disappeared without blowing. To an observer on the beach or in a boat, as Graeme was for most of this time, he would have been invisible—no one would have seen him approach or leave. The only reason I knew he was there is that I happened to have a high and favorable viewpoint. I think it's possible that there was a male down underneath the female and calf Graeme saw. But Graeme says that as the female returned to the surface, the sound diminished and remained about the same. That is an extremely important observation, because if you are listening with a shallow hydrophone to a whale singing, at the moment the whale comes to the surface, most of the energy from the singing is refracted downward by the warmer water near the surface and doesn't get to your hydrophone. The result is that when the whale is right at the surface, it sounds very feeble, then as it dives, the sound can travel directly to your hydrophone without being refracted away from it and the sound becomes louder. I'm still not sure that there wasn't a male singer that was out of sight down below or that the female didn't interpose her body between Graeme and a singing calf each time she happened to come to the surface. On the other hand, he may be absolutely right—maybe females do sing. If you take even a newborn chicken and give it enough testosterone, it will begin crowing like a rooster. You can make the female of many bird species sing a male song by injecting the right male hormones. So that might also be the case with whales. A female with enough male hormone might sing the male's song. Or another possibility is that it could have been the calf singing; it might have been a male calf."

No one has any idea how humpback whales make their sounds. Joking about how little we know, William Schevill, a distinguished elder statesman of whale biology, once said, "Perhaps they make their sounds by rubbing their vestigial hind limbs together." For all we know, they play their ribs like a concertina and their baleen like a pocket comb. I pursued the question with Roger.

"Don't they have a larynx or windpipe?"

"It used to be thought that whales didn't even have vocal cords. But now we know that certain Odontoceti have something very much like them."

"How about air pockets?"

"They have every kind you can name. They have an area of their windpipe that might be in some way involved. They have a plumbing system that's so fancy it could support any theory you like about how they generate sounds, but at present, any other theory would do, too. We just don't know where their sounds are coming from. The harmonic series associated with the sounds are certainly the kinds that would be made by a system based on air—closed pipes filled with air."

For a moment the creaking and moaning gave way to popping sounds and clarinet notes. "How about other passageways working like whistles or flutes?" I suggested. "The Aztecs had a large variety of whistles and flutes that could make many different sounds, depending on the air chambers or the chambers holding water and other fluids."

"Whistles, yes, but no flutes, because a flute is an open-ended pipe. But whales could be using any number of different sound-producing mechanisms, and some of their sounds are clearly just a train of pulses produced so rapidly that you and I perceive it as a tone. The tone A on the piano is 440 cycles per second, and we normally think of it as the kind of sound that might be produced by a flute, for instance. But you can also get a nice tone of A by taking 440 noisy soundbursts per second and listening to them. What you're hearing is the rate at which these little bursts of sound are being produced; and that rate is the note A on the piano. If you made it 238 bursts per second, you'd get middle C." Sweeping aside a row of invisible possibilities with one hand, he said, "One thing I can tell you is that when a whale sings, no air is released."

"What a mystery."

"It's one of the more intriguing little mysteries of our time."

Roger walked outside to adjust the antenna he had put up near a chunk of fused crystals, embraced by ferns, that sat on a block of lava on the grassy promontory just beyond the back porch. Ani said she had set a crystal down on the house's private beach out of respect for the wild dolphins, and it drew them. I did not pursue this. Two white rope hammocks hung between palm trees, and flowery terraces led to an open-air shower made of lava and other rocks. Thick white clouds churned fresh smoke above the horizon. One whale singer came on strong, like a yowling tomcat, while we fixed an impromptu dinner of mashed potatoes, broccoli, salad, and ice cream. Ani was wearing a new black sweatshirt with good drawings of a humpback mother and calf. Everywhere you looked in the multilevel, meticulously decorated house, primitive sculptures and paintings mixed with images of whales. There were whale sculptures, whale drawings, whale videos. Katy was wearing a silver ring on which two dolphins were entwined.

Roger took down his long, splayed-fingered antenna and found a better spot for it, at the side of the house, near a tree. It was a line-of-sight antenna, directed toward a buoy about three hundred yards offshore. With the buoy, worth only about $700, Roger was hoping that he could make a unique collection of a week's continuous recordings. When he returned, taking care to close the screen door snugly to keep out poisonous centipedes that rippled through the grass and could bite, we sat down to eat, serenaded by a concert both eerie and familiar.

ONE morning, though the seas were galloping and high, we stood on the promontory in back of the house, binoculars pressed to our eyes, searching the horizon for whales. Actually, all we were looking for was a "blow," the misty spout a whale leaves when it surfaces to breathe. This was not the only sighting cue we could use. Whale watchers have learned to look for a rolling animal and for a whitecap splash of flukes or flippers. A sperm whale throws its flukes very high into the air and their trailing edge has a big notch on it; humpbacks have multicolored flukes; a right whale has broad, lip-shaped flukes with a shallow notch. Whale scientists look for changing color under the water—say, the pale blue of humpback flukes near the surface. They look for "footprints" in the water, rings that look like slick footsteps, caused by animals swimming just below the surface. They look for a dorsal fin. The killer whale has a very tall, erect dorsal fin, whereas the southern right whale has no dorsal fin at all. But the most common guide is the blow, because it varies so much among the whales and can be seen at such a distance. In the dry Antarctic air, the blue whale shoots up a thin column that can rise a hundred feet and stay visible for thirty seconds. The sperm whale has a forward-canted, left-sided blow, easy to identify. Right whales and bowheads make a misty, V-shaped blow from their twin blowholes.

"There's a whale!" Roger said, pointing to a wedge of ocean just off the southern end of Molokini, a crescent-shaped island across the bay from the Mosses' home. "It's moving north along the island."

A moment later I saw a low, bushy balloon of vapor, the signature of the humpback. Early mariners used to think that the exhalations of whales were poisonous, a caustic mixture of brimstone and sulfur that could strip the flesh from any man who chanced too close. Perhaps the blood entering the lungs of wounded whales sometimes tainted their last breaths, giving them a fetid odor. But scientists who have been drenched by the breath of healthy whales say that it feels like a delicate mist; some report a faint odor of musk.

The clouds had begun to swarm again, and to keep ourselves dry and warm, we put on many layers of clothing over our swimsuits, then took green plastic trash bags and cut arm-and head-holes. No one else was crazy enough to be at the marina when the sky was like clotted milk and a blue veil of rain hung on the horizon. Roger steered the Zodiac out to where the waves were heaving, toward Molokini, where we knew that at least one whale would be singing. And what a song it would be! It was said that the shape of the island created lovely echoes when the whale and his listener were in just the right position. The farther we got from shore, the higher the waves became. High enough that Roger paused suddenly to teach me how to restart the engine if it should fail; he gave me the throttle and rudder, making sure I could steer straight and in circles. He was not planning on being washed over the side, but the wind could get right underneath a Zodiac and flip it, and the current could carry one some distance. Then we continued at speed. Over my shoulder, I watched a faint blue drape of storm approach the north end of Maui. The winds had begun to pick up again, the lunging waves shook froth from their mouths like runaway horses, and after each crest we skidded down into the bottom of a bowl, the sides of which grew steeper. Roger cut across them obliquely, like a surfer riding the inside of a wave, angling smartly from one crest to another. Although I had been in Zodiacs in rough seas in South Georgia and the Antarctic,

I had never been in one handled more expertly than this; we skidded across the sides of tall, muddy-blue waves to weave among the convulsive valleys where rising and falling waves met. Then water spumed over the bow, spumed a second time, and Roger turned sharply at a ninety-degree angle and headed straight back for shore. There was no use going on: It would be unsafe. If we hugged the coastline, the waters would be a little calmer. The suddenness of his decision to turn back surprised me, but then I realized that this small boat was one of the main tools of his trade and he had learned its limits and eccentricities, just as he had learned to read the many moods of the ocean. He could judge the difference between potential discomfort and potential danger. It is like that for me when I fly airplanes. On final approach, in a savage crosswind, you can reach a point where it is no longer possible to land safely, because you've used up the full travel of the stick and rudder. The oceanic sky has overpowered you, the limits of your craft have been reached, and there is no use going on. All you can do is search for an airport somewhere else.

"A whale scientist's work isn't always as balmy as I'd imagined," I said as we began the bouncy return to the marina, with the wind now against us.

"This is normal. You're always at the mercy of the weather, and storms seem to follow me." Roger had tied a panama hat on with a string under his chin, but the brim fluttered in the squall, and spray had thrown rivulets down his glasses. Running across the choppy waves, the boat bounced hard, and the ride jarred our kidneys and bones. But the ocean was a wild, beautiful tumult. I could understand why the painter J. M. W. Turner would have himself lashed to the mainmast of a ship and go out into the middle of a raging storm just to behold its color and fury. Below us somewhere in the gelatinous phantasmagoria of churning blue, the whales wouldn't be much aware of the storm. Their world, which has as much geography and real estate as ours, is distinctive. There are mountain ranges in their world, great gorges and rift valleys and sprawling prairies, and even hot springs and volcanoes. We forget that the ocean floor includes some of the tallest mountain ranges on earth—we just don't see them. And there are the magnetic features, about which we know so little. Because we don't steer along the magnetic web of the planet, we forget that other animals do. In some underwater valleys, the magnetic signals are polarized in one direction; in some harbors the signals are bound to be stronger or weaker, or perhaps even jangled by power plants and motorboats. Whales navigate through a rich, complicated landscape at a stately pace, slow as zeppelins, majestic and alert.

When we were at last back at the marina, cold, tired, and wet, we loaded the Zodiac onto a waiting trailer and headed for a nearby fast-food restaurant to get a hot breakfast. Roger ordered scrambled eggs and a rasher of bacon. Both arrived in nearly the same dull resiny color. The coffee was strong enough to trot a mouse across.

"What was it like the first time you heard whales singing?"

"I was in Bermuda, as a guest of the late Frank Watlington, an engineer who worked for the Lamont Geophysical Field Station. He used to go out towing hydrophones when the Navy was firing off explosives and record the sounds far away. But when he did this during humpback season, he often heard the songs of whales, which fascinated him. One April day, he played them to me in the engine room of a wooden minesweeper just like Cousteau's boat, the *Calypso*. And although the boat was very noisy and loud, out of his tinny speaker came incredible sounds. I had never heard anything like them. They riveted my attention as nothing ever had before. These were superb recordings he had made on bottom-mounted hydrophones that the Navy was using for purposes of listening to enemy submarines and that sort of thing. Later, he gave part of his tape collection to me. It's some of those sounds that the world has heard since on the record *Songs of the Humpback Whale.*"

"Why do the songs move you so?"

"Why is spending the afternoon standing on your feet and tiring out your calves in a museum to see great art worth it? Why do you spend thirty dollars in an evening to go hear music? I don't know. To me it's a marvelously evocative performance that comes from the most unexpected quarter. It would be the same as walking by your cat and having it start humming a tune to you. Humpbacks have been singing longer than human beings have existed."

"What is the most beautiful encounter with singing whales you can remember?"

"Oh, that's easy," he said, stretching his long legs out into the aisle and settling against the booth wall, a mug of coffee in his hands. Looking somewhere in the middle distance, he shed the present easily, as if it were nothing more than a light sweater. "Lying in the cockpit of a boat at night off Bermuda," he said, "with a faint gentle breeze and the mast sweeping across and clouds of stars above you, listening to the sounds of whales, which are sort of flooding up out of the ocean through the earphones you're wearing as you become part of the same rhythm that the songs dance to. The songs are set by the rhythm of swells in the oceans. If you listen to whales when you are being borne on the sea, you can feel that the rate at which they're producing a given phrase is about the same as the rate between the swells that are coming by. What an extraordinary, compelling experience that is! You never tire of it. The ocean is the greatest of all echo chambers—there's nothing like it on land. And when you listen over a pair of headphones to whales under perfect recording conditions in deep ocean, it's really as though you were listening from within the Horsehead Nebula, or some galactic space that is otherworldly, not part of anything you know, where the boat itself is floating. Once, for example, on an early fall night, I was coming back from the

Arctic, where I had been working on bowhead whales in a boat at sea. As we flew down across the Canadian Arctic, we were beneath an arc of northern lights, which were pure green and bell-shaped. We and the plane were the clapper of this bell, with the green light over us. And for the first time in my life I felt that I was in the position of that whale that is singing to you when you're in the boat and listening to it. That's the kind of space that is somehow illuminated, depicted, made sensible by the hydrophones. It gives you a special impression of the sea. We all love the ocean's beautiful sparkle blue, but beneath it, down deeper, whales are moving with slow, drifting currents, whales that are great, gentle cloudlike beings, not just some *meaty animal.* Everything the whales do is so slow, so deliberate, outside the normal time sense of the human world. When you watch whales for an entire afternoon, you don't realize what they're doing. You see things that look very slow and graceful. Only later, when you've looked at your day's notes might you put it together and say, 'Oh my God, this animal was playing. That's what I was seeing, but I was seeing it at a speed much slower than I'm used to.' Whales teach us a new sense of time."

In a nearby booth, a young man wearing an electric-blue T-shirt on which the letters M-A-U-I were arranged in the rough shape of the island was reading a local newspaper. The headline and a drawing announced yet another occasion on which a whale had saved the life of a human being: in this instance by reportedly driving off sharks that were heading for a fallen surfer. Do whales have emotions like ours? I wondered. How intelligent are they? Do they have minds of the sort that would be familiar to us?

After all, mind is such an odd predicament for matter to get into. I often marvel how something like hydrogen, the simplest atom, forged in some early chaos of the universe, could lead to us and the gorgeous fever we call consciousness. If a mind is just a few pounds of blood, dream, and electric, how does it manage to contemplate itself, worry about its soul, do time-and-motion studies, admire the shy hooves of a goat, know that it will die, enjoy all the grand and lesser mayhems of the heart? What is mind, that one can be *out of one's*? How can a neuron feel compassion? What is a self? Why did automatic, hand-me-down mammals like our ancestors somehow evolve brains with the ability to consider, imagine, project, compare, abstract, think of the future? If our experience of mind is really just the simmering of an easily alterable chemical stew, then what does it mean to *know* something, to *want* something, to *be*? How do you begin with hydrogen and end up with prom dresses, jealousy, chamber music? What is music that it can satisfy such a mind, and even perhaps function as language?

"Remember those 'brutal facts' you were talking about?" I said. "I've been thinking a lot about the mind of whales. How self-conscious do you think whales are?"

Roger turned his fork over and nudged his slices of bacon into a kelplike dune, cut off a section, and chewed it thoughtfully. "There are reasons to suspect that the brains of whales—and I'm including dolphins—are equal to or of even greater complexity than the brains of human beings. These complexities must serve some important role in the lives of the whales and dolphins. But nobody has a clue as to what that role is, not the slightest idea, not even a persuasive theory. I will go out on a limb and say that the most interesting question in biology today is what dolphins are using their complex brains for; I can't think of anything that would be more interesting to know. You can say, 'Well, maybe they just have a large brain; why not?' Well, I can tell you why not. It's because brains are extremely expensive to maintain and operate. For example, during the first few weeks of life in a human being, whose brain-to-body ratio is not very unlike that of a newborn dolphin, the brain requires about a third of the metabolism of the whole body just to run it. It's a very costly thing to have. So you don't just kind of end up having a fancy brain. You have a fancy brain because there's a very important reason why you need one. It is selected for, and as soon as the advantage that is conferred by having it is gone, you'll lose it and lose it fast. What this means is that there must be something that dolphins and whales are doing with their brains that's fundamental to their lives.

"Here's one of the standard unsupported guesses: They're using them for fancy acoustic functions—by making a few clicks, they can not only hear how far it is to the bottom in many directions but they can also figure out its structure and how soft it is and how many fish are hovering above it and which others are buried in the mud and so on. Yes, those are all very important functions. But equally complex tasks are done by bats with brains that are probably a thousandth the mass of the brains of dolphins. And I can't believe that dolphins' brains are so inefficient that they have to be so much more complicated just to equal what can be done in a brain the size of a pea or much smaller. So I don't think that's going to solve the question. No, there's something they're using their large brains for that, I suspect, is completely different from what we use ours for. Ours, basically, serve and interact with two things: one, our opposable thumbs and grasping simian fingers, which, with our brain, make possible eye-hand coordination; and two, language and all that language does for us. Do whales have a language? Well, as I said, if there is a language to the songs of humpback whales, it's very monotonous. They're repeating themselves endlessly, saying the same, perhaps very complex, thing over and over, for months at a time. So it won't do to say that they have a language that is in any sense equivalent to or similar to our language, if they use all of its complexity and structure to say just a very few things. You could say that the song is analogous to a carrier frequency in a radio and that basically it is the minor modifications in the song that carry the message. I somehow think that's unlikely, because whales tend to be alone when they're singing, not in social groups, not in contact with other whales. When a whale comes near a singer, the singer instantly shuts up, and often a fight will ensue. That suggests that the song is a simpler thing, either a challenge or a wooing call. But it doesn't explain the big brains. I think the brains of whales are being used for things we have no intuitive understanding of whatsoever, yet what they're used for is critically important to the life of the whales. It must deeply affect their reproductive fitness. It must be crucial to their survival. But we don't know what it is."

Turning sideways, he leaned back against the outer wall of the booth and propped one sneakered foot up on the bench seat. "You could ask, Why do human beings have such huge brains? There are lots of theories, but to me the one that's most appealing is that human beings dwell in long-lived societies in which they have contact for years with the same individuals and family groups, and these groups are constantly exchanging favors, with the idea that if you give a favor you will get one in return, then you have to wait around and collect on the debt. This process is sometimes referred to as 'reciprocal altruism,' and although nobody has found a means by which just plain true altruism could be selected for, reciprocal altruism could very well be accepted and selected for. A classic example of reciprocal altruism is that you are drowning and I reach down and grab a stick and hold it out and you grab it and I pull you to shore. I've done you the most important favor of your entire life, and you owe me a big one. All I had to do is bend over, pick up a stick, and extend my arm. And now, oh my gosh, what can I expect from you?"

A pink-and-white-uniformed waitress with a bouffant hairdo appeared suddenly with a heavy pot of coffee and poured something like crude oil into Roger's mug. He thanked her and continued: "Why, tremendous things, for a tiny investment on my part. But I might have to wait a long time for you to come up with a reward large enough to express the depths of your gratitude. You can get a social system going based on reciprocal altruism, but it will only work in groups in which associations last for a very long time. It doesn't work in groups in which you have a total despot at the head who will just beat you senseless if you don't pay up. It works in groups more like human groups, and may in fact be like whale and dolphin groups. The smarter you get the smarter you have to be, because eventually that kind of system invites cheating. So let's say, for example, that I discover a beautiful bush of blueberries as we are walking along together. And at the moment, I owe you. I say to you, 'Ah, Diane, look at this marvelous bush of blueberries. Because of what you did for me last week, these are yours, all yours. I'm not going to take any of them.' You begin eating them, with gratitude, and you're glad to have them all to yourself. But the reason I've really done that is that I've noticed another one in the distance that is better than this bush, and I want to keep you away from it. So I wander off until I'm out of sight and then quickly devour it, while you're left with the lesser meal. You have to be able to detect in me little signs that tell you I'm lying. And that requires some very sophisticated analysis of what my true motives may be. If reciprocal altruism invites cheating, then you must become a deft detector of cheating, and if you get good at detecting cheating, then I have to get better at cheating in more subtle ways. What you end up with is a brain racing in its evolution toward greater and greater complexity and sophistication to be able to detect and to employ cheating. You'll quickly end up with animals that have fancy brains. That could be true for dolphins. They certainly exist in long-lived social groups in which they have opportunity to repay reciprocal debts.

"But they may need their brains for reasons much more complex than that. Think of how important myths are in our cultures. Think of all the similarities that myths have, think how memorable those elements are, and how they control the lives of the people who hear them. There may be some kind of need for myth in the vertebrate brain, whether it's located in the head of a whale or of a person. Nobody really knows."

After breakfast, before returning to Kīhei, we paid a visit to Spear Venus at his shop, Venus Electronics, where Roger ordered a special tape recorder with features he needed for recording whales. A whale enthusiast, Spear had worked with Roger in the past, observing and filming whales. His brother owned a local television station. Drifting into an alcove at the back of the shop, which was a small gallery of signed Salvador Dali prints, Roger discussed with Spear the possibility of a donor buying an FM radio station so that he could make ultra-high-quality stereo recordings from a bottom microphone in deep water, then broadcast the songs. People all over the world would be able to tune in to Whale Hawaii and hear nonstop singing.

"What would a station cost to buy?" he asked.

Spear adjusted one corner of a Dali print. "Oh, I would think around a hundred thousand dollars."

"You could sell it by subscription," Roger explained, "and scramble the signal. People could have it as background music in their house. Every now and then, a whale would come by and sit right on the mike and sing and blow everybody's mind. Look, I want to make long-term recordings of humpbacks," Roger explained. "But if you want to get into it commercially, I can't think of anyone better."

Spear stroked his mustache. It was an idea that appealed to him both environmentally and commercially, but he was getting ready to retire and hoping to travel the world with his wife and two small children. But he agreed to think about it and lend a hand setting it up, if the money became available. Whale Hawaii: a steady pour of whale songs streaming around the world above water, so that human beings could hear them, like neighbors picking up on a party line.

At last, we returned to the Mosses' house, where Roger continued work on the buoy. The winds were growing loud and unruly but surely the next day the squalls would have moved on like a flock of migratory birds.

THE following morning, when the winds ebbed a little, we went out in a Zodiac piloted by Colin, a young, fair-skinned Englishman with heavily freckled ears and sunburned neck, chest, and arms. At regular intervals, explosions came from the nearby island of Kahoʻolawe, where the U.S. Navy was practicing bombing. According to Hawaiian legend, the island looks like a humpback, which is why the whales keep returning. At Molokini, Roger dropped a white hydrophone into the water on a long black line and put on a headset. Smiling, he handed the headset to me. Painfully loud whale songs surged through both earphones. Three whales were singing the same song somewhere beneath us, their voices blending and mixing. A storm began prowling Maui. The ocean was cobalt blue, like an Oriental glaze, with gray clouds reflected in it. At times it was the color and texture of whale skin.

"I think he's starting back up," Roger said.

"How can you tell?"

"From where the singer is in the song—at *rattle, rattle, rattle*," he said. "I think it's the coming-up section, but I don't know this year's song very well yet."

The apparently silent ocean filled with white curds as it reflected the plunging storm clouds. The hydrophone drifted below the boat on its long lead like an electrode in a heart. Molokini's structure created a natural amphitheater, which concentrated the sounds. A slow hooting began, like that of a barn owl. It seemed to come from every direction and reminded me that Roger's doctoral work, at Cornell, was on how owls locate their prey, which was as much through sound as vision, he discovered.

"What is that strange hooting?"

Roger smiled. "A singer. It's very close by."

"But in what direction? It seems to be coming from all over."

"The boat transmits the sound to you from all its interior surfaces. It's as if you were sitting in the center of a loudspeaker."

Now I can understand how Greek sailors of the ancient Mediterranean, bewitched by eerie singing, thought it came from Sirens. Although there are no humpbacks reported in the Mediterranean today, an intriguing possibility is that humpbacks once thrived there, among other whales, and were indeed the Sirens of Greek myth. At night, far from land, under a mantle of stars, lonely sailors could have heard the plaintive songs of the humpbacks but would not have been able to tell where the music was coming from as it swirled around inside the wooden hull of their boat, wrapping them in a cocoon of lamentation and desire. Whale songs can continue for many hours, even days, so that becalmed sailors could have grown unnerved and then drowsy, as the singing both bedeviled and enchanted them, and could have fallen asleep with Siren voices tugging at their dreams. Whales may well have been the mythic unicorns, too. Narwhals, which live in Arctic regions, grow long, tapered, spiraling tusks that exactly fit the description of unicorn horns.

Not only have whales generated two of our most beguiling Western myths, they frequent the myths of far-flung cultures, from the aborigines of Australia to the Quechua of Peru. The Inuit consider themselves the "people of the whale," an idea that figures in their creation myths and religious life. In *Whales*, Jacques Cousteau reports that "the Koryak people of Siberia ... hold astonishing meetings during which they confess to whales any sins they have committed, any taboos they have broken, any evil thoughts they may have had." Throughout history, Leviathan, as the whale has often been called, embodied the monstrous grandeur of the unknown, nature at its most primeval and unplumbable, the rampaging beauty of the oceans, the magical realm where the ordi-

nary and the sacred meet. When Melville describes a whale breaking the surface, a figment of fused grace and power, bursting from
its cryptic world into the world of humans, he writes with un-
ashamed worship: "Rising with his utmost velocity from the furthest depths, the Sperm Whale thus booms his entire bulk into
the pure element of air.... In those moments, the torn, enraged
waves he shakes off, seem his mane." Whales live enigmatic lives,
in that realm impenetrable to our gaze. Small wonder they've
seemed magical and strange. Until recently, we couldn't even enter their world long enough to see them completely. And scientists still aren't able to travel with them sufficiently to learn of
their wanderings and relationships. Almost everything we know
about whales we have had to learn from dead animals or from the
occasional stranding of confused or sick ones. In rare, privileged
moments, we enter their world, and then only briefly and shal-
lowly, to watch through the murk or to eavesdrop.

Colin leaned over the side of the Zodiac and put his head
underwater, holding his nose, then came up dripping, his short
blond hair swept into a punk style. Momentarily disturbed, the
water surface went back to being slick as whale skin and mottled
by reflected clouds.

"Sounds close," he said.

But close might have been a mile or more away. Turning a
slow circle, I scanned the horizon. Somewhere a whale was singing, and would surface to breathe, but I saw no sign of it. "How
do they arrange their bodies when they're singing?"

"Most of the time they're head-downward," Roger explained
as he untangled the hydrophone wire. "But when they're at the
surface, breathing, they're horizontal, and they don't interrupt
the performance of the song to breathe. They pace themselves the
same way a human singer does, catching their breath between
phrases. A whale normally breathes at the same point in the song.
But sometimes one will breathe at an inappropriate moment—

catch a breath in the wrong place. When that happens they don't stop the performance, and so songs with and without breathing in inappropriate places will sound the same. I don't sing, for example, 'Glory, glory [breath, breath] hallelujah.' I manage to breathe while producing the song, so as not to interrupt it. Whales do the same thing, and to me that suggests their singing is a conscious performance. They're good singers who don't mess up a song with awkward breaths. When they reach the surface, they often make a surface ratchet sound, sort of like a slowly opening creaking door; and I suspect that most of the time they start singing right after the surface ratchet, when they throw their tail into the air—'peak their flukes,' as it's called—and make the first phrase as they dive. Sometimes singing can last for periods of several hours, or even for more than a day. Once, off Hawai'i, in a place where one seldom encounters whales, my former wife, Katharine, and I found a singer who was already singing when we began recording, and when we quit, deep into darkness eleven hours later, it was still going nonstop. Here, around Maui, where the whales are always interacting—getting into fights, chasing each other—a song rarely lasts for more than two hours, because another whale comes along and cuts it. A song stops when the singer is interrupted by another whale, a boat, a swimmer—any kind of stimulus that is curious or threatening and needs the singer's attention."

Roger was covered in bruises and Band-Aids. One fingertip was still shining from a patch of spilled Krazy Glue. As he recorded a song, he closed his eyes and his mouth fell open, as if he were asleep. A straw hat with an Hawaiian-print band kept the sun from his eyes. His unbuttoned shirt revealed a freckled chest; his legs were lightly freckled, too, and he was wearing maroon shorts. A pair of reading glasses dangled from a cord around his neck. A speedboat cruised by, playing loud rock music, its partying crew unaware of the concert in full swing below them. After it had passed, we moved to the windward side of Molokini, where its coral-covered wall drops six hundred feet.

I put on a snorkeling mask and fins and slipped over the side, into a school of fifty Moorish idols—a black-yellow-and-white fish with a small puckered mouth and a long spear trailing from the top of the head—and swam toward the wall, where brain coral ribboned like disembodied minds and parrotfish flashed blue-green spangles. Taking a gulp of air and diving a few feet, I heard the moaning of whales again, but this time louder and accompanied by gurglings and creaks. Then a trumpeting sound—half elephant, half monkey—surged into a two-stage grunt that started low and swung high, followed by a stuttering lawnmower that changed to a finger being dragged across a taut balloon, then a suite of basso groans and a badly oiled garden gate creaking open. Turning a slow circle, I looked for the singer, whose voice was everywhere, but saw only raccoon butterfly fish (bright yellow, with black masks) and a blooming garden of coral. I felt as if I'd fallen into the middle of a millifori paperweight. This singer, warbling with such panache, was most likely a male. I could not see him, but his eerie song sent shivers down my back and made my ribs gently chime as it filled the waves with waves of music. Linda Guinee, of Roger's lab, and Katharine Payne, now a researcher at Cornell, had recently discovered an astonishing new fact about humpbacks: They use *rhyme* to help them remember their long songs. Floating in what might be a whale's epic poem, I marveled at its strange embroidery. Each time I dove a few feet under the surface, I heard and felt the radiant booming again, and wished I could hold my breath for hours, stay down and listen with the whole ocean cupped to my ear like a single hand.

But at last, too tired to keep diving, I climbed into the boat, and we cruised back to Maui. Rainbows formed in the spray at either side of the Zodiac. The siren song followed us for some distance, then vanished among shore sound as we approached the marina. Thrilled to have felt the singing wash over me, I yearned to be near a whale in its own element, to watch its habits closely.

Though that would be difficult with the shy humpbacks wintering at Maui, would it be possible elsewhere?

Half of Roger's whale study revolved around humpbacks and their songs. Studying them in Hawai'i, hemmed in by the constant jangle of tourists, speedboats, and hotel chains, made relentless demands. The other half of his whale study took place on the coast of Patagonia—at an outpost far from noise and society. There, mother right whales raised their babies, eager males came courting, and it was possible to observe whale families going about their daily routine. When I said goodbye to Roger in Hawai'i, I knew that we would meet again—first at the Long-Term Research Institute, and then in one of the wildest and most remote places on Earth.

ON WATER

THOMAS FARBER

The rip pulled us toward the lava at the north end of
　　　　the beach
and we had to swim hard to stay there ...

We ducked the biggest waves that caught
us inside. A quick breath, then down to kick along the
sand toward the blue haze outside, the waves cracking,
　　　　pressure
from the white water hissing over us, a cold shadow. We
　　　　surfaced
on the other side, looked at each other and laughed,
surprised again to have made it into the sunlight and air.
　　　　　　　　　　　　　　　　　—Tino Ramirez

CALL me Queequeg. Out once more to surf at Tongg's, the
lineup perhaps two hundred and fifty yards offshore. Storm clouds
above the Koʻolaus and over past the cathedral-like mass of Diamond Head, rain beards—gray, grayer—dropping from the low
sky, and then suddenly a squall is on us, boards and riders blown
downwind, paddling hard into the chop and spray just to hold

position. A simultaneous abrupt absence of light: furrows, folds, flanks, buttresses, and crevices of Diamond Head obliterated, waves almost black. *Wai* and *kai*, fresh and salt water, rain and sea. Song of the water planet (Earth-the-misnomer). But then, faster than we can adjust to the change, the sun's reappeared, the water's jade green, and, saying he has to get home, Wendell paddles ewa toward Sans Souci beach.

Wendell. 'Local' Chinese, in his late fifties/early sixties. Former airline mechanic, grew up in Honolulu. The year before, Wendell arrived one morning—spontaneously generated as if summoned by the waves—out at Tongg's, riding high on his massive ten footer, paddling easily, surgical tubing around his waist as a leash. Unorthodox, but effective. No one else there that day, we sat bobbing on the swell, shafts of the boards erect before us, thick plume of smoke rising from the cane fields down on the Wai'anae peninsula. Watches and clocks irrelevant mechanisms of measure here, time organizing itself into sets and lulls, sets and lulls, Wendell speaking of the change in the color of the water since he was a kid, the loss of clarity/kelp/shellfish. We sat silent for a while, gently rising and falling, Diamond Head always again compelling our attention, like the landform obsessing Richard Dreyfuss in *Close Encounters*. Sometimes, clouds scudding behind the volcano's vast bulk as we lifted and dropped, sometimes it seemed we were the fixed point, Diamond Head that must be moving.

"WATER remains a chaos," Ivan Illich writes, "until a creative story interprets its seeming equivocation. . . . Most myths of creation have as one of their main tasks the conjuring of water. This conjuring always seems to be a division . . . the creator, by dividing the waters, makes space for creation." Illich also writes that "to keep one's bearing when exploring water, one must not lose sight of its dual nature." Deep and shallow, life-giving and murderous, etc., etc.

Reading water. "Water represents the unconscious," says the psychologist at the party. The surface the boundary between consciousness and unconsciousness. Water in this view thus a form of seductive regression, representing the purely instinctive. As Heraclitus cautioned, "It is fatal for the soul to dissolve in water."

For instance, naturalist Ann Zwinger, entering the "peaceful, cradling ocean," looking up from below at the surface, "a silken tent in the underwater wind, gray blue with moving ovals," is dazzled by the "interlocking lozenges of light," the "scintillating northern lights in an aqueous sky..."

Or consider the vision of author Joan Ocean, who, in seeking a name that conveyed "no male lineage," took on the first word that came to her. As she notes in *Dolphin Connection*, it "was easy to spell, easy for other people to remember, unusual ..." What's in a name? It was not until seven years later that she first experienced a "symbiotic love for the ocean.... I accepted completely my personal connection to it, and my responsibility to preserve and respect all of the vast life forms that resided within it." This epiphany came "by 'absorption,'" after she had for the first time been in the water with (captive) dolphins. Soon, Joan Ocean wanted to be a dolphin, which for her meant "to be weightless and buoyant," to "move within the changing currents of water, to feel the earth turn, to slide on the waves, and be surrounded by the varied and unique concerts of sea animals. To play in the sparkling shafts of sunlight and bubbles, to feel the pull of the moon and the stars ... to have seventy percent of the planet as your intimate and cozy home."

Ocean does not mention, however, that dolphins are predators—of squid, lantern fish, shrimp, etc.—and that they have their own predators, including the eighteen-inch "cookie cutter shark," which uses suction to extract large discs of dolphin flesh. More, deep-water dolphins school because it increases their capacity to protect themselves and/or to feed successfully. Lone Ranger dolphins, James Dean dolphins? Apparently not in the Pacific. Nonetheless, Joan Ocean has experienced "commingling with particles of the water," has come to believe that telepathic interspecies messages can be "conveyed on this air-water conduit."

Liquid eyes. For Claudel, "that unexplored pool of liquid light which God put in the depths of our being." And, by extension: "water is the gaze of the earth, its instrument for looking at time." Water perhaps also being the earth's instrument for looking at us. And/or, our instrument for us to look at ourselves. As Melville wrote, Narcissus could not grab hold of the "tormenting, mild image he saw in the fountain, plunged into it and was drowned. But that same image we ourselves see in all rivers and oceans. It is the image of the ungraspable phantom of life." Put another way, the story of Narcissus suggests that the images of the self we see in water are not only seductive, but lethal.

Reading water. Dylan Thomas' "carol-singing sea," for example. Or that sentient, conscious ocean in Stanislaw Lem's science fiction novel *Solaris,* which "lived, thought, and acted," capable, as Victoria Nelson observes, not only of reading the hearts of the scientists observing it but "able to manufacture and send back to them the incarnation of their deepest desire." One studies the ocean on the planet Solaris, then, only at enormous risk. And always, of course, there are the limits of perception: the ocean on Solaris, Lem seems to be saying, is beyond human ken, whatever the human yearning for "Contact." (Poet Robinson Jeffers, looking west from Carmel, for years studied "the hill of water" which is "half the/planet: this dome, this half-globe, this bulging/Eyeball of water" with "eyelids that/never close," what Jeffers termed "the staring unsleeping/Eye of the earth." And, he concluded, "what it watches is not our wars.")

Reading water: "teach us to see the sea wave by wave," Pablo Neruda writes. Not a bad aspiration, though Neruda himself is quick to figurative language: the ocean's "gifts and dooms," the "spent comet" of the wave's "scorn and desire." The need of the poet, like Lem's scientists, to make Contact. To name the qualities of even Earth's ocean, Lem seems to be arguing, thus reveals our hungers. Takes us to the limits of our capacities. And beyond.

TO TURN one's back on the land, to enter the proximate wilderness of the sea, sets coming in from forever. The familiar blast of mist as a wave drops down on a pocket of trapped air. Surf beating on, vaporizing over, the reef. And what's being left behind as one pushes off? Flickering TV light in the windows of the highrises along the shore at sunset, testimony to the human capacity—need—to rival and miniaturize the larger creation. NFL football, Oprah, Brokaw, Pavarotti. The community of modern man, but in Hawai'i there is a sadness on the land. The drumbeat of development, future shock, a pace of environmental change faster and more extensive than even *Homo sapiens* can absorb. Yet one more golf course/development/resort, home-grown legislators cashing out, cashing in. "Straddling the Tropic of Cancer amidst the trackless waters of the North Pacific," writes Patrick Kirch, "the Hawaiian chain is the most isolated archipelago in the world…. Once a colonizing plant or animal had managed to pass through 'the sieves of overseas transport' … it more likely than not found the environment free of competitors. A process of adaptive radiation and speciation followed." Thus the awesome impact of man's imported plants, animals, and farming: for instance, perhaps half the species of Hawaiian land birds became extinct during the 1,500-year Polynesian era before European contact. (Numbers: at present, 70 percent of nonmigrant native birds, 50 percent of native insects, and hundreds of species of native plants are extinct, 50 percent of the survivors are now candidates for the federal endangered species list. Some 75 percent of species extinctions recorded in the United States have occurred in Hawai'i; 25

percent of all U.S. rare and endangered plants and animals are in Hawai'i.)

Radiation, speciation. In 1916 a three-year-old elephant, Daisy, captured in what was then Rhodesia, made a 20,000-mile sea voyage to arrive at Honolulu. Though Daisy was a sensation at first, in time she became difficult to handle, was chained to trees for weeks at a time. By 1933, her keepers feared her, were reluctant to feed her or clean her area. When the public protested a plan to execute Daisy, her original keeper said he'd care for her without salary. Three days after he resumed work, however, Daisy picked him up with her trunk and gored him with her tusks. Police marksmen then shot and killed her.

Radiation, speciation: humans, those late arrivals, also an adaptive species. But native Hawaiians? Oh, to talk of them is perforce to acknowledge the past. "The death of a culture," argues Victoria Nelson, "like the death of a star, lasts longer than anyone can possibly imagine. The sadness, the echoes and ambiguities, persist for hundreds of years." According to David Stannard, the native Hawaiian population fell from more than five hundred thousand to forty thousand in the one hundred years after first contact with the west, "bodies eaten alive by the white man's venereal syphilis, consumed by the fires of his influenza, gored by his tuberculosis." Whites, for Stannard, thus the real cannibals of the Pacific. This karma, these ghosts. Such violation, human and environmental. *Extinction is forever*, says the sticker on the rent-a-car.

Radiation, speciation. Like a number of the migrants who now come to Hawaii, who fear a grim future for the islands, who feel they know how to parse the past, like them I arrive, depart, and arrive again on a Boeing 747, that leviathan of man's technology. The airplane meal is offered to me too, though I usually bring my own food. A pure spirit—I may be reading up on ecology during the in-flight film—I'm further blessed with *Homo sapiens'* peculiar gift, the capacity to exempt myself from what I most deplore.

*   *   *

> I once knew a writer who, after saying beautiful things about the sea, passed through a Pacific hurricane, and he became a changed man.
>
> —*Joshua Slocum,* Sailing Alone Around the World

Glassy, that state of grace: no wind, no noise, board shooting along, waves perfectly defined, absolutely themselves, their shape not affected by any other force, a realm of clarity and ease. Water thick as milk, as cream. As porridge.

A windless winter day, after a month of cold. Very heavy rain, each drop making a small crater on the ocean surface, but despite the cumulative impact of so many minute explosions the net effect is to calm the water, to eliminate all other normal movement or pattern—ripple, chip, groove, rill. In the torrential downpour, each successive incoming wave seems smooth, sheer, immaculate, pure as the formula of the textbook curve.

Poet Philip Larkin: "If I were called in/To construct a religion/I should make use of water." Not to think of believing in the Almighty or not believing in the Almighty one way or the other, but then to hear the words on one's lips after two hours in the surf: "Thank you, God." For what? Oh, for this pulsing, undulating, shimmering, sighing, breathing plasma of an ocean. For the miracle of warm water. For rideable waves and no wind.

Watching water. Clouds: God in Genesis separated "the waters from the waters"; clouds/vapor/rain are the water above the firmament. According to Louis Ginzberg, "On the second day of creation, the waters rebelled against this separation. . . . The waters destined to be up high refused to leave the embrace of the waters resting below, and they embraced each other more closely . . . weeping."

Clouds: water vapor in air condensing into minute drops because of falling temperature. Part of the miraculous yet daily cycle of evaporation and precipitation enabling the life of the planet, this process of heat absorption and release providing the requisite thermal stability. Extraordinary, the role of the sun in transmuting water, occasioning its metamorphosis, distilling it, ridding it of impurities, even converting salt to fresh water. Extraordinary, the role of the sun, but hardly obvious. As Christophe Girot explains, "Aristotle had a theory of a central fire that heated the waters of the ocean which rose and condensed inside vaults beneath the mountains. These immense reservoirs ... were thought to feed torrents and rivers." Not until the eighteenth century did the astronomer Halley hypothesize the atmospheric cycle of water. Now, as Girot points out, the cycle has become quantifiable, predictable, but the vocabulary of physics, meteorology, and hydrology describing our reading of water sometimes also obscures or even diminishes what is most miraculous. It is still true, as it was in the Middle Ages, that water "is the alchemical mediator between fire and earth." Sunset over the ocean, in any case: clouds giving would-be artists yet another course in perspective.

Watching water. Toward 10:00 P.M. Just-past-full moon behind over the Ko'olaus, rain clouds coming around the corner of Diamond Head in front of us as we sit on the seawall, palms swaying, surge breaking, waves black with white foam. Suddenly, an enormous lunar bow materializes—fluorescent green, almost phosphorescent. Makes itself known, comes into our ken, arching down from the rain clouds toward the horizon, slowly widening on the left to include red and orange tones.

Time stops, as if such beauty is in no hurry to move with more than serenity; one feels a strange calm, gratitude for the privilege of being a witness. And then the bow is gone, leaving an effort to retain what the eye saw, a yearning for what is already beyond telling.

WATER, according to photographer Guy Motil, is "opaque, transparent, reflective, or a combination of all these." As light enters water, various parts of the visible spectrum are affected differently. The longer red wave lengths are quickly filtered out—absorbed—in shallow water, converted into heat, shorter wavelengths absorbed only in deeper water (though even blue light, which penetrates most easily, reaches no more than 1,000 meters). Also, photographer David Doubilet writes, sunlight is transformed when it enters the sea; in the deep blue, other colors change. "Red becomes black, blue veins look green. Some yellows become mustardy, others stay bright." (A photographer's underwater flash, supposedly 'like' or 'containing' the values of sunlight, thus 'restoring' the surface spectrum, which of course doesn't exist here, thus allowing images on film that the human eye in water cannot see.) (Cannot see, that is, even from inside a mask, since the human eye, adapted for air, loses its focusing power in water.)

Consider, then, the depth of the vast lake of the Pacific off the Kona coast of the Big Island of Hawai'i. Deep water, bluer than longing. And, in the vast wind shadow of Mauna Loa (nearly 14,000 feet above sea level, running down to a base more than 12,000 feet below sea level), the surface startlingly calm, flat, silent. Below this liquid mirror, *aqua incognita*, a filled but empty space except for countless tiny diatoms, just-visible transparent microplanets. All quite unlike the teeming primal soup of the reef with its variety of colors/shapes/strategies/urgencies, what Ted Mooney called "the sea's blunt fecundity." In this deep blue, all alone, one as if inevitably begins to catalogue its qualities, to search for appropriate prepositions, verbs, nouns. All right, one is *in* it. *Surrounded* by it? *Engulfed* by it? Or, yes, it's *transparent*, but of course one's visibility is quite limited. Or, is this blue a *void?* Can something be nothing? Or, what's the *scale*, anyway. No help there: no referents in no matter what direction. But if not scale, what of *vector?* The diatoms, for example: *floating? dropping?*

(held) in suspension? All these questions unanswered as enormous broad shafts of light spiral . . . *up from down under,* as if somewhere down there a gala film opening is being celebrated. Remake of *Alice in Wonderland,* perhaps.

Back to the surface for air, up through the quicksilver interface, having overcome the quite palpable tug from below, and ... there's life. Dorsal fins approaching: as if to confuse things further, the play of dolphins, the endless circling wheel of their surfacing and diving. And here they are, more or less: squadrons, armadas, flotillas, echelons, convoys, holding just below in formation, in a display of skill, the Blue Angels of the deep blue. "Check this out," they seem to be saying, exhibitionists of this liquid Sahara. Forget the spinning, individual dolphins over and again surging up through the surface as if for a toke of gravity, try these group routines to make you *ooo* and *ahhh* like the skating of the Rockettes at Rockefeller Center. So you look: there they are, perhaps thirteen of them, one/four/two/four/two, front to back. But even as your eye sees this, the formation alters both depth and angle, though without visible movement, so that as the image is perceived it is already in jeopardy or is in fact lost. Another image taking its place at a different distance, or perhaps now the formation has also changed, is now one lead dolphin and a football-shaped cluster behind. Student body left. Even the MTV-trained eye now beginning to rebel against such transitions. At which point, click, a small pod is within touching distance, dolphins angling, right eyes staring, one's own eye now staring at the cookie-cutter shark bites, which seem enormous even as one reminds oneself: *water magnifies.* Further confusing the eye/mind dialogue. The dolphins then not suddenly but suddenly, that is, without apparent use of any force, both simultaneously alongside and heading away, spiraling down in one of those primary patterns, the formula governing growth of the chambered nautilus/proportions of the human body/patterns of leaf growth/efficiency of projectiles in air.

At which point, click/click, spiral dissolves, squadron again holding just below and ... *shitting*. Now what, you might ask, what's the message? Choose one:

    a. it is normal for dolphins to shit; they think nothing of it, nor should we;

    b. dolphins shit in front of others only rarely; this is a great honor; in fact, one should reciprocate;

    c. though twenty to forty feet below, the dolphins are shitting on one, so to speak.

(Dolphin feces may contain sexual pheromones or other chemical traces, which would explain why they seem at times to intentionally make passes through their school's field of excrement. Or: such passes may simply be some kind of a game, etc....)

Oops, now flukes are moving, dolphins having in a moment shifted planes, down and away into what is both transparent and invisible. *Gone*, by God. There only the moment before, but, from the very start of contact, threatening to move beyond one's capacity to apprehend them. Their very presence, constantly intimating the boundary of perception, having induced ongoing visual confusion—focus! focus!—as well as a form of despair at the nonstop effort to retain an image of them on the retina.

Alone in the endless blue, one searches for something to cling to. Data, for instance: what species were they? "No problem," comes the answer from the deep: "imagine, say, *Balinese* dolphins." Which is to suggest, not just play, but shadow play.

(As for the apparent difficulty of the human eye in taking in the immediate presence of dolphins, the unsettling sensation that the dolphins must be using their sonar to disrupt one's capacity to see or remember, this is no accident. According to Kenneth Norris, if a "dolphin is among enough others that look very much like it, if all face the same general direction and move in generally the same way," then the attack will fail. Part of this has to do with the incapacity of a vertebrate's eye to track more than six or eight objects at any given moment, part to do with the extraordinary coordination of the dolphin school, which can outmaneuver its attackers by group behavior even as it denies the predator any coherent point of reference.)

*   *   *

The corpses of men float face upward, those of women face down, as if nature wished to respect the modesty of dead women.

—*Pliny the Elder*

Drowning, the thing itself. Third leading cause of accidental death in the United States—5,400 in 1984, primarily children and young adults, four out of five of them males—and an estimated 50,000 near-drownings annually. Given hot tubs, boating, and the popularity of water sports, experts believe that half the population is at risk of drowning each year.

In a way, however, it's odd that we can drown at all; babies, Watson argues, "swim, naturally and easily, long before they ever learn to sit up or crawl" and "behave calmly, gazing around with wide open eyes, showing no sign of fear, paddling easily up to the surface whenever they need to breathe. They never ever try to do so with their heads underwater. It seems to be only later that we lose these instincts and become more prone to drowning. Which seems unnecessary, because as a species we are unique among land animals in that we have a 'dive reflex,' a marked reduction in heart rate and oxygen consumption, which takes over automatically as soon as water touches our faces. We all have rudimentary webs between our fingers and thumbs, and as many as 7 percent of human beings ... are still born with distinctively webbed feet." More, we eat vegetables that are nearly entirely water, and we ourselves are as waterlogged as fish, two thirds water—ten to fifteen gallons in most of us (human brains three quarters liquid, bones more than 20 percent liquid, the just-formed human fetus nearly entirely water). Also, it's true that we are hairless mammals, like dolphins and hippos—water creatures all. And that our bodies, like those of marine mammals, are insulated with subcutaneous fat, making us both buoyant and streamlined. And that, like dolphins, we can produce a variety of nasal sounds, perhaps a function of the breath control diving requires. (In Europe, various doctors, believing that newborns are aquatic creatures and that the transition from womb to world includes a powerful shock of gravity, have apparently been birthing babies in water tanks in hospitals. One, it seems, has also delivered babies in the Black Sea, with a nearby pod of dolphins to telepathically instill their intelligence in the babies.)

Nonetheless: you can drown in a tablespoon of water. Some people panic as they inhale that first quantity of water, which causes the larynx to go into violent spasm—laryngospasm—and though there's no water in the lungs, or very little, they asphyxiate, die because of the lack of oxygen. It happens to babies and to those who panic in the water. Such drowning is called "dry drowning," and occurs in something like 15 percent of all cases.

The second kind of drowning, including the actual aspiration of a quantity of water, is often more gradual, with fatigue over time as opposed to this initial panic. You are out in the ocean, for example. You get more water in your lungs. Humans take in oxygen, get rid of CO_2. If we can't, the acid in the body increases, and as it does you get sleepy. Just before you become unconscious, besides the burning feeling of suffocation, there may be delirium because the brain begins to swell. You may feel a wave of relief, a sense of return to the amniotic. ("I myself almost drowned," a doctor explains. "I felt, finally, that life is a struggle but that death would be easy. The ease of it was making me feel buoyant. When I saw a boat coming to save me, I felt dejected because I was being pulled back into the maelstrom that was life.")

Also, drownings in fresh and salt water are not the same. The body's chemical composition is very similar to that of salt water, so if your lungs fill up with salt water you can aspirate more of it than you can fresh water. But if you have salt water—i.e., blood—on one side of those square miles of membrane that are the lungs, and fresh water on the other, the effort to balance the electrolytes (potassium, sodium, chloride) deranges your blood very fast. Thus, when you die in salt water, you suffocate because oxygen can't get across the membranes. But fresh water changes the blood chemistry faster, and that is what kills you. There is still oxygen across the lungs, but you die because your membranes are letting salt leak out of the blood and into the water you swallowed. Your heart starts to fibrillate and then stops. Speaking of the spirit, a prisoner in Alexander Solzhenitsyn's novel *The First Circle* remarks that it is better to drown in the ocean than in the puddle. Given the physiology involved, it appears that the prisoner could have been speaking of the body as well. (Much of this medical knowledge has been gained from studies with laboratory animals: rats and dogs. Increasing man's knowledge of drowning through animal experimentation is not, it seems, for the weak of heart.)

IMPARADISED. Verb transitive—to put in or as in paradise ... to make supremely happy. A cold day, for Hawai'i, below 70, water temp 73, 74. An old woman shivers, tests the water. "This isn't paradise," she says. No. But not for want of trying. From the Hawaiian Tel. white pages: Paradise Finance/Paradise Implants/Paradise Laundromat/Paradise Termite and Pest Control/Paradise Towing/Paradise Used Furniture.

Life on, by, the water. History is, as they say, written by the victors, but it is also a Rorschach test: we read in it what we are able to see. By 1870, after a century of contact with Europeans, there were 50,000 native Hawaiians, down from a population that may have been more than 500,000. There was now also leprosy, which Hawaiians called ma'i pākē, Chinese disease. Transmitted by the imported Chinese laborers or not, leprosy as the Hawaiians well knew came from outside. Despite the developing science of bacteriology, no vaccine had been devised for the recently discovered *Bacillus leprae*. Many *haoles*, Gavan Daws explains, believed leprosy was associated with venereal disease or a form of it: Hawaiians were promiscuous, their leprosy thus "as much a judgment as a disease." (Of course, Captain Cook had brought syphilis with him to Hawai'i, knew it.) Though only one hundred whites contracted leprosy in Hawai'i in the nineteenth century, it seemed to some merchants to threaten the "total destruction of civilization, property values, and industry." At the personal level, this could mean terror. Sanford Ballard Dole's wife, Ana, "led a private life dominated by such a dread of leprosy that she would not go from room to room in her own house without covering the doorknob with a handkerchief." (Though an infectious disease, leprosy is in fact one of the least communicable.)

In 1865 the Hawai'i legislature began transporting the afflicted to the Kalaupapa settlement on Moloka'i, a remote peninsula ringed by high cliffs. Within fifteen years more than a thousand had been sent; in all, more than eight thousand. Many refused to work; there was robbery of the sick and dying. Thus, the cry emanating from Kalawao was "A'ole kānāwai ma kēia wahi"—"In this place there is no law." Though many whites believed that without segregation Hawai'i would become a "nation of lepers," native Hawaiians were not repelled by the afflicted, seemed in fact to consider segregation worse than the disease. More, Daws writes, "hundreds of healthy Hawaiians, faced with the exile of a friend or relative ... chose to go too, to help, to kōkua.... In the early days, there were as many kōkua as there were people with the disease." This though in the 1870s "never less often than two or three times a week, someone died." (Daws also writes that in the

early history of the settlement there was only a single white kōkua—
and of course Father Damien, the Catholic priest.) (Not only were
there very few suicides at Kalawao, but apparently some Hawaiians even sought to simulate the marks of the disease.)

Against this backdrop, there is the famous story of Koʻolau
the leper. In 1893, at Kalalau Valley on the island of Kauaʻi, the
cowboy Koʻolau shot and killed the haole sheriff, Stolz, who sought
to transport him to Molokaʻi. Koʻolau then also shot and killed
three of a party of eighty soldiers who came after him, and soon
after disappeared with his wife and child. It was only four years
later that Koʻolau's corpse was found. In 1906 his wife, Piilani,
published an account of the death of her husband and child. As
it turns out, they never left the Kalalau Valley, but remained in
hiding in what Piilani called "the gloom of the mountain forest,"
where "we were as wild things." After nearly two years their son
died of leprosy: "How can I tell of the grief that overcame the
parents, alone in the wilderness?" Piilani writes. Worse, she could
see her husband begin to fail. A year later, "in the middle of the
night when the Milky Way turns, the light in the house that was
Kalua-i-Koʻolau was extinguished.... There is a season for blus-
tery winds, there is a season for gentle breezes, there is a season for
the rains to drench and for the rays of the sun to swelter. There is
a season for everything, but there is, after all, only one season,
death." Auwē, auwē.

THE photographer underwater, seeking to deepen the mystery.
Fins, goggles, and a camera strapped to his wrist, often down five
to twenty feet underwater, in the path of a collapsing wave, reef
perilously close, or with a forty-five to fifty-foot humpback surfacing nearby, yet again at Makapuʻu in the clouds and fog of
aquatic turbulence or in the deep, still, blue-black of Kealakekua
Bay.

Twenty years of this, and it has been, as they say, a learning experience. "As a large outside wave approaches," he explains, "you dive under and feel the pull of it passing over you, and then as the wave breaks the spray blown off the top of the wave comes down like an instant of heavy rain." Or, "The key to survival in rough water is that there is tranquillity down below. Of course, this creates a problem, since inevitably you have to return to the surface." Photographing surfers, he says, is true reflex photography—"I just have to react and trust my reactions. Not only do the surfers move through my visible space in a matter of seconds, but that space itself is in constant flux, with a visibility of one hundred feet in one instant and three feet the next." And, "The waves are extremely steep at Half Point as they break over a shallow reef. I am about twenty feet toward the shore from a group of board surfers and body surfers. The coral reef is about five feet beneath me. A wave approaches and one of the boards shoots down the face, heading directly toward me. I take one exposure, then dive for safety, but the oncoming wave has sucked much of the water and the depth is now only two or three feet. Clinging to the reef, I feel the wake from the skeg [fin] of the board as it passes inches from my head. Wheeling around, I hit the shutter as the board skims across the face of the wave." And, of a school of āholehole sighted outside at Hanauma Bay in somewhat calmer water, he says: "It was like a wall of fish. At times it would encircle me. I'd swim through it and it would open up like a tunnel."

Searching to photograph dolphins and humpbacks ("The whale stuff has been difficult," he reports, laconically), his commitment has as usual been labor intensive, requiring him to swim great distances, to paddle a kayak for miles. "I was a little reluctant to use weight belts in a bottomless ocean," he reports, though of course he ends up doing so in an effort to get down deep quickly, to be able to photograph marine mammals at their level or even from below. "Dolphins move at human speed or even faster," he notes, "but whales move in what seems to be slow motion.

Even when they breach it seems that they are taking forever, rising simply on pure power."

The photographer searching the horizon for sign of a whale's blow, for days at a time finding nothing at all, distances between occurrences of life surprising, almost confusing. Scanning the waves over and again for some swirl that might suggest recent movement in the water, for bubbles that might indicate life below, for shadows just beneath surface, focusing and refocusing the eyes to discern what is no more substantial than a wisp of smoke, since "if something is visually persistent in the water it is usually human or dead." And, "If you're not looking within 45 degrees of where a whale or dolphin comes up you won't see it unless you hear it. You really have to be looking at one to see it. The result is that you really start seeing—imagining—things."

Yet of course all his water photographs are seeing as a form of imagining. "The large marine creatures," he says, "fill me with awe. In their presence I am transposed into a mythological realm, and they are the spirits or gods of this world." Feeling this even as he swims endless in search of them, paddles in search of them, waits for them in the broiling sun. Submerges in pursuit yet another time. This fusion of close observation of the physical world, a passionate specificity, and the heart moved to wonder.

Mastery, surrender. The photographer in the dangerous 'Alenuihāhā Channel, getting overwhelmed by the current. "I paddled hard," he says. "It seemed the first half hour I wasn't making any progress toward land. There was a little bit of doubt. I wouldn't say I panicked, but I felt fear." Or, on being in the water with whales: "There is something frightening about proximity to something that big, also the knowledge that you are in the presence of a superior being." Or, on the subject of sharks. Laconically, again: "I haven't seen any recently." And, finally: "Of course I realize how completely helpless I am out there. Each time I go out I am placing my life into the hands of something infinitely more powerful than I am. It is only by the grace of the sea that I return."

Portrait of the artist: late forties, 5 feet 8 inches/140 pounds, pure will at least where the ocean is concerned. (Only) one good eye, sleeps on a ... water bed. Wife and infant daughter, garden teeming with bananas, avocados, corn, radishes, peppers, pineapples, mosquitos. Dawn chorus of roosters just down the way, everything leafy and green, greener. A dazzlingly battered nearly antique Toyota station wagon being loaded yet one more time with water gear. Find the door that opens.... This being the artist at work off the Kona coast of the island of Hawai'i, a rural area where the forces of nature are inescapably imminent, land still being born through volcanic eruptions, ocean always reshaping, reclaiming, the land. Beneath and in the wind shadow of the huge, long, high wall of Mauna Loa, under the vast vault of the sky, in this boundless ocean, the photographer is the Loch Ness monster of his own photos, sea creature just beyond our field of vision. Diving down yet one more time as broad shafts of light radiate up from below, hair streaming behind as he disappears into the murk, streams of air bubbles trailing from his fins, the contrails of his energy. (To stay near him in the water, this recommendation: play the infant dolphin, stay close to what would be his dorsal fin, ride on the pressure waves created by his movement in the water. No worry, it will take only the occasional flip of your fluke.) Back at the surface, a breath before another passage through the liquid mirror, the photographer becomes one of the chimeras he follows, is transformed into the kind of mirage he stalks. See—imagine—him in his kayak in search of a whale, trying to locate that huge needle in that huger haystack, paddling into the sunset and so beyond our capacity to make him out any longer, paddling relentlessly toward the horizon until he is no more than a filament in one's eye, as hard to apprehend or to contain as any force of nature, the artist now at least as elusive as what he has for so long, so intensely, pursued.

*   *   *

"The ocean is closed."
        —*Sign at a Miami Beach hotel, noted by Lewis Lapham*

Wendell riding high on his ten-foot board that day off Diamond Head, the two of us gently rising and falling on the swell, lull in no hurry to end, Wendell speaking of the headline in the morning paper: a sewage plant down the coast had once again been dumping vast amounts of raw waste into the ocean. Sewage, nuclear wastes, drift nets, the plan to build new breakwaters and groins at Waikīkī and to pour tons of sand to "save" the beach. To kill the reefs, destroy the surf. "You know," Wendell observes as we sit there waiting for—being there for—the next set, "you know, there is just no end to man's greed."

Man's greed: "God gave Noah the rainbow sign, no more water but the fire next time." Well, maybe not. Maybe water once again. In the late 1960s, scientists came up with something called polywater, which possessed a very low freezing temperature and a very high boiling point. There was apparently some initial fear that polywater, in contact with natural water, might take it over until the earth became … completely unable to support life. This seems just the kind of thing that Kurt Vonnegut had in mind in *Cat's Cradle's* famous ice-nine, a different kind of ice, which could "teach" ordinary water to stack and lock in a new way, to reform, to structure itself to melt at, say, 130 degrees Fahrenheit. Such a water as this, of course, would mean the end of all life on Earth.

*   *   *

… in ancient times, you could sleep in the sea.
        —*Paul Eluard*

Ubi sunt? Surfer in the south swell in a power stance, driving left. An unmistakable stance, to anyone who has seen photos of the great surfers of the sixties, pictures of this man and others when they were eighteen/twenty/twenty-five. The good news is that this man is still in surfing shape. And the other news? Oh, that he is no longer the young man he once was, whatever wisdom he's achieved along the way. *Ou sont les vagues d'antan.* . . . In the morning paper, four weekend water deaths are reported, one of them a man on the Big Island who "*disappeared in the ocean.*"

Funeral of a surfer in Honolulu, canoes heading out off San Souci beach to strew his ashes on the waves. Story of one of the last Micronesian master navigators, who not long ago apparently took his small sailing craft out for one last voyage and failed to return. All this evoking Queequeg, who one gray morning told Ishmael "that while in Nantucket he had chanced to see certain little canoes of dark wood, like the rich warwood of his native isle; and upon enquiry he had learned that all whalemen who died in Nantucket were laid in those same dark canoes, and that the fancy of being so laid had much pleased him; for it was not unlike the custom of his own race, who, after embalming a dead warrior, stretched him out in his canoe, and so left him to be floated away to the starry archipelagoes; for not only do they believe that the stars are isles, but that far beyond all visible horizons, their own mild, uncontinented seas interflow with the blue heavens, and so form the white breakers of the milky way. He added, that he shuddered at the thought of being buried in his hammock, according to the usual sea custom, tossed like something vile to the death-devouring sharks. No: he desired a canoe like those of Nantucket, all the more congenial to him, being a whaleman, that like a whale-boat these coffin-canoes were without a keel; though that involved but uncertain steering, and much leeway adown the dim ages."

Once washed, Ivan Illich writes, the dead in traditional Indo-Germanic cultures journeyed until they waded or were ferried across a body of water which took away the memories of all who crossed. These memories were then carried to a well of remembrance named for Mnemosyne, mother of the Muses. Drinking from her waters, living mortals, coming back from a dream or vision, can recount what they have learned. "Philo says that by taking the place of a shadow the poet recollects the deeds which a dead man has forgotten. In this way the world of the living is constantly nourished by the flow from Mnemosyne's lap through which dream water ferries to the living those deeds that the shadows no longer need." (Solitary drinker in the bar drowning his sorrows: drowning in memories.) (Souse—to plunge into water or other liquid, to steep, to pickle. Slang: to intoxicate.)

In early 1991, a seventy-two-year-old retired electrical engineer died while surfing off Spanish Beach in northern California. "That's what he did," his widow said. "He surfed. He'd just go out there and wait for the waves. If he had a profession, I guess that was it."

What a way to go, no? Right on the face of the waters. ("In the beginning God created the heavens and the earth. The earth was without form and void, and darkness was upon the face of the deep; and the Spirit of God was moving over the face of the waters.") When *I* die, please, scatter my ashes on the face of the waters. *Warm* waters, too, as I head off. Let me cycle and recycle in the tropics forever and ever, lest the residue of my flesh and bone cry out—ashes that were my teeth now chattering, ashes that were my lips now turning blue—lest the residue that was me haunt the living by crying out from the briny deep for ... something like a wet suit against the dreadful chill, against the dreaded chill factor. No. Make it easy on all of us: let the waters be warm.

And don't mourn for me. I'll be in touch ... when it rains. When it pours!

CALL me Queequeg. One is not always at one's best. There have been times on land, particularly after too many days in our smog-filled post-modern urban centers, when the human capacity for affection and ingenuity has.seemed to fail to hold its own with the human capacity for ... well, you know. This may be a form of species-fatigue, a special hazard of *Homo sapiens* in maturity, the kind of thing that sends Gulliver, back at last in the land of the Yahoos, out to his stable for hours yearning for the horse-like Houyhnhnms, those creatures of true reason. In fact, when first restored to humankind, picked up by a ship, Gulliver is so repulsed that he plans to go overboard and swim for his life. Even years later Gulliver writes, "My Reconcilement to the Yahoo-kind in general might not be so difficult, if they would be content with those Vices and Follies only which Nature hath entitled them to. I am not in the least provoked at the sight of a Lawyer, a Pickpocket, a Colonel, a Fool, a Lord, a Gamester, a Politician, a Whore-monger, a Physician, an Evidence, a Suborner, an Attorney, a Traytor, or the like . . . But, when I behold a Lump of Deformity, and Diseases both in Body and Mind, smitten with Pride...."

In such a state of dismay, one may seek to return to what Melville called "the watery part of world." One thinks of Verne's brilliant and cultivated Captain Nemo, free in his submarine from the power of the despots who destroyed his country and family, free to avenge their loss, to be the benefactor of radical causes. Free, that is, until the maelstrom consumes him and his crew. It being true for all of us that there have been times in or on the ocean when all one feels is threat, the ocean not singing but snarling. Its message? That there is no point in trying to escape from its undertow, nothing to be gained in trying to be safe, in being too conscious. In being conscious at all. There is, for instance, no wit in the water. No respect for, say, the language of James Joyce. This is the ocean as Nature speaking, death the bottom line. (This is also the flip side of the ocean's siren song, the one that inveigled back into the deep brine reptiles and mammals who'd already safely made it onto shore. Various reptiles, nearly two hundred million years ago, and several waves of land mammals beginning some sixty million years ago.)

Imperfect creatures, creatures of aspiration, inadequately or too well evolved—though surely some kind of success story—nonetheless we are completely at home in neither environment ("When men come to like a sea-life," Samuel Johnson said, "they are not fit to live on land.") Leaving us, often, in turmoil, and yearning. As Melville's Ishmael says at the opening of *Moby Dick*, "Whenever I find myself growing grim about the mouth; whenever it is a damp, drizzly November in my soul; whenever I find myself involuntarily pausing before coffin warehouses, and bringing up the rear of every funeral I meet; and especially whenever my hypos get such an upper hand of me, that it requires a strong moral principle to prevent from deliberately stepping into the street, and methodically knocking people's hats off—then I account it high time to get to sea as soon as I can." Where, we remember, Ishmael was not entirely in his element.

"THE wind speaks the message of the sun to the sea," writes Drew Campion, "and the sea transmits it on through waves. The wave is the messenger, water the medium."

On the east side of the Big Island of Hawai'i, the rain endless, 400 inches a year, soft, quiet, calming. Falling, dropping. Just north of Hilo at Honoli'i Park in the afternoon humidity, mosquitos swarming, the surfers jump into the cold water of Honoli'i Stream—a river, really—and are carried out right to the break. Conservation of energy.

Surfers as centaurs, as matadors. Teenage girl springing to her feet up off the board: Minoan dancer vaulting the horns of a bull. The ideal of the great waterman, the master surfer who has no commercial ties, surfs for the thing itself, who does not search for the waves but is, rather, found by them. Syncopation of the surfer, against the beat of the wave. Surfing is carving, they say; surfing is shredding. Surfers and time, slowing the wave down, speeding it up. The recurring mystery of moving toward the approaching wave instead of fleeing from it. Then taking the drop, trying not to wipe out. Impact zone. Boneyard.

At Mākaha on Oʻahu, several older surfers on long boards sweep back and forth, elegantly, deliberately, like dinosaur herons or cranes from the Pleistocene, kids on short boards playing like porpoises, doing 360s as they hit the backwash from the shore-break off the steep beach, and then, unbelievably, not stopping but surfing the backwash out against the flow, weaving through the incoming human traffic. Such artistry eliciting more and more and more from the waves until, in from so unutterably far away, the waves finally *expire.* As they would have anyway, this exuberant grace a gain without sacrifice of anyone or anything, a rare—impossible?—interaction of humans and the environment. Beyond the laws of physics: nothing lost.

These children at play, singing the song of the sea. What Whitman called the "inbound urge" of the waves. Pulse of the planet. This light, this air.

One's life passes before one's eyes. That is, just how much of your life would you give to be in such a medium in such a way?

EPILOGUE: THE TREE ON ONE TREE HILL

W.S. MERWIN

IF YOU happen to be an expert in some distinct field of learning such as the order Physallidae or cuneiform script, no doubt there are sections of the British Museum that seem to be not just repositories but models of human knowledge, reflecting, proving, serving as emblems of its orderly and progressive nature. The institution originated, after all, in the middle of the eighteenth century and is still haunted by the spirit of that age—in Europe—of achievements at once grand and contained, a time marked there by a faith in symmetry and an adulation of Reason—a word that those generations used to describe their peculiar view of what they thought was everything.

But in straying from the familiar exhibits into the surrounding maze of corridors, even the expert may come to feel that the particular confined area that had seemed to be the mind itself, the orderly spot to which whole lifetimes of study have been dedicated, is little more than a makeshift arrangement in a corner of what any child can see is an attic of empire. While passing the sarcophagi and the glass cases, the sense of human knowledge may seem neither definite nor near at hand. In our time, in the greater part of the Museum, even the expert is as ignorant as the rest of us, and much of what has been so assiduously and ruthlessly acquired and compiled there in the name of knowledge remains, and is likely to remain, utterly unknown to almost everyone. The contents of Sir Hans Sloane's original gatherum for which the Old Montagu House was acquired, in 1753, to become the British Museum, were referred to as "curiosities." And where, precisely, as one wanders through the halls, is human knowledge now, that goal of curiosity? We do not even know whether the question is really characteristic of our lifetime or only seems to be because it occurs to us. The Museum conceived of as an extended memory has become just as certainly one of the mansions of oblivion.

For almost two centuries, much of what Sydney Parkinson managed to convey of what he knew, from having seen it at first hand, lay in the dark in the Museum, along with other relics of Captain James Cook's first circumnavigation of the earth on the bark *Endeavour*, between August 1768 and July 1771. There are certain things that a few of us know now only because Parkinson saw them and drew them, painted them, noted them down. They are among the things we know about Parkinson himself. But they are constant reminders also of the limits of what we can pretend to know about what we are seeing, and about what he saw and about the young man himself.

By now, at least, this is not so because of neglect. Scholars since the 1950s have been bringing attention to the artists and naturalists who sailed on Cook's voyages. The work of Averil Lysaght in particular helped to put together all that we are likely to find out, in a factual way, about Parkinson's life. In 1983, the Natural History section of the British Museum, in association with the University of Hawaii Press, published a volume, edited by D. J. Carr, which included essays on Parkinson, on the *Endeavour* voyage as a whole, the successive landfalls and what the

English found there, and reproductions of more than two hundred drawings and paintings by Parkinson, as well as some finished after his death by other artists working from his drawings and color notations. Two years later, Yale University Press published two sumptuous tomes edited by Rudiger Joppien and Bernard Smith, *The Art of Cook's Voyages*, which contained further discussion of Parkinson's life and work. Alecto Historical Editions is preparing a publication of line engravings made from Parkinson's drawings. A facsimile edition of his sketchbook is in production, and meticulous study of his work is continuing in England and Australia. We are able to catch glimpses now of what Sydney Parkinson saw for the first and last time.

We take it for granted that what we see becomes part of what we know even though we may not remember it. The effect of what we know on what we see is not so easy to distinguish, though it may be just as influential. Parkinson's paintings of birds, his earlier ones in particular, reveal as much about the prevalent contemporary conventions for looking at—or conceiving of—birds as they do about any living creature. Of course, most of his models were not alive at all. They had been shot, as a matter of course, and stuffed, or had their "skins" pickled in alcohol, to be washed out later, dried and propped up for their portraits. For us, come to that. Sometimes it was other portraits that were the models. In either case, any passerine bird was likely to be depicted clutching a chunk of branch, generally inconveniently thick for its grasp, and usually shaped like part of an S broken off somewhere, with a sprig and leaves sprouting as though startled from its upper end. The bird often looks as though it had been caught at the moment of trying to recover from paralyzing cramps, except that it is hard to imagine, from the picture, that those appendages could ever move at all. We can notice this even in one of Parkinson's paintings of a bird whose kin he must have seen often, alive, in England: a wheatear (*Oenanthe oenanthe*), which, perhaps from exhaustion, had made the mistake of alighting near human company, off the coast of Spain, on September 4, 1768. The nearside wing (the only one visible) is as stiff as a paper knife and appears to be clamped to the side of the bird, which is evidently just toppling forward from one branch of a generic blasted bush. There is no doubt that what has been set before us is less a bird than a convention that was solid enough to keep well and be brought out when the subject *bird* came up. It was something learned, and so in at least one sense known, and art historians can trace its scant variations from decorative friezes around the Mediterranean Basin, and heraldic symbols and designs on fabrics, through most of two millennia in the West. It was taught. It is possible to guess with some confidence where Parkinson had acquired his own artistic influences, including this one. And there is evidence of his passing the convention on to his thirteen-year-old pupil, Ann Lee, the year before he sailed with Cook. Both his original painting of a yellow bunting (*Emberiza citrinella*) and her copy have survived. The convention is obvious in them both: it is flat, static, and its virtues are primarily decorative. They do not so much reveal life, or a life, as provide something agreeably reminiscent of it, an acceptable abstraction. Something interposed, so that where the convention is the pervasive rule, to the person in whose culture it has become a habit, it is what the real thing looks like.

It looks dead. Whatever that is. Rigid, glazed, aware of nothing. Never to stir again. It suggests not life but ornament, usage for human pleasure, and not an original with its own flight and senses. But we look at the convention too, now, in the light of things that we have come to know, so we see something different from what was apparent to those for whom it may once have seemed, indeed, natural.

It is never entirely possible to separate what we are seeing from what we know or imagine we know. We look at Parkinson's paintings and drawings knowing things about the world and about him that Parkinson did not know when he made them, and we may think we see things in the work that were not visible to Parkinson.

What we think we see there may not be mere fancy. One does not have to know anything about the painter Carol Fabritius, a pupil of Rembrandt's, on entering the room in the Mauritshuis where his painting of a goldfinch on a perch in a plaster wall is hung, to be struck at once by a startling power in that single frame among so many. It flows into the room, dominating it like a musical chord reverberating from an unknown place, touching and commanding everything there. It would be best, in fact, to see that painting for the first time without knowing anything about the painter, so that there could be no doubt that it was simply what one was seeing there on the wall that was having that effect, unmixed with any suggestive knowledge that one might have brought to it. Having seen it then, that watchful imminence and radiant otherness in the form of a goldfinch, it will not be altogether surprising to learn that the painting (which bears a date in the painter's hand) was completed in the same year and within a few months of the date of the painter's sudden death, at thirty-two, in Delft. According to one version, he was killed when a powder magazine blew up, destroying also his studio and many of his paintings. According to another, he was walking home at night with friends, and the explosion killed them all as they passed the door of the magazine. However it happened, it occurred as a blast and a flash of light, and once one knows that, one is likely to think one sees it prefigured in the luminous presence that emanates from the painting. One may recall as well the role of the goldfinch in medieval Europe as a symbol of eternal life, and may feel that both forms of knowledge—the symbolic one that certainly figured in Fabritius's intellectual storeroom, and the premonitory one of which he would not have been consciously aware—must have been urgent in the painter's mind and found their way onto the canvas. It looks like a living bird there, perched on the bent rod fixed into the wall above the wooden feedbox, a fine chain keeping it from flying away. But it looks more intense than life, as life usually appears to us. That is how it looked to Fabritius just before it all disappeared.

It requires no indulgence in pathos to note that paintings and drawings are all showing us worlds that have vanished. That is something we know about them that we tend to forget because we want to, and besides, the illusion created by the image in front of us asks us to forget such knowledge for a moment and allow the image itself to be the present. We know, in more ways than may at first occur to us, how much of what Sydney Parkinson saw and drew and painted for us ceased almost at once to be there. His paintings and drawings are all of them testaments of youth, the work of a very young man. He was twenty-two or -three—we cannot be sure—when he sailed with Cook, and he did not live to complete the voyage, but died of malaria after the *Endeavour* left Java, and was buried at sea at the end of January 1771. Knowing that, there is a persistent temptation to foresee it in what he left, in the colors of the flowers he painted, the mouths of the fish, the opened seeds, the bent neck of a girl at work scraping bark, as though it must have been visible as he portrayed those things. At the very end, before the fever stopped him, he was drawing boats, the Malay sailing vessels that he had seen in the Sunda Straits and off the coast of Java. *Mayangs*, they were called. The drawings are faint, rather tentative sketches. Many of the boats have large brushes of tassels or radiating discs of fiber at the ends of the booms or fixed in the rigging: spirit antennae, talismans that had been bought from sorcerers for safety and good fortune on the unpredictable way. He was also drawing another kind of sailing vessel, one that he had not set eyes on but had only heard about and imagined. That was the so-called flying proa, of whose speed Western sailors had spoken again and again with amazement. Magellan's chronicler, Pigafetta, in 1521, had been only the first to tell of the proas, and for over two hundred years explorers had marvelled at them. On Spanish maps, the islands where they were built were named "Islas de Las Velas"—Islands of the Sails. No doubt Parkinson, having read the accounts, was hoping to see those flying proas. But by the time he was born, the boat builders had been all but exterminated by Europeans, by the Spaniards in particular. Their islands—the Marianas—and what few proas may still have been sailing, lay far from the course of the *Endeavour*, and Parkinson's drawings of their sails and shapes are late guesses at something he would never see.

His own survival among us, though, rests upon his portraits of what he was seeing for the first time and knew he might not, and probably would not, see again. It is the condition of art to see things that way. And his youth and relative lack of sophistication meant that even if he had stayed home, he might have wakened day after day to things that he realized he had never seen before. He was living, besides, at a time when a growing number of people in Europe were becoming aware that the world teemed with things that they had not yet beheld. Parkinson's brief lifetime, and the first two years of the *Endeavour* voyage in particular, were a moment when the sense of that unseen world suddenly became much clearer and more suggestive. When the *Endeavour* sailed from Plymouth, European botanists supposed the flora of the earth to consist, "by fairly safe calculation," Linnaeus said, of something less than ten thousand species. The Linnaean system for cataloguing these was a bright new instrument that filled the natural scientists with hopes of giving every living thing its true name and place in the scheme of things at last. By the time the *Endeavour* had spent a few days anchored off Rio de Janeiro, Parkinson could not keep up with the new material set before him to paint, and the naturalists of the expedition, Daniel Solander (a favorite pupil of Linnaeus and an assistant at the British Museum) and the

Finn Hans Sporing, were stretching the system to include biological manifestations that were wholly new to them.

Expeditions long before the *Endeavour* had taken artists with them to bring back records from life. Wilfred Blunt, in one of the essays in D. H. Carr's Parkinson volume, mentions the artistic accounts of Thutmose III's campaign in Syria, in the fifteenth century B.C., and what he describes as "the first known florilegium," which was carved in limestone at Karnak. Later travelers and explorers arranged to be accompanied by artists, or regretted the lack of them, in their own verbal chronicles. But on the *Endeavour* expedition "no people," John Ellis wrote to Linnaeus, "ever went to sea better fitted out for the purpose of Natural History." The complement of naturalists and artists sailing on board was largely due to the interests, originality, and wealth of Joseph— later Sir Joseph—Banks, who was himself just twenty-five at the time of the sailing.

For anyone following the hatching of curiosity in eighteenth-century England, or indeed Europe, Banks is an interesting phenomenon. He was a member of the landed gentry, with enough money to do anything he pleased, and his wealth, in the course of his lifetime, continued to increase. "I have a sufficiency," he wrote in Tahiti, as he proceeded, against Cook's wishes, to add a young Tahitian, Tupaia (who also died on the voyage), to those sailing on the crowded *Endeavour*, "and I do not know why I may not keep him as a curiosity, as well as some of my neighbors do lions and tygers at a larger expense than he would probably put me to."

Banks was driven by curiosity—it became inseparable from his ambition. As a child, he had been intrigued by Gerard's *Herbal* and had collected bugs and butterflies and shells with an uncommon ardor that led him into a growing fascination with the natural world as a whole, or at least the study of it. He went to Harrow and Eton, where the acquisition of the classical European languages was expected of everyone, but his overriding passion continued to be the Natural Sciences, and above all botany. When he went on to Oxford and found no one there to teach him the subject, he simply went to Cambridge, hired a professor of botany and brought him back. The Latin authors never became his familiar ground, and according to the criteria of the time, he remained a semiliterate man. His own idol was Linnaeus.

When Banks was eighteen, his father died, and he came into an estate that made him completely independent. According to portraits and contemporary accounts, he was good-looking, and everyone agreed that he was charming. He was full of energy, enthusiasm, a passion to know the things he was interested in and those who were engaged in the study of them. He bought a house in London, and instead of traveling on the continent to see the ruins of antiquity, he sailed to Newfoundland to collect insects and botanical specimens. He was still in his early twenties when he was admitted to the Royal Society, and it was the Royal Society that proposed to the Admiralty that he, "together with his suite, being seven persons more, that is, eight persons in all, together with their baggage, be received on board of the ship, under the command of Captain Cook." The "persons" (there were more than seven in the suite before the *Endeavour* sailed) included two young servants from Lincolnshire, probably from Banks's estates, two Negro servants, as well as the naturalists, a draftsman named Alexander Buchan and, of course, Sydney Parkinson. There were also Banks's two greyhounds, which may have been considered part of the caravan of baggage.

Parkinson had been introduced to Banks the year before by James Lee, a botanist with a vineyard nursery garden at Hammersmith. It is not hard to imagine something of the meeting—its contrast of characters, at least. Lee, a sober, industrious, Scottish businessman, a Quaker, at once reserved and deferential, in conversation with the lively, talkative, self-assured young Oxonian, heir to large estates in Lincolnshire. And Parkinson—we know his face had been marked with smallpox, and we have one, and only one, portrait that is known to be of him (another, said to be a self-portrait, in oils, is oddly amorphous). The one portrait was included as the frontispiece in the posthumous edition of Parkinson's *Journal*, published by his elder brother, Stanfield. It shows a very thin, long-faced, earnest young man, wrapped tightly in the clothes of the time, and sitting up stiff and straight at a plain table, holding in his right hand a piece of paper, and gazing beyond it at the grave nature of things. Some plant—perhaps a fern, since the drawing must have been made in Scotland—dug from its life is lying at the edge of the table, as though it were the subject of a drawing in his hand. We have the impression of someone intensely serious, self-effacing, unflagging and yet fragile. Not one for many words, no doubt, nor for idle amusement, but obviously reliable and probably likeable, or at least no trouble to get along with. Banks might not have been surprised to learn that he, too, was a Scot and a Quaker.

It may seem incongruous to us that the Quaker Lee ran a well-known vineyard nursery, but Sydney's father, Joel, embraced a similar combination: he was a Quaker and a brewer. The eighteenth century had not yet been afflicted with Victorian logic. Sydney grew up in or near Edinburgh. We know that he was still very young when his father died, that he was apprenticed to a woollen draper, "but taking a particular delight in drawing flowers, fruit, and other objects of natural history," his brother Stanfield tells us, "he became soon so proficient in that style of painting, as to attract the notice of the most celebrated botanists and connoisseurs of that study." There is a good deal of foreshortening in this account, obviously, and we have no real details of the early manifestations of Sydney's passion for drawing the forms of the natural world, but it seems likely that his family was eager to nurture his talent and encouraged it, sending him to study with the French painter William De La Cour, who opened in 1760, in

Edinburgh, the first public art school in Great Britain. One can imagine that the opening of such a school in Edinburgh might have appealed to serious, modest, middle-class families with some aspiration and a Scottish regard for education, and that they might have been rather proud to have Sydney enrolled there. Then, when he was nearly twenty, his mother moved with the boys to London. The Friendly Society must indeed have befriended the widowed Mrs. Parkinson and helped to keep the family's means of livelihood from melting away in the years after the death of Sydney's father, and they may have helped to make it possible for Sydney and his brother to acquire as much education as they did. Then, when the Parkinsons moved to London, a selection of Sydney's flower drawings was exhibited at The Friendly Society's house there, in 1765 and 1766. Mrs. Parkinson may have already known her fellow Scot and Quaker, James Lee, before moving to London. Lee soon engaged Sydney to tutor his gifted thirteen-year-old daughter, Ann, in painting and drawing.

Banks was sufficiently impressed, by Lee's recommendations and by the young man's paintings, to employ him to do paintings of some of the zoological specimens that he had collected the year before on his expedition to Newfoundland and Labrador, and copies of paintings of tropical birds and mammals that had been made originally for the former governor of Ceylon. Clearly he was pleased with the results and with what he saw of Sydney, for he went on to enlist him among his "gentlemen" for the *Endeavour* voyage.

A good deal of what Sydney had done for Banks by then might be described as painting from death: stuffed animals and birds, skins and copies. There had been little incentive to go beyond accepted convention. It is not that there were no conceptions of paintings besides those that Sydney had grown up with, but we know little of what he had actually seen when he sailed with Cook. He owned a copy of Hogarth's *Analysis of Beauty*. But

painting the natural world from life, to evoke its life—such work
as Dürer's, for instance—would he have been aware of it at all?
With remarkable exceptions, it was in botanical illustration that
representation of the natural world, in Europe, had come closest
to a portrayal of it as a living presence, and many painters probably unknown to Parkinson had been important in developing that
tradition. Dürer, it is true, had put before us flowers and leaves
and plants growing in their lives, and indeed in their social lives,
whereas botanical illustration for the most part had set forth the
individual plant in isolation from its surroundings, its kin, and
even from much of the rest of its body: abstracted, projected, held
up as a type, in company with the dissected organs that make it
typical. It, too, like the portraits of stuffed animals, often presents
us with a view of life in the form of death, of life, in a sense, after
death. But the botanical subjects were likely to be closer to their
lives than were the dried or pickled skins brought back from another continent a year before. There was an urgency in the botanical portrayal of flowering stems and fruit cut off or dug up and
brought to the artist's table, a need to try to reproduce the textures of surfaces before they grew dim, the colors before they faded, the grace of leaves and stems and petals before they wilted. For
when the painting was done, the subject would finally be lifeless,
and there would be only the portrait in its place. For Parkinson,
the months on the *Endeavour*—the rest of his life—would be filled
with this kind of urgency. It would overwhelm him as the voyage
lengthened, and he would not be able to keep up with the growing rush of subjects set before him day after day in the Great
Cabin, where the naturalists and Sydney's fellow artists convened
to work and confer every morning at eight, stayed at it until two,
then returned to it from dinner until twilight. After that, according to one of these colleagues, Sydney "frequently sat up all night
drawing for himself or writing in his journal."

In fact, there was more than one journal in which he wrote.

After Parkinson's death, his employer, Banks, simply appropriated his effects until the end of the voyage. And thereafter, an unknown number of Parkinson's papers, including notes, drawings of people, landscapes, trees and plants, and a very full personal journal, known and admired by his fellow "gentlemen" on the voyage, remained in Banks's keeping and were never seen again. A bitter quarrel arose between Banks and Sydney's surviving elder brother, Stanfield, over Sydney's effects, a dispute that does small credit to Banks. But he did hand over some of Sydney's "working papers," which Stanfield, against the combined efforts of Banks and Hawkesworth, the official historian of the voyage, proceeded to assemble and publish with his own preface and the portrait of Sydney, looking frail and somber. That is what is known as "Parkinson's Journal" and, apart from a few stiff letters and some notes written on paintings and drawings, it is virtually all that remains to us of Sydney's sleepless efforts to put into words the new things he was seeing. We cannot even be certain whether particular comments in the published "Journal" are Sydney's own or were inserted by his brother or by Kenrick, the professional editor when the material was published. But there was some quality in the account that led the reviewer in *The Gentlemen's Magazine*, in January 1785, to greet the publication of the "Journal" with warm praise, remarking that it represented "a superiority over those contemporary voyagers" who had "departed from the simplicity of Nature." Some of Sydney's notes on light and color, written on drawings as the *Endeavour* sailed among the islands of the South Pacific, indicate how acute and subtle his attention to the visible world had become even while the conventions of "composing" landscape remained with him, and how eager he was to seize what he saw as it slipped past and dissolved before him. They give a hint of what we have lost in his more personal journal, the observations that have not reached us after all.

But the impulse behind his fuller journal was also awake in

his drawings and paintings, and though some of them, too, have disappeared, many have survived—very many indeed, in view of the circumstances in which they were produced and the time that has passed since then. Between the *Endeavour*'s sailing from Plymouth in late August 1768 and Sydney's death between Java and Africa two and a half years later, he produced almost a thousand botanical drawings, nearly three hundred of them finished as paintings, and almost three hundred more drawings and paintings of birds, fish, other animals, and insects, besides roughly a hundred drawings of people, landscapes, and boats—most of these last, in particular, drawn literally from life. And there was an undetermined number of drawings that would be finished, painted, or copied by others, and in some cases, ascribed to others altogether.

From the sheer volume of his work, it is clear that he must have been engrossed in an all but constant effort of attention, an attempt to portray forms of the living world that until then had been unknown to him. And he was trying to represent the lives from which most of his subjects had just been deprived. The colors would very soon dim, and in a matter of hours would be gone. The textures would follow, and the shapes. He must have made fervent demands upon his talents and his skill and whatever he knew about painting. He developed an ability to draw very rapidly what was put in front of him, and yet few of his drawings—and virtually none of his botanical illustrations—give the appearance of haste. When he was in too great a hurry, he left the drawings unfinished, supplying the essential shapes and details, painting in crucial areas of color, indicating the rest in careful notes.

He worked in circumstances, furthermore, that required the closest possible concentration on the evanescent objects before him. Most of his work was done at sea in the Great Cabin, with the other "gentlemen" and, no doubt, officers of the *Endeavour* present at the same table, often in bad weather, with the bark pitching and rolling ("seldom was there a storm," Banks wrote,

"strong enough to break up our normal study time"); in the midst
of almost continuous motion, he was portraying an illusory still-
ness. When they lay at anchor and he took his easel, pencils, and
brushes ashore, the conditions were not necessarily much better.
In Tahiti, the flies were so thick that they "ate the colours off the
paper as fast as they [could] be laid on," Banks recorded, and even
when Sydney's chair and table were set up under a kind of mos-
quito net, a fly trap had to be put inside it "to attract the vermin
from eating the colours."

We know from his figure paintings, his depiction of groups
in canoes or on land, that his attention to what he was seeing, and
his feeling for it, was growing more direct and intimate in the
course of the voyage. Wilfred Blunt finds some of the work "mechanical," but to an amateur's eye, the drawings of native peoples,
from this distance, are fresh and poignant glimpses of an irretriev-
able world, and many of the botanical paintings, including some
that were never finished, have a luminous sharpness, an arresting
depth, a kind of personal authenticity independent of their scientific accuracy. We know from his writings that Parkinson sympa-
thized with the native peoples they met, that he regretted
profoundly the violence that the uninvited Europeans insisted they
"had to" visit upon their hosts in order to establish the "peace"
and circumstances that would allow them to go about their own
purposes. He was interested in the languages encountered on the
voyage, compiled work lists and made intelligent deductions about
the relationships between the various tongues.

All, needless to say, from the point of view of someone outside, and from outside, coming to the subject and its world from a
great distance. At Tolaga Bay in Aotearoa (which Europeans would
call New Zealand), he wrote, "the country about the bay is agree-
able beyond description," and then, revealing the European, the
appropriative itch to tamper, added "and with proper cultivation
might be rendered a kind of second Paradise." He saw it perforce,

at least consciously, from the viewpoint of an eighteenth-century Englishman, a *ratere*, as the Tahitians said: a stranger. One extreme of the alien approach to all this otherness was put quite succinctly by J. R. Foster, a Prussian botanist, apparently a very disagreeable man and an inferior artist, who sailed on Cook's second voyage. "We were to make it," he wrote, "the object of our special care and attention that ... nothing would remain unexplored on those shores, and that their natural history should be imparted to the learned world so described and illustrated that no one in future would have any desire to go back again to those regions and examine anything afresh." It was, in effect, an ambition to obliterate whatever was different by recording it, and the South Pacific, when Foster saw it, filled him with a mixture of covetous excitement and a despair at the wealth of the unknown: "everywhere ... such treasure houses of Nature were laid before my eyes. I therefore saw that all regions to which we were to go would abound in the same riches." Foster was perhaps more candid than he realized about the Europeans' attitude toward the world they had not known to claim. But they would return. The real objective of the *Endeavour* voyage included sounding out possibilities for colonization, and discovering another great southern continent (Australia was not big enough to count), but the expedition's purpose was generally given out to be astronomical study, a project to observe the Transit of Venus from the antipodes in order to determine the earth's distance from the sun. And for their astronomical proceedings, the British built a fort on Tahiti and named it Fort Venus.

(It is worth noting, in that regard, that the fort supposedly was built, at least in part, to protect the foreigners' instruments and other possessions from the natives, whom the English had found to be deficient in respect for ownership of property. A revealing objection, considering that, in the attitude underlying the voyage, in the show of force with which the Europeans landed, in their building forts on land not theirs, claiming territories used by others and in most of their writing about their acquisitive ventures for at least two centuries afterward, the Europeans showed so little respect for the indigenous inhabitants' rights to their very homelands.)

Of course the British were not the first to bring the greed and diseases of Europe to the islands of the South Pacific. The English, preoccupied for almost two hundred years with the investment and reduction of North America, were relative newcomers to this other, vaster region. The Portuguese, the Spaniards, and the Dutch had been to many parts of the area long before the British showed up, and in some places, whole European imperial structures had been established and superseded before the British came. It should have been easy for representatives of other European powers to guess the true purpose of the *Endeavour* voyage, but Cook was at pains to see that they found no evidence of it nor of where the vessel had been, when he did eventually put in at the Dutch port of Batavia, on Java.

As it happened, the astronomical instruments on the *Endeavour*, and the timing of the voyage, were important for making imperial claims among the islands of the South Pacific. Other European nations may have known their way around parts of that ocean and laid waste whole cultures and archipelagos, but it was only in the latter eighteenth century that navigational instruments became precise enough to allow accurate maps indicating beyond further doubt the location of small islands among those distances, placing them in a grid at last, bringing them into the net.

The Linnaean system for classifying and naming the natural world was an analogous development, a product of the same urge and the same moment—the moment that Sydney Parkinson was painting. He was observing another Transit, in fact, except that the light that disappeared behind the new system of knowledge would not emerge again. The world that the Europeans "discov-

ered" began to vanish as they set eyes on it, and to decompose at
their touch. Their words for what they wanted from it, even as
observers, are telling: they must "seize it," "capture it" once and
for all, to "take home"— for home was somewhere else, somewhere already known and intrinsically different.

There had been a number of attempts by Europeans to describe the life surrounding and permitting human life on some of
the islands of the South Pacific before Cook and Banks and their
naturalists came to see it. In some ways, the most remarkable of
those precursors was the German-born Georg Everard Rump
(1628–1702), who came to be known as Rumphius, a resident of
Java and then of the island of Ambon from the time he was twenty-eight until his death.

But Rumphius had found words for the world around him
in a manner that would have seemed obsolete, cumbersome, and
exasperating to the later naturalists on the *Endeavour*, and to others of their generation eagerly following the great pioneer of rational, scientific classification, Carl Linnaeus. Rumphius had had an
ordinary middle-class German seventeenth-century education, evidently, which would have included the Roman naturalist Pliny,
and Aristotle, whose procedure of definition and whose view of
the structured relations of life as whole would in time become the
basis of Linnaeus's system. And Rumphius, in compiling the
seven-hundred-odd illustrated chapters of his *Herbal* of Ambon,
in twelve books, and his further thesaurus of shells, stones, sea
creatures, minerals, and other "curiosities," wrote originally in
Latin, and provided names in that language, as other European
naturalists and botanists had done since the days of Rome. It was
by then, for Europeans, the language of "everywhere" and so the
tongue of nowhere. It was an articulate abstraction, a dead grammar. Some of the Latin names Rumphius ascribed to flora were
known and used by the naturalists on the *Endeavour*, and some
are still in use, "grandfathered" in before the present system. But

Rumphius was writing and often drawing from life in a sense that was eclipsed in the century that followed him—at least in anything that pretended to be scientific illustration. He described plants and animals in their lives and as they appeared in the human consciousness of which they had become a part. It was an approach that would return to use in the nineteenth century, just as it was beginning to be apparent that life as a whole had become threatened by the human species. And after finishing the first (lost) draft of his *Herbal* in Latin, Rumphius rewrote the entire work in the Dutch that had become his vernacular, and his words convey a sense that he is not standing outside the world he is portraying but is an intimately and endlessly concerned part of it, as it in turn is a part of the ceaselessly attentive motion of his own mind.

"The front of these Wanderers," he writes of hermit crabs, "is shaped like a little Crab, while hindermost they look like a whelk, and they live in the houses of strangers, which is why their origin is uncertain and, likewise, their shape.... One of the claws, usually the right one, is always larger than their entire body [and] has been shaped by its house in such a way that it can close the selfsame door with it as if with a shield.... These little quarrelsome creatures have caused me much grief, because when I laid out all kinds of handsome whelks to bleach, even on a high bank, they knew how to climb up there at night, and carried the beautiful shells with them, leaving me their old coats to peep at." (E. M. Beekman trans.)

This was not the kind of exactness nor indeed the kind of concern that Linnaeus, his disciples, or most of the world they heralded were interested in. There is surely no need to magnify the name of Linnaeus and his system and what they have accomplished. He and his method evolved from a craving of his species to possess a sense of the order of life, to occupy a commanding position in a pattern of existence that they alone understood, and therefore they alone, in the long run, would control. It is no essential detraction from the originality and genius of Linnaeus to suggest that the basic wants of his own kind demanded a system such as the one he provided, and that if he had not developed it, no doubt someone else would have done so. And it is as well to notice that the system is not identical with the lives it codifies, though it ascribes names to them and says where they belong in its scheme of things. It is itself an illusion, and the perfection it aspires and pretends to is bound to life primarily through its source in the unsatisfied nature, the innate imperfection of human desire, ambition, and anxiety. Out of that comes its goal and its procedure, which are the same: the deduction of structure and the labor of separation. Of role from role, species from species, life from life. And abstracted from these abstractions, the isolated human species with its relative knowledge remains the mirror of the unknown.

Within the system of classification and naming that Linnaeus evolved, the first word of the Latin name indicates the genus, the second the species, and the third, if any, the variety. The species name in some cases indicates the place where a specimen was found, the place that was believed to be its origin, but what mattered more was its place within the biological hierarchy of the system, and often one or both names commemorated naturalists associated with describing the species, or patrons of the enterprise, far removed from the unchristened lives to which the names were attached. To Linnaeus's immediate heirs, his system must have been without question a part of the pursuit of truth itself, and certainly it is possible to view it as a necessity. But such a view, such a pursuit, indeed, tends sometimes to assume that a perfect and accessible truth can exist in separation from life itself, which is never finished, never in that sense perfect, but arises continuously out of the unknown. Of course, those who are utterly dedicated to such a pursuit can be impatient with a portrayal of life such as Rumphius was attempting, in which the observer is not an abstracted manipulator of a process, but a wondering presence whose wholeness is the completeness of existence. They may find it useless and therefore inconsiderable, an embarrassment that they may call romantic.

Still, the difference is relative. Rumphius inevitably had observed from his own distance. Though Ambon became his home as the Pacific never was home to Cook's naturalists, and though he must have conducted much of his life in the tongues of the islands, he described the life around him in the languages of Europe, and he approached it with a mind formed on the other side of the Earth. Which meant that he wrote first of all, and as a matter of course, for the minds of Europeans. He translated what he saw into European terms, insofar as that was possible. He would have been doing something of the kind, though, in any language, since that is the way language works: on the one hand to evoke and identify, and on the other to be about something else, to stand in its stead, to take its place and so to interfere. It is a kind of knowledge that at once informs seeing and impairs it. It exists because of a knowledge of separation, and in partially healing the separation, it confirms it, perpetuates it, proves it. It is at once a power and an indication of helplessness, incompleteness, necessity. But between Rumphius and the disciples of Linnaeus and what they represented, as between the artisans of the Renaissance and the producers of the Industrial Revolution, in which the Linnaean outlook would come to be taken for granted, there was a leap, however one may describe it, after which there would, of course, be no going back. The Linnaean system was one of its manifestations, and one way that Sydney Parkinson would have seen it working itself out was in the heated preoccupation with new names.

For it was only the names that were new and not the subjects, which had been there for a long time before there were Europeans to "discover" them. Yet again and again, the novelty of the names was and still is ascribed to the subjects themselves, and

so we speak of "new species," meaning forms of life that are our
elders but that have only recently entered our awareness. For the
purposes of immeasurable memory, the act of naming has always
been deeply important, though for a long time there have been
some who have noticed that a name at once indicates and obscures its object. But naming is a part of language, of the ceaseless,
inevitable ambivalences involved in conversing with the world and
about it. Day after day, and evening after evening, as Sydney sat
drawing, the Great Cabin of the *Endeavour* must have been filled
with a revolving discussion of names, Latin syllables that would
identify each example that he was portraying and would place it
in a hypothetical scheme of existence, without its life. Sydney,
sketching and painting the specimens they were talking about,
must have heard the names eddying around him, but from what
we know of the voyage and of his temperament, it seems unlikely
that he said much. After all, he was not a naturalist himself. And
the cabin contained, more or less intact, a small section of the
behavior of the species *Homo sapiens* var. *Brittanicus* of that period, a hologram of the class structure of England. Banks represented the gentry. Cook was the commander of the expedition, but
was Banks's social inferior, and their complicated relationship had
been harmoniously established at the start of the voyage. Parkinson was Banks's employee, and though he was one of the "gentlemen," was socially a nobody. This unquestioned order of things
extended to the assumed relations of Europeans to the native residents of the places they visited, and no doubt it seemed as immu-
table and inevitable as the movements of the heavenly bodies that
they were recording.

By the time of the *Endeavour* voyage, the Linnaean enterprise of naming the species of the natural world as each was found
had become as feverish as the communications of the time allowed, and the process continues today with scarcely abated intensity. Most of the drawings and paintings reproduced in Carr's

volume on Parkinson are accompanied by a succession of botanical names that have been ascribed to the species since the late
eighteenth century, and a brief history of the ascriptions. The
principal participants in discussions of nomenclature in the Great
Cabin would undoubtedly have been Linnaeus's favorite pupil,
Daniel Solander, Banks himself, the impassioned amateur, and
his secretary, the Finn Hans Sporing, with the ultimate authority
resting with Solander. And in view of the volume and unfamiliar-
ity of the material that was set before him, Solander seems to have
done remarkably well. The names that he arrived at reveal again
and again that he knew what he was looking at, what classification
was appropriate to it in the Linnaean system, what its nearest of
kin were. Some of the names he ascribed to species are still current, and perhaps more would be if the full results of his labors
had been published soon after the *Endeavour* returned to England.

It was not, after all, mere coincidence that Solander and the
preoccupation with naming should have formed so central a part
of a voyage whose ultimate purpose was colonial occupation. As
the history of magic indicates, finding the "real" name of anything is a way of claiming and establishing power over it. In itself
it is an act of appropriation, an annexation, and the moment of
such naming of the flora and fauna of the South Pacific coincided
with the final and most pervasive era of European imperialism,
the nineteenth century. And Foster need not have worried about
Europeans even having the desire to go back again to the natural
world he would see at the end of the eighteenth century. Individual species would survive, but that apparently inexhaustible fabric
of flora and fauna, like the world of the flying proas, would not be
there to go back to.

At the time, what Cook's crew wanted to go back to was
merely England. As the *Endeavour* cleared the northernmost tip
of Australia, Banks said they were "pretty far gone with the longing for home which the Physicians have gone so far as to esteem a

disease under the name of Nostalgia; indeed I can find hardly anybody in the ship clear of its effects but the Captn.[,] Dr. Solander and myself, indeed we three have pretty constant employment for our minds which I believe to be the best if not the only remedy for it." The quantity of Parkinson's output would suggest that he, too, had "pretty constant employment for his mind," but the captain, Dr. Solander, and Banks were evidently immunized as well by their unappeased craving for what was still unknown to them, unseen, unnamed. The others longed for a Europe they thought they remembered, in which nothing of the voyage, nothing that they had "discovered," nothing of the moment through which they were sailing had been known, or seen, or named.

What Europe—England, Scotland—meant to Sydney Parkinson we can scarcely guess. In the published "Journal" he tells almost nothing of his more private feelings, and it seems unlikely that his lost, more complete journal would have revealed anything more intimate. For one thing, it seems that the journal, as it was written from day to day, may have been available to others of the company in the Great Cabin. And for another, there is Sydney's own shy and reticent temperament. Of his attachments in England, we know of his mother and brother and Lee, and of a cousin, Jane Gomeldon, a woman some years his elder, widowed, to whom he wrote that he had "spared no pains during the voyage, to pick up everything that is curious for thee." Besides the leaves and petals fading in front of him.

Other sicknesses besides Nostalgia, rising out of memories of Europe, lay in wait for them. On the Great Barrier Reef, the *Endeavour*, one quiet night, was badly damaged by a spur of coral. Sea water soaked part of the carefully stowed herbarium—it was only the beginning of the harm they found, and they were lucky to have survived at all. They managed to make temporary repairs to the bark by themselves, on the Australian coast, but Cook knew that the hull was in no condition to brave the crossing of the

Indian Ocean and the long sail northward back to England without a major overhaul. Despite a distrust of the imperial Dutch, the port of Batavia on Java seemed the best place for the job, and he put in there on October 9, 1770. Five days later, Sydney Parkinson sent off two letters to England on a departing vessel, one to a Quaker friend, Dr. Fothergill, and the other to his cousin, Jane Gomeldon—the first letters from the *Endeavour* to reach England—saying that all was well.

So it was, more or less. They had all narrowly escaped death on the Great Barrier Reef. They had "done great things this voyage," Sydney wrote to Fothergill, "having been very successful in discoveries of Land, in Astronomy & Natural History, having got an amazing number of new subjects that way; our Crew has been very healthy & we have hardly lost any of them yet, but I am sorry to inform you that your faithful servant Richmond is no more, he & another black Servant of Mr. Banks's died at Tierra del Fuego. I felt the loss of him very much." The servants had helped themselves to the entire rum ration of Banks's Tierra del Fuego shore party, and had frozen to death. And Sydney's fellow artist, Alexander Buchan, who suffered from epilepsy, had died in Tahiti and had been buried at sea, to the astonishment of the Tahitians. There had been one suicide on the voyage, two drownings, one death from consumption, and one from venereal disease—which Cook's crews, like those of other European vessels, spread through the Pacific. But everyone felt they had come through remarkably well: all told, eight of the eighty-five who had left Plymouth had died before the *Endeavour* reached Java, where the Dutch had established themselves by ruthless force almost two hundred years earlier.

Batavia was the seat of Dutch power in the Indies. After they had seized the original port of Jakarta in 1619, they had built their own capital there, laying it out like a Dutch city with a network of canals. The mud along the waterways, Banks wrote, "stinks intolerably, as indeed it must, being chiefly formed from human ordure of which … the Canals every morning received their regular quota, and the more filthy recrements of housekeeping." The fetid water and the swamp around the city were full of dysentery and malarial mosquitoes, and one by one the crew of the *Endeavour* came down with one disease or the other until "everyone on shore and many on board were ill," Banks recorded. Solander and Banks himself sickened; Sydney Parkinson worked on at his botanical drawings and sketches of boats, but already in the letter to Dr. Fothergill in mid-October, he spoke of being "so confused and fluttered about at present that my mind is not settled," referring perhaps to the onset of the "intermittents"—the fevers of malaria.

Not only Banks and Solander but Cook himself fell sick. Some twenty-seven officers and men of the *Endeavour* would die as a result of calling at Batavia. It is impossible to form a clear picture of the life in the ship's company during the months there, though we know that Banks and Solander, at least, could afford to rent houses out of the city in the hills, and hire nurses, and apparently for that reason they survived. Parkinson might have rented a house in the hills and hired a nurse, too, if Banks, before taking off, had troubled to pay him the wages that were due him when the *Endeavour* reached Java. Life must have been miserable indeed for most of the crew and officers of the vessel, lying sick and feverish while the bark was overhauled in the foul-smelling harbor, and knowing nothing of the local languages. It appears that there was some cinchona bark—quinine—in the ship's medicine chest, but who used it and to what effect we do not know. At the end of Parkinson's sketchbook, there are a few notes about monies paid and monies owed him, and a surprisingly long list of books that, it seems, he had with him on the voyage, including many volumes of poetry: Shakespeare, Virgil, Pope, Dryden, Homer, Ovid, Chaucer and Spenser, La Fontaine, Cervantes. (Joppien and Smith have suggested that he may have compiled the list as he prepared to make his will.) He managed to produce a surprising number of botanical drawings—many of them sketches that were finished later by others—as well as his ethereal outlines of boats, at Batavia, but by the time the *Endeavour* sailed from Java on the day after Christmas, 1770, his work was finished. They sailed west for the coast of Africa. He must have been racked with fevers, growing weaker day by day. The islands of Tahiti and England must have seemed equally evanescent, and all the shores that he had painted.

Among his drawings and paintings, "mechanical" or luminous, stored away there in the patched hull of the veteran collier, there was one of a tree overlooking Matavai Bay on Tahiti, where they had lain at anchor in a happier time. A huge, dark, ancient tree, the One Tree on One Tree Hill. Out on the bay, the vessel floats like a shadow, and on the far shore is the fort that the British had built for the pursuit of knowledge. A young Tahitian woman is poised in the act of walking along the path under the tree, heading toward the bay with a load of breadfruit, probably, suspended from a stick on her shoulder. A man, possibly a sailor, is striding in the same direction, carrying a rolled mat. Two men, evidently Europeans, one with a notebook and staff, have climbed the slope under the tree and are looking up into its branches, towering far above them. Perhaps they are Banks and one of his "gentlemen." And in the shade of the tree, in a tricorner hat, someone is sitting with a pad on his knee. It seems likely that it is Parkinson himself as seen from a little distance, by Parkinson. It is an ancient tree, far older than anything else in the painting, but everything is there in the same time. The Parkinson who drew the tree as we see it has been specific about its botanical identity. It is an *Etoa casuarina equisetifolia*: the first word, in this case, is Polynesian, and the second, "casuarina," is a legacy of Rumphius, alluding to the wing of a cassowary.

In England, the tree would be copied from Parkinson's drawing by John James Barralet, who had never seen it. Barralet made
the copy for Hawkesworth's official edition of *An Account of
Voyages Undertaken by the Order of His Present Majesty, 1773*, a
work commissioned by Banks. When Hawkesworth asked Banks
whether he should make acknowledgment of those materials of
Parkinson's that he was using, Banks replied, "as for Drs. [a reference to Fothergill] intention of saying that Parkinson's materials
have been used by you I am strongly of the opinion that that
should not be." In Barralet's pencil copy of Parkinson's scene,
there is an erasure at the foot of the tree where the seated figure
had been.

A month out of Java, at the age of twenty-five or -six, Parkinson joined the subjects he had painted.

A NOTE ON HAWAIIAN SPELLING

The spelling of Hawaiian words has evolved a great deal since the language was given a standardized alphabet by American missionaries in the 1820s. At present, throughout the state of Hawai'i, efforts are being made to compensate for the harm done to the language by more than a century of disparagement and distortion. One such effort involves correcting faulty spellings that have come into common usage, and reestablishing the inclusion of diacritical marks in written Hawaiian words. The glottal stop (represented by a reversed apostrophe) and the macron (a bar over a vowel indicating greater than normal duration and stress) affect meaning as well as pronunciation. A common example is shown in the pairs of words *ko'u* (my) and *kou* (your) and *malama* (light) and *mālama* (care). In this book, every attempt has been made to conform to the spellings of the *Hawaiian Dictionary*, by Mary Kawena Pukui and Samuel H. Elbert, and *Place Names of Hawaii*, by Mary Kawena Pukui, Samuel H. Elbert, and Esther T. Mookini. The reader will see that, as a rule, Hawaiian terms are not italicized and, as is common practice in the islands, diacritical marks are not used when a Hawaiian word is altered by English grammar or inflection (thus, "Islands of Hawai'i" but "Hawaiian Islands") or in proper names, such as the names of some organizations and institutions.

READINGS IN HAWAII'S NATURAL HISTORY, INCLUDING SELECTED FIELD GUIDES

Twentieth Century

Armstrong, R.W. (ed.). *Atlas of Hawaii*. 2nd edition. Honolulu: University of Hawaii Press, 1983.

Berger, A.J. *Hawaiian Birdlife*. 2nd edition. Honolulu: University of Hawaii Press, 1981.

Bertsch, H., and S. Johnson. *Hawaiian Nudibranchs*. Honolulu: The Oriental Publishing Co., 1981.

Carlquist, S. *Island Life: A Natural History of the Islands of the World*. Garden City, NY: Natural History Press, 1965.

Carlquist, S. *Island Biology*. New York: Columbia University Press, 1974.

Carlquist, S. *Hawaii: A Natural History*. Lawai, HI: Pacific Tropical Botanical Gardens, 1980.

Cuddihy, L.W., and C.P. Stone. *Alteration of Native Hawaiian Vegetation: Effects of Humans, their Activities and Introductions*. Honolulu: University of Hawaii Press for Cooperative National Park Resources Studies Unit, University of Hawaii, 1990.

Culliney, J.L. *Islands in a Far Sea: Nature and Man in Hawaii*. San Francisco: Sierra Club Books, 1988.

Degener, O. *Plants of Hawaii National Parks Illustrative of Plants and Customs of the South Seas.* Ann Arbor: Braun-Brumfield, 1973.

Devaney, D.M., and L.G. Eldredge. *Reef and Shore Fauna of Hawaii: Protozoa through Ctenophora.* Honolulu: Bishop Museum Press, 1977.

Fielding, A. *Hawaiian Reefs and Tidepools: A Guide to Hawaii's Shallow-Water Invertebrates.* Honolulu: The Oriental Publishing Co., 1979.

Fielding, A., and E. Robinson. *An Underwater Guide to Hawaii.* Honolulu: University of Hawaii Press, 1987.

Frierson, P. *The Burning Island: A Journey through Myth and History in Volcano Country, Hawai'i.* San Francisco: Sierra Club Books, 1991.

Gosline, W.A., and V.E. Brock. *Handbook of Hawaiian Fishes.* Honolulu: University of Hawaii Press, 1960.

Hardy, D.E. *Insects of Hawaii.* Vols. 10-12. Honolulu: University of Hawaii Press, 1960-1981.

Harrison, C.S. *Seabirds of Hawaii: Natural History and Conservation.* Ithaca, NY: Comstock/Cornell University Press, 1990.

Haselwood, E.L., and G.G. Motter. *Handbook of Hawaiian Weeds.* 2nd edition, revised and expanded by R.T. Hirano. Honolulu: University of Hawaii Press for Harold L. Lyon Arboretum, 1983.

Hobson, E.S., and E.H. Chave. *Hawaiian Reef Animals.* Honolulu: University of Hawaii Press, 1972.

Kanahele, G.S. *Kū Kanaka—Stand Tall: A Search for Hawaiian Values.* Honolulu: University of Hawaii Press, 1986.

Kay, E.A. (ed.). *A Natural History of the Hawaiian Islands: Selected Readings.* Honolulu: University of Hawaii Press, 1972.

Kay, E.A. *Hawaiian Marine Shells.* Honolulu: Bishop Museum Press, 1979.

Kepler, A.K. *Hawaiian Heritage Plants.* Honolulu: The Oriental Publishing Co., 1983.

Kepler, A.K. *Trees of Hawaii.* Honolulu: University of Hawaii Press, 1990.

Kimura, B.Y., and K.M. Nagata. *Hawaii's Vanishing Flora.* Honolulu: The Oriental Publishing Co., 1980.

Kirch, P.V. *Feathered Gods and Fishhooks: An Introduction to Hawaiian Archaeology and Prehistory.* Honolulu: University of Hawaii Press, 1985.

Lamb, S.H. *Native Trees and Shrubs of the Hawaiian Islands.* Santa Fe: Sunstone Press, 1981.

Lamoureux, C.H. *Trailside Plants of Hawaii's National Parks.* Hawaii Volcanoes National Park: Hawaii Natural History Association, 1976.

Macdonald, G.A., A.T. Abbott, and F.L. Peterson. *Volcanoes in the Sea: The Geology of Hawaii.* 2nd edition. Honolulu: University of Hawaii Press, 1983.

Magruder, W.H., and J.W. Hunt. *Seaweeds of Hawaii: A Photographic Identification Guide.* Honolulu: The Oriental Publishing Co., 1979.

McKeown, S. *Hawaiian Reptiles and Amphibians.* Honolulu: The Oriental Publishing Co., 1978.

Merlin, M.D. *Hawaiian Coastal Plants and Scenic Shorelines.* Honolulu: The Oriental Publishing Co., 1977.

Merlin, M.D. *Hawaiian Forest Plants.* 3rd edition. Honolulu: The Oriental Publishing Co., 1980.

Minasian, S.M., and K.C. Balcomb III. *The Whales of Hawaii.* Honolulu: University of Hawaii Press for the Marine Mammal Fund, 1991.

Morgan, J.R. *Hawaii: A Geography.* Boulder: Westview Press, 1983.

Munro, G.C. *Birds of Hawaii.* Honolulu: Tongg Publishing Co., 1944.

Neal, M. *In Gardens of Hawaii.* Honolulu: Bishop Museum Press, 1965.

Norris, K.S. (ed.). *Whales, Dolphins, and Porpoises.* Berkeley: University of California Press, 1966.

Norris, K.S. *The Porpoise Watcher.* New York: W.W. Norton, 1974.

Norris, K.S. *Dolphin Days: The Life and Times of the Spinner Dolphin.* New York: W.W. Norton, 1991.

Pratt, H.D., P.L. Bruner, and D.G. Berrett. *A Field Guide to the Birds of Hawaii and the Tropical Pacific.* Princeton: Princeton University Press, 1987.

Pryor, K. *Lads Before the Wind: Adventures in Porpoise Training.* New York: Harper & Row, 1975.

Pukui, M.K., E.W. Haertig, and C.A. Lee. *Nānā I Ke Kumu (Look to the Source).* Vol. I. Honolulu: Queen Liliuokalani Children's Center, 1972.

Riedman, M. *The Pinnipeds: Seals, Sea Lions, and Walruses.* Berkeley: University of California Press, 1990.

Rock, J.F. *The Indigenous Trees of the Hawaiian Islands.* Tokyo and Rutland, VT: Tuttle, 1913–1974.

Rotor, P.P. *Grasses of Hawaii.* Honolulu: University of Hawaii Press, 1968.

Sauer, D. (ed.). *Na Waiwai Hawaiʻi No Keia La: Hawaiian Values for Today.* Proceedings, Waiaha Ku Kana Conference, Honolulu: Waiaha Foundation, 1988.

Shallenberger, R.J. (ed.). *Hawaii's Birds.* Honolulu: Hawaii Audubon Society, 1984.

Sohmer, S.H., and R. Gustafson. *Plants and Flowers of Hawaii.* Honolulu: University of Hawaii Press, 1987.

Stearns, H.T. *Geology of the State of Hawaii.* 2nd edition. Palo Alto: Pacific Books, 1985.

Stone, C.P., and J.M. Scott (eds.). *Hawaii's Terrestrial Ecosystems: Preservations and Management.* Honolulu: University of Hawaii Press for University of Hawaii Cooperative National Park Resources Studies Unit, 1985.

Stone, C.P., and D.B. Stone (eds.). *Conservation Biology in Hawaii.* Honolulu: University of Hawaii Cooperative National Park Resources Studies Unit, 1989.

Titcomb, M. *Native Use of Fish in Hawaii.* 2nd edition. Honolulu: University of Hawaii Press, 1977.

Titcomb, M. *Native Use of Marine Invertebrates in Old Hawaii.* Honolulu: University of Hawaii Press, 1978.

Tomich, P.Q. *Mammals in Hawaii: A Synopsis and Notational Bibliography.* Revised edition. Honolulu: Bishop Museum Press, 1986.

van Riper, S.G., and C. van Riper III. *A Field Guide to the Mammals in Hawaii.* Honolulu: The Oriental Publishing Co., 1982.

Wagner, W.L., D.R. Herbst, and S.H. Sohmer. *Manual of the Flowering Plants of Hawaii*. Honolulu: Bishop Museum and University of Hawaii Press, 1990.

Zimmerman, E.C. *Insects of Hawaii*. Vols. 2–9. Honolulu: University of Hawaii Press, 1948.

Nineteenth Century and Earlier

Bassett, M. *Realms and Islands: The World Voyage of Rose de Freycinet in the Corvette* Uranie *1817–1820*. New York: Oxford University Press, 1962.

Beaglehole, J.C. *The Exploration of the Pacific*. Palo Alto: Stanford University Press, 1966.

Beaglehole, J.C. *The Life of Captain James Cook*. Stanford: Stanford University Press, 1974.

Beaglehole, J.C. (ed.). *The Journals of Captain James Cook on His Voyages of Discovery*. Cambridge, England: Printed for the Hakluyt Society at the University Press, 1955–1967.

Beckwith, M. *The Kumulipo: A Hawaiian Creation Chant*. Honolulu: University of Hawaii Press, 1972.

Beechey, F.W. *Narrative of a Voyage to the Pacific ... in the Years 1825, 1826, 1827, 1828*. London: Colburn and Bentley, 1831.

Bellwood, P. *The Polynesians: Prehistory of an Island People*. London: Thames and Hudson, 1978.

Bingham, H. *A Residence of Twenty-One Years in the Sandwich Islands....* Hartford: Hezekiah Huntington; New York: Sherman Converse, 1847.

Bird, I.L. *Six Months in the Sandwich Islands*. Reprint of the 1875 edition. Honolulu: University of Hawaii Press for Friends of the Library of Hawaii, 1964.

Bishop, S.E. *Reminiscences of Old Hawaii*. Honolulu: Hawaiian Gazette, 1916.

Bloxam, A. *Diary of Andrew Bloxam, Naturalist of the* Blonde *on her Trip from England to the Hawaii Islands, 1824–25*. Honolulu: Bishop Museum Press, 1925.

Briggs, L.V. *Experiences of a Medical Student in Honolulu and on the Island of Oahu, 1881.* Boston: David D. Nickerson, 1926.

Broughton, W.R. *A Voyage of Discovery to the North Pacific Ocean ... Performed in his Majesty's Sloop* Providence *and Her Tender, in the Years 1795, 1796, 1797, 1798.* London: Cadell and Davies, 1804.

Campbell, A. *A Voyage Round the World from 1806 to 1812.* Facsimile of the 1822 American edition. Honolulu: University of Hawaii Press, 1967.

Charlot, J. *The Kamapuaʻa Literature.* Laiʻe, Hawaii: Institute for Polynesian Studies, Brigham Young University, 1987.

Cheever, H.T. *Life in the Sandwich Islands, or the Heart of the Pacific as it Was and Is.* New York: Barnes and Co., 1851.

Coan, T. *Life in Hawaii.* New York: Randolph and Co., 1882.

Coats, A.M. *The Plant Hunters: Being a History of the Horticultural Pioneers, Their Quests and Their Discoveries from the Renaissance to the Twentieth Century.* New York: McGraw-Hill, 1970.

Dampier, R. *To the Sandwich Islands on H.M.S.* Blonde. Honolulu: University of Hawaii Press, 1971.

Dana, J.D. *Corals and Coral Islands.* New York: Dodd and Mead, 1872.

Dixon, G. *A Voyage Round the World: But More Particularly to the North-West Coast of America....* London: Goulding, 1789.

Dodge, E.S. *Beyond the Capes: Pacific Exploration from Captain Cook to the* Challenger, *1776–1877.* Boston: Little, Brown, 1971.

Douglas, D. *Journal Kept by David Douglas During his Travels in North America....* London: Wesley and Son, 1914.

Ellis, [Surgeon] W. *An Authentic Narrative of a Voyage Performed by Captain Cook and Captain Clerke ... During the Years 1777, 1778, 1779, and 1780....* London: Printed for Robinson, Sewell and Deberett, 1792.

Ellis, [Rev.] W. *Polynesian Researches during a Residence of Nearly Eight Years in the Society and Sandwich Islands.* New York: J. and J. Harper, 1833.

Ellis, [Rev.] W. *Journal of William Ellis: Narrative of a Tour of Hawaii, or Owhyee.* Rutland, VT, and Tokyo: Tuttle, 1979.

Golovnin, V.M. *Around the World on the* Kamchatka, *1817–1819.* Honolulu: University of Hawaii Press, 1979.

Gulick, A. *Evolutionist and Missionary John Thomas Gulick.* Chicago: University of Chicago Press, 1932.

Handy, E.S.C., and E.G. Handy. *Native Planters in Old Hawaii: Their Life, Lore and Environment.* Honolulu: Bishop Museum Press, 1972.

Harvey, A.G. *Douglas of the Fir.* Cambridge: Harvard University Press, 1947.

Hillebrand, W.F. *Flora of the Hawaiian Islands.* Facsimile of the 1888 edition. Monticello, NY: Lubrecht and Cramer, 1981.

Jarvis, J.J. *Scenes and Scenery in the Sandwich Islands and a Trip through Central America 1837–1842.* Boston: Munroe and Co., 1844.

Jennings, J.D. (ed.). *The Prehistory of Polynesia.* Cambridge: Harvard University Press, 1979.

Johnson, R.K. *Kumulipo: Hawaiian Hymn of Creation.* Honolulu: Topgallant, 1971.

Kaeppler, A.L. *Artificial Curiosities.* Honolulu: Bishop Museum Press, 1978.

Kamakau, S.M. *Ruling Chiefs of Hawaii.* Translated from the Hawaiian. Honolulu: Kamehameha Schools Press, 1961.

Kamakau, S.M. *The Works of the People of Old: Na Hana a ka Poʻe Kahiko.* Translated from the Hawaiian. Honolulu: Bishop Museum Press, 1976.

La Pérouse, J.F.G. *A Voyage Round the World Performed in the Years 1785, 1786, 1787, and 1788, etc.* Reprint of the 1799 edition. New York: Da Capo Press, 1968.

Lisiansky, U. *A Voyage Round the World in the Years 1803, 4, 5, & 6. . . .* London: Printed by J. Booth, 1814.

Lyman, C. *Around the Horn to the Sandwich Islands and California, 1845–1850.* New Haven: Yale University Press, 1924.

Macrae, J. *With Lord Byron at the Sandwich Islands in 1825, Being Extracts from the MS Diary of James Macrae, Scottish Botanist.* Honolulu: n.p., 1922.

Malo, D. *Hawaiian Antiquities (Moʻolelo o Hawaiʻi)*. Translated from the Hawaiian by N.B. Emerson, 1898. Honolulu: Bishop Museum Press, 1951.

Menzies, A. *Hawaii Nei 128 Years Ago*. Reprint of the 1792 journal. Honolulu: Privately printed, 1920.

Montgomery, J. (ed.). *Journal of Voyages and Travels by the Rev. Daniel Tyerman and George Bennet Esq., deputed from the London Missionary Society to Visit Their Various Stations in the South Sea Islands, China, India &c. between the Years 1821 and 1829*. Boston: Crocker and Brewster, 1832.

Morrell, B., Jr. *A Narrative of Four Voyages to the South Sea, North and South Pacific Ocean, Chinese Sea, Ethiopic and Southern Atlantic Ocean, Indian and Antarctic Ocean from the Year 1822 to 1831*. New York: J. and J. Harper, 1832.

Nordoff, C. *Northern California, Oregon, and the Sandwich Islands*. Centennial reprint of the 1874 edition. Berkeley, CA: Ten Speed Press, 1974.

Parke, W.C. *Personal Reminiscences of William Parke*. Cambridge, England: Printed at the University Press, 1891.

Portlock, N. *A Voyage Round the World ... in 1785, 1786, 1787, and 1788 ....* London: Printed for Stockdale and Goulding, 1789.

Price, A.G. (ed.). *The Explorations of Captain James Cook in the Pacific, as Told by Selections of His Own Journals, 1768–1779*. New York: Dover, 1971.

Pukui, M.K. *ʻŌlelo Noʻeau: Hawaiian Proverbs & Poetical Sayings*. Honolulu: Bishop Museum Press, 1983.

Reynolds, J.N. *Voyages of the United States Frigate* Potomac *Under the Command of Commodore John Downes During the Circumnavigation of the Globe in the Years 1831, 1832, 1833, and 1834*. New York: Harper and Brothers, 1835.

Sharp, D. (ed.). *Fauna Hawaiiensis: Being the Land Fauna of the Hawaiian Islands*. Cambridge, England: The University Press, 1899–1913.

Simpson, G. *Narrative of a Journey Round the World, During the Years 1841 and 1842*. London: Henry Colburn, 1847.

Sinclair, I. *Indigenous Flowers of the Hawaiian Islands.* London: Sampson Low, Marston, Searle, & Rivington, 1885.

Stanton, W. *The Great United States Exploring Expedition of 1838–42.* Berkeley: University of California Press, 1975.

Stewart, C.S. *Journal of a Residence in the Sandwich Islands During the Years 1823, 1824, and 1825 ....* Facsimile of the 1830 edition. Honolulu: University of Hawaii Press, 1970.

Strauss, W.P. *Americans in Polynesia 1783–1842.* East Lansing: Michigan State University Press, 1963.

Taylor, F.W. *A Voyage Around the World in the United States Frigate Columbia, Attended by Her Consort the Sloop of War* John Adams *and Commanded by Commodore George C. Read.* 2nd edition. New Haven: H. Mansfield, 1842.

Turnbull, J. *A Voyage Round the World.* London: Printed for Richard Phillips, 1805.

Vancouver, G. *A Voyage of Discovery to the North Pacific Ocean and Round the World.* Reprint of 1798 edition. New York: Da Capo Press, 1967.

Viola, H.J., and C. Margolis (eds.). *Magnificent Voyagers: The U.S. Exploring Expedition, 1838–1842.* Washington: Smithsonian Institution Press, 1985.

von Kotzebue, O. *A Voyage of Discovery into the South Sea and Bering's Straits ... in the Years 1815–1818, etc.* Reprint of 1821 edition. New York: N. Israel/Da Capo Press, 1967.

Whitney, H.M. *The Hawaiian Guide Book.* Facsimile of the 1875 edition. Rutland, VT: Tuttle, 1970.

Wilkes, C. *Narrative of the United States Exploring Expedition, During the Years 1838, 1839, 1840, 1841, 1842.* Philadelphia: Lea and Blanchard, 1845.

Wilson, W.F. (comp.). *David Douglas, Botanist at Hawaii.* Honolulu: New Freedom, 1919.

SELECTED ORGANIZATIONS INVOLVED IN THE CONSERVATION OF HAWAII'S NATURAL HISTORY, AND OTHER SOURCES OF INFORMATION

Animal Rights Hawai'i
P.O. Box 1313
Kea'au, HI 96749

Bernice Pauahi Bishop Museum
P.O. Box 19000-A
Honolulu, HI 96817

Conservation Council for Hawai'i
P.O. Box 2923
Honolulu, HI 96802

Earthtrust
2500 Pali Highway
Honolulu, HI 96817

Environment Hawai'i
733 Bishop Street, Suite 170-51
Honolulu, HI 96813

Environmental Center
2550 Campus Road, Crawford 317
University of Hawaii
Honolulu, HI 96822

Global Environment Change
    Initiative
Sea Grant Extension Service
Marine Science Building 205
University of Hawaii
Honolulu, HI 96822

Greenpeace Foundation of Hawai'i
P.O. Box 10909
Hilo, HI 96720

Haleakalā National Park
P.O. Box 369
Makawao, HI 96768

Hawai'i Academy of Science
P.O. Box 19073
Honolulu, HI 96817

Hawai'i Audubon Society
212 Merchant Street, Room 320
Honolulu, HI 96813

Hawai'i Coastal Zone
  Management Program
Office of State Planning
State Capitol, Room 410
Honolulu, HI 96813

Hawai'i Conservation Biology
  Initiative
1116 Smith Street, Room 201
Honolulu, HI 96817

Hawai'i Dept. of Land and
  Natural Resources
Division of Forestry and Wildlife
1151 Punchbowl Street
Honolulu, HI 96813

Hawai'i Dept. of Land and
  Natural Resources
Office of Conservation and
  Environmental Affairs
1151 Punchbowl Street, Room 131
Honolulu, HI 96813

Hawai'i Environmental
  Education Association
P.O. Box 1236
Honolulu, HI 96807

Hawai'i Green Movement
P.O. Box 61508
Honolulu, HI 96839

Hawai'i Institute of Marine
  Biology
P.O. Box 1346
Kaneohe, HI 96744

Hawai'i Nature Center
2131 Makiki Heights Drive
Honolulu, HI 96822

Hawai'i Volcanoes National Park
P.O. Box 52
Hawaii National Park, HI 96718

Hawaiian Botanical Society
Botany Department
3190 Maile Way
University of Hawaii
Honolulu, HI 96822

Hawaiian Entomological Society
Department of Entomology
Gilmore Hall 310
University of Hawaii
Honolulu, HI 96822

Hawaiian Malacological Society
P.O. Box 22130
Honolulu, HI 96822

Hawaii's Thousand Friends
305 Hahani Street, #282
Kailua, HI 96734

Honolulu Botanic Gardens
50 N. Vineyard Boulevard
Honolulu, HI 96817

Honolulu Zoological Society
151 Kapahulu Avenue
Honolulu, HI 96815

Ho'omaluhia Botanic Garden
50 N. Vineyard Boulevard
Honolulu, HI 96817

Koke'e Natural History Museum
P.O. Box 100
Kekaha, HI 96752

League of Conservation Voters
Environmental Legislative Network
1030 Aoloa Place, #102B
Kailua, HI 96734

Life of the Land
19 Niolopa Place
Honolulu, HI 96817

Lyon Arboretum Association
3860 Manoa Road
Honolulu, HI 96822

Maui Zoological and Botanic
Gardens
200 High Street
Wailuku, HI 96793

Moanalua Gardens Foundation
1352 Pineapple Place
Honolulu, HI 96819

National Park Service
Pacific Area Office
300 Ala Moana Boulevard
Honolulu, HI 96850

National Tropical Botanical
Garden
P.O. Box 340
Lawai, HI 96765

Native Hawaiian Legal
Corporation
1270 Queen Emma Street, #1004
Honolulu, HI 96813

Native Hawaiian Plant Society
P.O. Box 5021
Kahului, HI 96732

Natural Resources Defense
Council
Hawai'i Office
212 Merchant Street, #203
Honolulu, HI 96813

The Nature Conservancy of
Hawai'i
1116 Smith Street, Suite 201
Honolulu, HI 96817

Oceanic Institute
Makapuu Point
Waimanalo, HI 96795

Outdoor Circle
1110 University Avenue, Suite 205
Honolulu, HI 96826

Pele Defense Fund
P.O. Box 404
Volcano, HI 96785

Protect Kahoʻolawe ʻOhana
1942 Naio Street
Honolulu, HI 96817

Rainforest Action Group
   (Big Island)
Box 341
Kurtistown, HI 96760

Rainforest Action Group (Maui)
385 W. Kuiaha Road
Haiku, HI 96708

Rainforest Action Group (Oʻahu)
Porteus Hall 346
University of Hawaii
2424 Maile Way
Honolulu, HI 96822

Sea Grant Extension Service
1000 Pope Road, MSB 205
Honolulu, HI 96822

Sierra Club Hawaiʻi Chapter
P.O. Box 2577
Honolulu, HI 96803

Sierra Club Legal Defense Fund
212 Merchant Street, Suite 202
Honolulu, HI 96813

U.S. Environmental Protection
   Agency, Region 9
Pacific Islands Contact Office
300 Ala Moana Boulevard,
   Room 1302
Honolulu, HI 96813

U.S. Fish and Wildlife Service
Office of Environmental Services
300 Ala Moana Boulevard,
   Room 6307
Honolulu, HI 96813

USDA Forest Service
Institute of Pacific Islands
   Forestry
1151 Punchbowl Street,
   Room 323
Honolulu, HI 96813

Waikiki Aquarium
2777 Kalakaua Avenue
Honolulu, HI 96815

Waimea Arboretum and
   Botanical Garden
59–864 Kamehameha Highway
Haleiwa, HI 96712

Wildlife Society Hawaii Chapter
P.O. Box 4632
Honolulu, HI 96813

ACKNOWLEDGMENTS

I would like to thank several friends without whom this book would not have come about: Lisa Erb, whose love for the forests of the Hawai'i volcanoes region led me deeper into them than I would have gone without her encouragement; Tom Farber, who taught me many new things about the sea and the writer's life; and Pat Matsueda, editor and friend. Thanks also to Kathy Matsueda for typing, editing, and good cheer.

And thanks to Tim Schaffner, Chris Merrill, Howard Boyer, and the authors and publishers whose generous permissions to use copyrighted material made this book possible:

Diane Ackerman, "The Moon by Whale Light" from *The Moon by Whale Light* by Diane Ackerman. Copyright © 1991 by Diane Ackerman. Reprinted by permission of Random House, Inc.

Kenneth Brower, "The Pig War" from *The Atlantic Monthly*, August 1985. Reprinted by permission of the author.

John L. Culliney, "Hawai'i at the Edge." Printed by permission of the author.

Gavan Daws, "The Islands of Life" from *Hawaii: The Islands of Life*, Honolulu: Signature Publishing, 1988. Reprinted by permission of the author and The Nature Conservancy of Hawai'i.

Thomas Farber, "On Water." Printed by permission of the author.

Pamela Frierson, "Kīlauea, Desert and Rift" and "Sacred Darkness" from *The Burning Island*, San Francisco: Sierra Club Books, 1991. Reprinted by permission of Sierra Club Books.

James D. Houston, "Fire in the Night" from *Image*, the Sunday magazine of the San Francisco *Examiner/Chronicle*, October 1990. Reprinted by permission of the author.

Maxine Hong Kingston, "A City Person Encountering Nature" and "A Sea Worry" from the *New York Times*, 1978. Reprinted by permission of the author.

Peter Matthiessen, "Kīpahulu: From Cinders to the Sea" from *Audubon*, May 1970. Reprinted by permission of the author.

W. S. Merwin, "The Tree on One Tree Hill" from *Mānoa: A Pacific Journal of International Writing*, Spring 1991. Reprinted by permission of the author.

"Cooling the Lava" from *The Control of Nature* by John McPhee. Copyright © 1989 by John McPhee. Reprinted by permission of Farrar, Straus and Giroux, Inc.

Victoria Nelson, "Into the Archipelago" from *My Time in Hawaii: A Polynesian Memoir*, 1990. Reprinted by permission of the author.

"Captain Cook's Porpoises" is reprinted from *The Porpoise Watcher* by Kenneth S. Norris, by permission of W. W. Norton & Company, Inc. Copyright © 1974 by Kenneth S. Norris.

ABOUT THE AUTHORS

Diane Ackerman's five books include *Jaguar of Sweet Laughter: New and Selected Poems*; *On Extended Wings*, a memoir about learning to fly; and *A Natural History of the Senses*. She is currently a staff writer for *The New Yorker* and lives in upstate New York.

Kenneth Brower has written and traveled extensively in the South Pacific and Hawai'i. His books include *Galápagos: The Flow of Wildness; The Starship & the Canoe; The Wake of the Whale; Micronesia: The Land, the People and the Sea;* and *Song for Satawal*. He currently lives in California.

John L. Culliney is a noted marine biologist who teaches biology and marine science at Hawaii Loa College on the island of O'ahu. Formerly associated with the Marine Biological Laboratory at Woods Hole, Massachusetts, he is the author of *The Forests of the Sea, Exploring Underwater,* and, most recently, *Islands in a Far Sea: Nature and Man in Hawaii.*

Gavan Daws, Australian born, has lived in and written about Hawai'i for many years. His books about the Islands include *Shoal of Time*, *Holy Man: Father Damien of Molokai*, and *Land and Power in Hawaii*. He has been a member of the United Nations Commission on the Scientific and Cultural History of Humankind and a Fellow of the Academy of Humanities in Australia.

Thomas Farber's books of fiction and nonfiction include *Tales for the Son of My Unborn Child*, *Curves of Pursuit*, and *Compared to What?* A former writer-in-residence at the University of Hawaii and a frequent visitor to the islands, he has been a recipient of John Simon Guggenheim Foundation and National Endowment for the Arts fellowships for fiction, and is a former Fulbright Scholar for South Pacific Studies.

Pamela Frierson grew up in Hawai'i and has made her home on the Big Island. A former reporter and editor for the news journal *Hawaii Observer*, she has written extensively about issues concerning Native Hawaiian rights and the environment. Her recent book is *The Burning Island: A Journey through Myth and History in Volcano Country, Hawai'i*.

James D. Houston is the author of five novels, including *Love Life* and *Continental Drift*. Among his several nonfiction works are *Californians: Searching for the Golden State* and *Farewell to Manzanar*, co-authored with his wife, Jeanne Wakatsuki Houston. A frequent visitor to Hawai'i, he has recently finished two documentary films on Hawaii's people and land with noted island musician Eddie Kamae.

Maxine Hong Kingston, one of America's leading novelists, lived for a number of years in Hawai'i. Her books include *Woman Warrior,* which won the National Book Critics Circle Award, *China Men,* and *Tripmaster Monkey.*

Peter Matthiessen's books on natural history include *The Snow Leopard*, which won the National Book Award, and *Sand Rivers*, which won the John Burroughs Medal. He is also the author of *The Cloud Forest: A Chronicle of the South American Wilderness; Blue Meridian: The Search for the Great White Shark; Far Tortuga; In the Spirit of Crazy Horse; African Silences;* and many other books, novels, and short stories.

John McPhee's many books of essays, on a range of subjects, include *The Control of Nature, Rising from the Plains, Table of Contents, In Suspect Terrain, Basin and Range, Coming into the Country, The Survival of the Bark Canoe,* and *Encounters with the Archdruid.* He is a staff writer for *The New Yorker.*

W. S. Merwin is one of America's most distinguished poets and translators. His recent publications include *The Rain in the Trees, Selected Poems,* and *Sun at Midnight,* a selection of poems by Muso Soseki, co-translated with Soiku Shigematsu. A long-time resident of the island of Maui, he is an active supporter of the campaign to save the Wao Kele O Puna rain forest from a controversial geothermal development project.

Victoria Nelson spent many years in Hawai'i, as a teacher and as an explorer through archaeology and writing. She has written stories, essays, and translations and is co-translator of *Letters and Drawings of Bruno Schulz.* Her most recent book is *My Time in Hawaii: A Polynesian Memoir.* She now lives near San Francisco.

Kenneth S. Norris is one of the world's foremost authorities on cetaceans. He recently retired as professor of natural history at the Long Marine Laboratory of the University of California at Santa Cruz. His books include *Whales, Dolphins, Porpoises; The Porpoise Watcher;* and, most recently, *Dolphin Days: The Life and Times of the Spinner Dolphin.*